Sereno Edwars Todd

The American Wheat Culturist

Sereno Edwars Todd

The American Wheat Culturist

ISBN/EAN: 9783744660242

Printed in Europe, USA, Canada, Australia, Japan

Cover: Foto ©Thomas Meinert / pixelio.de

More available books at **www.hansebooks.com**

THE

AMERICAN
WHEAT CULTURIST.

A Practical Treatise

ON THE

CULTURE OF WHEAT,

EMBRACING A BRIEF HISTORY AND BOTANICAL DESCRIPTION OF WHEAT,
WITH FULL PRACTICAL DETAILS FOR SELECTING SEED, PRO-
DUCING NEW VARIETIES, AND CULTIVATING ON
DIFFERENT KINDS OF SOIL.

Illustrated with Numerous Engravings of a Practical Character.

BY S. EDWARDS TODD,

AGRICULTURAL AND HORTICULTURAL EDITOR OF THE NEW YORK TIMES, AND AUTHOR
OF "THE YOUNG FARMER'S MANUAL," ETC., ETC.

NEW YORK:

' TAINTOR BROTHERS & CO.,

229 BROADWAY.

1868.

—

CONTENTS.

CHAPTER I.

PREFACE.

My apology for writing a book on wheat is simply my desire to aid farmers in their efforts to produce more bountiful crops of this kind of grain. For more than forty successive years, I have had more or less practical experience in the culture of wheat. I have studied the habit of the wheat plant far more, perhaps, than the great mass of farmers have considered the subject to be of any practical importance. I have investigated the failures of the wheat crop, and endeavored to discover efficient and practical remedies.

I have excluded from the book every subject that might leave the ambitious young farmer in doubt; and have simply made a record of my own practical experience. There are scores of successful farmers who know most of what is contained in these pages. But the great mass of young farmers, who are just taking the places of their fathers, have yet to learn the important fundamental principles laid down in this work. Thousands upon thousands of active men, who know little about the practical part of raising wheat, will find in the following pages exactly the information they *must have*, before they can raise a bountiful crop of this kind of grain.

Some of the articles were prepared originally by my pen, for the Independent, New York Observer, New York Times, and American Agriculturist. But after publication in those papers, they were rewritten and revised. I herewith desire to give honorable and honest credit for anything that has appeared in those periodicals and in this book also.

With a few exceptions, the illustrations were originally prepared by myself for this book. The use of cuts on pages 11, 25, 27, 28, 29, 30, 39, 99, 406, 407, 408, 415, has been kindly afforded by Moore, Wilstack & Baldwin, Cincinnati, O., and 62 Walker St., New York City, publishers of "Klippart's Wheat Plant." I have quoted a few pages from his work; and I sincerely hope every reader will procure a copy, as it will be found an excellent introductory treatise to this book.

I have aimed to bring out in these pages all the facts on wheat culture that young farmers will be ambitious to know. If they will peruse this book with care, they will find an answer to nearly every question that they may wish to have answered about wheat. Although my instructions are strictly elementary, they are by no means superficial. Mere theories have been discarded. My aim has been to tell farmers how to raise good wheat, where their predecessors failed to get fair crops. If they follow my directions, success will crown their efforts.

I have frequently referred to my first and second volumes of The Young Farmer's Manual. The first has met with an excellent reception. The second is just issued; and is following the first. This Wheat Culturist may be called a third volume, as they are intimately connected with each other.

Illustrations of certain farm implements have been introduced for the express purpose of directing beginners where to procure reliable tools and machines that stand preëminently the highest in our country.

Read the Index and Table of Contents.

SERENO EDWARDS TODD,

Office New York Times, New York City.

THE WHEAT CULTURIST.

CHAPTER I.

INTRODUCTION TO WHEAT CULTURE.

> " The sire of gods and men with hard decrees,
> Forbids our plenty to be bought with ease ;
> And wills, that mortal men inured to toil,
> Should exercise with pains, the grudging soil."

UNREMITTING diligence is the price of material luxuries. The beautiful compensation principle seems to pervade the entire domain of all animated existence. Well-directed skill and industry are always crowned with a satisfactory reward. To do something—to make something—to give material substances a variety of forms—to produce something useful out of certain useless substances, is a consideration worthy of our highest ambition. There is an indescribable satisfaction in doing something. There is a charm in industry. The man who toils through a long summer's day to catch a single trout experiences an enjoyment when partaking of his frugal meal which he could never feel were the same fish taken by other hands. And the same is true of him who cultivates the soil to secure his daily bread. Were a field of wheat to spring up spontaneously, and were we not required to break up the stubborn ground and cultivate it, and put in the well-selected seed, existence would not bring half the pleasures which it now proffers so freely. The all-wise Creator foresaw that it would always be better for every man, woman, and child to have something to do, than to spend their days in idleness. For this reason, if we would have fine wheat for making excellent bread for ourselves and children, we must labor for it.

It has been suggested by some writers that the difficulties attending the production of delicious fruits, and fine grain, seem to increase with developments in arts and science. As our day is, so shall our knowledge be. Our ancestors cultivated wheat with but little difficulty. As soon, therefore, as scientific men were competent to devise remedies for the insect and other enemies in checking the growth of the wheat crop, the foes appeared. Science has taught us that, if we would have ripe fruit, we must destroy the insects which will devour the young fruit or kill the tree. And science has taught us that, when we would grow wheat, as we are unable to exterminate the hordes of insects that would feed upon the crop, we must cultivate and enrich the soil so as to make the plants grow faster than the insects can eat.

CHEMICAL STRUCTURE OF WHEAT.

In common parlance, when wheat is alluded to, the bran and the flour only are spoken of. The bran is the tough skin that envelops the part that makes the flour. Then, when we discourse farther of wheat, we say that the part that makes the flour is composed principally of starch and gluten.

Now, if with a sharp knife we slice up a kernel of wheat into thin sections, and examine it with a glass of greatly magnifying power, the various parts will appear similar to the accompanying illustration, which represents a portion of a kernel of wheat highly magnified. The part of the kernel represented by *a a* shows an exceedingly thin portion of the external part of the bran. The section represented by *b* reveals a second layer filled with minute pores. At *c* is a third layer, much more delicate than either of the others, which is so exquisitely fine, that its presence can scarcely be detected, even by the aid of

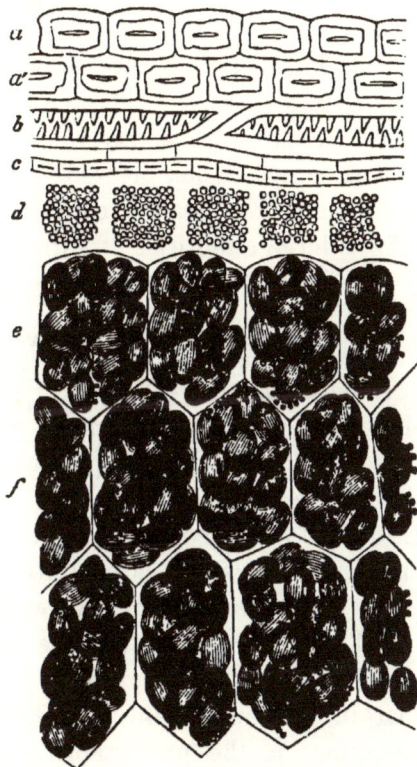

Fig. 1.--Section of a kernel of wheat highly magnified.

a good glass. The part of the illustration at *d*, represents the portion of the kernel which is composed principally of gluten. "These four layers constitute the bran. The gluten in the cells, *d*, appears to be a faint yellowish substance, very small grained, and oily to the touch and smell. The cells in which the gluten is formed are rather larger than any of the cells of the three layers just described, the walls of which are perhaps more delicate than any others in the entire kernel." Directly beneath the cells of gluten, d, lies the albuminous portion of the seed, which consists of hexagonal prismatic cells, which are filled with ovoid granules of starch, shown at e. These granules of starch, f, are enveloped in several layers of cellulose, or cell membrane, which, when heated to excess in water, burst and exude the starch contained in them. Gluten affords large quantities of nitrogenous matter.

Influence of Climate on Plants.

A writer in the "Portland Press" gives some facts to show that a northern climate, within certain limits, is better adapted to those plants which yield food, than the warmer climate, where the same plant is indigenous. In order to succeed most satisfactorily, he thinks southern plants must be carried to a latitude north of the place where they grow. He writes:

"That a northern climate is more conducive to health than a southern one, is generally admitted; but that its influence upon the vegetable kingdom is more propitious to the perfectability of plants necessary for the sustenance of man and of beast, is a proposition perhaps not so generally noticed and adopted as it should be. In these cold northern regions we sometimes need to be apprised of facts which will rebuke the spirit of discontent, and make us more reconciled to the climate in which Providence has cast our lot.

"The influence of climate upon plants is unquestionable. Those carried from the North to the South generally deteriorate; those brought from the South are generally improved by the transfer. In the process of vegetable acclimation, nature indicates that plants should emigrate toward the fields and gardens of northern cultivation, rather than that northern cultivators should emigrate toward south-born plants. The process, indeed, is slow, but it is sure. Tropical plants, which once could hardly exist beyond a vertical sun, have, by acclimation, been transferred to temperate latitudes, and made to yield larger and better fruits than they ever were capable of yielding in their native soils.

"In general it is true that *all cultivated plants yield the greatest products, and these of an improved quality, near the northernmost limit in which they will ripen.* This is true of all the farinaceous plants, such as rice, maize, wheat, rye, oats, barley, and millet; of all tuberous and bulbous roots, as potatoes, carrots, beets, turnips, parsnips, and radishes; of all lint plants, as cotton, hemp, and flax; of the salad family, as cabbage, lettuce, endive, and spinach; of all the grasses, from timothy and redtop to lucern and the clovers, red and white; of all the gourd family, from pumpkins and squashes to cucumbers, gherkins, and musk and water melons; of all delicious and pulpy fruits—as apples, pears, peaches, nectarines, grapes, plums, cherries, currants, gooseberries, and strawberries. It is also equally true of sugar cane, sorgo, and tobacco. Each and all of these most important products of the earth are improved by northern acclimation, and when brought as far into the high latitudes as they can be made to grow and mature, are found to produce in the greatest perfection and of a more excellent quality. The reason is this: the hot sun of a southern sky forces the plants into a rapid fructification before they have had time to concoct their juices. The growth in stalk, vine, and foliage is too much for the composition of fruit."

It is stated by respectable authority, that wheat raised in Virginia is better for making white bread than northern grain. The wheat grown in Missouri and in California yields a flour that commands a higher price in market than the northern wheat. The flour of the California wheat is said to yield a larger percentage of gluten than wheat that was grown in latitudes north of the latitude of California.

I pen these suggestions simply for the purpose of awakening in young farmers a spirit of investigation, with a view of encouraging them to take critical observations on every subject connected with the cultivation of this valuable grain.

GROWING WHEAT THEN AND NOW.

The question is asked with no little solicitude, why farmers cannot raise as good wheat at the present time as they did fifty years ago? Then, a crop of wheat was as sure as a crop of Indian corn; and, in numerous instances, three bountiful crops of wheat were taken from the same field, in three successive seasons. I well remember, when a small lad, that my father raised three crops of wheat in one of his fields in three successive years; and the third year, the growing grain seemed heavier than either of the preceding crops. Then, with miserable cultivation, and only a small quantity of inferior barnyard manure, a farmer could count upon a heavy crop of first-rate wheat, with almost absolute certainty. But now, many of our best farmers have met with so many serious failures and disappointments in their wheat crops, that they are sometimes exceedingly loath to try again.

The true causes of failure have not, as yet, been satisfactorily unravelled. It is a remarkable fact, that the product of good wheat has not only diminished, but the quality of the grain has greatly deteriorated. Then, it was a common occurrence to see an entire crop of wheat as fair and plump as the best qualities of seed grain at the present day. Scientific farmers and intelligent laborers have been anxiously inquiring after the cause; and one has assigned the ravages of the midge as the main cause, while others have attributed the failure of crops to the increased severity of climatic influences following the removing of our extensive forests. Besides these causes, others have assigned another, to them, plausible cause, which is the diminution of those elements of fertility in the soil which are essential to the formation of the grain. But all these reasons have been satisfactorily refuted, in most instances, when taken alone. We must, therefore, attribute the failure—not to any single cause—but to a variety of such causes as have been mentioned, operating together to the great injury of the wheat crop. There is one observation in which I think every intelligent farmer will coincide with me, which is this: If a piece of new land be sowed with choice seed wheat, and a dense forest protects the field during the winter, and if the midge do not injure the growing crop, the yield will be about as bountiful as crops were forty years ago. These hints suggest what is required in order to succeed in raising a bountiful crop of wheat.

In the year 1861–62, I was ruralizing in Monroe Co., N. Y., when I penned the following suggestion, touching the culture of wheat in the wheat-producing part of the State:

In the county of Monroe, thirty or more years ago, raising wheat was attended with remarkably good success. Indeed, wheat was *the* great staple with farmers for many successive years. Many old farmers with whom I conversed, pointed out to me whole farms, here and there, and many large fields, where the yield was seldom less than forty bushels of most beautiful wheat per acre; and, in many instances, the yield would be fifty bushels. But at the present time, on the same soil, the yield is expressed by any number from eight to thirty bushels per acre.

"We cannot raise wheat now, as we could once," was the oft-repeated expression among old farmers; and the reason assigned, usually, was the "insects—the wheat midge makes such ravages in the crop." Thirty or forty years ago, they had all the advantages of a most excellent virgin soil, which was as well adapted to wheat as any other crop; and had there been proper care exercised with reference to keeping the soil in a good state of fertility, by making and applying as much barnyard manure as was practicable, there never would have been such a decrease in the number of bushels per acre, as farmers now talk of. Old farmers have told that "here on these fields we once could raise three crops of wheat in succession, and the third would be fully equal to the first." Of course, under such a system of farm management, the most productive soil that can be found in the country would fail to produce a remunerating crop, after so many years of hard cropping. I was assured that thirty years ago they were sure of a good crop of wheat, even when the soil was very poorly cultivated. But now wheat was the most uncertain crop that they attempted to cultivate.

WINTER WHEAT—*Triticum Hybernum.*
SPRING WHEAT—*Triticum Œstivum.*

> " In the rich soil, clean wheat we sow;
> Out of the soil, fine wheat we grow;
> In measureless store, we garner the sheaves
> When the kernels are ripe, and dry the leaves;
> Out of the sheaves, pure wheat we beat;
> Out of the chaff, we winnow the wheat."
>
> EDWARDS.

Wheat is one of the most excellent of our cereal grains. *Botanically*, wheat is one of the grasses. But, from time immemorial, the wheat plant has been cultivated for its excellent and fine grain.

The *origin* of wheat is not positively known. Still, there is good reason for the belief, that, when " the Lord God made every plant of the field before it was in the earth" (Gen. ii. 5), wheat was one of the finest productions of His hands. And, there is no doubt, that this esculent grain constituted a good proportion of the best food of the antediluvians.

The first allusion to wheat in sacred history is in Gen. xxx. 14, during the patriarchal age, by which we may infer that wheat was raised by the servants of Jacob. And, when the Lord sent the destructive plague of hail on the land of the ancient Egyptians, Moses has told us, Ex. ix. 32, that " the wheat and the rye were not smitten." In Numbers xviii. 12, wheat is alluded to among the offerings of the Israelites. In the days of the prophet Samuel, and during the reign of David and Solomon, this grain is alluded to in such a manner as to convey the idea that wheat was a kind of grain of great value and excellence. See Ps. cxlvii. 14, where "the finest of the wheat" is spoken of as one of the crowning blessings which the God of Israel lavished on his obedient people. And when Solomon dipped his graphic pen to portray the excellent graces of the Church, nothing would convey a more impressive and exalted idea of the beauty which he would describe than "a heap of wheat set about with lilies." (Cant. vii. 2.) Solomon sent wheat to Hiram, King of Tyre, when he was erecting the Temple. And in numerous other places in the Bible, from Genesis to Revelations, wheat is alluded to in a manner to convey the idea that it was the finest of the cereal grains, which rendered the most excellent food, not only for the poor, but for the rich and distinguished characters of the age.

There is another idea concerning wheat worthy of especial notice, which is, that the wheat plant flourishes in proportion to the intelligence and condition of the agriculture of the people. This is especially true as to the condition of agriculture. If the agriculture of a nation is in a low state, but little or no good wheat will be found there. On the contrary, where the people are industrious, well civilized, and their agriculture is in a good condition, in most latitudes, good wheat—either winter or spring wheat—is, or may be, raised with profit, provided the climate is congenial to the production of this cereal.

Wheat an Emblem of Civilization.

After alluding to the wheat plant as an unequivocal emblem of civilization, enlightenment, and refinement, J. H. Klippart, in his "Wheat Plant," writes that:

"As truly as did flocks of sheep in the primitive ages lead the shepherds to the threshold of that truly magnificent science, Astronomy, just so certainly did the wheat plant in yet earlier ages induce man to forget his savagism, abandon his nomadic life, to invent and cultivate peaceful arts, and lead a rural and peaceful life. There is not on the vast expanse of the face of the globe a savage, barbarous, or semi-civilized nation that cultivates the wheat plant. In the settlement of New England, the Indians called the plantain the 'Englishman's foot;' and in the infancy of society wheat may have been similarly regarded as springing from the footsteps of the Persians or Egyptians.

"The ancients, who had burst the bonds of savagism, and scarcely more than escaped from the confines of barbarism, and through the magic influence of the fruit of the wheat stalk, barely reached the threshold of civilization, retained a grateful memory of the plant, which was the prime cause of their amelioration. They erected temples and instituted an appropriate rite for the worship of the goddess Ceres, who was by them regarded, not only as the patron goddess of the crops, but the propitiator of sound morals, and the promoter of peace and peaceful avocations.

"In their traditions of the wars of the giants, the ancient Germans have a legend, the purport of which is, that Thor, the agriculturist, obtained possession of the soil from Winter, who had depressed, brutalized, scattered, and destroyed the inhabitants with his chilling blasts and storms of sleet and snow, and drenching

showers of rain, upon condition that he would introduce harmony, peace, and fellowship into social life by
the culture of straw-producing plants.

"The culture of the wheat-bearing plant compelled
the cultivator to abandon the wild or nomadic life which
it is not unreasonable to suppose he must have led; and
the time which otherwise would have been spent in
roaming through the forests, was now spent in contriv-
ing indispensable implements. First and prominent
among these were the plough and harrow—rude beyond
question in mechanical structure, and uncouth in appearance, yet they were the first peaceful, and at the
same time utilitarian products of civilization.

"Thus has the culture of this straw-growing plant
caused savages to abandon their barbarous customs—
has fixed in friendly communion many nomadic and
rival hordes—inaugurated the greatest era the world
ever saw, the era from which the human race may date
its incipient civilization—the era of labor. The continued
culture and increase of this plant has from the very
commencement called into action all the resources of
civilized nations. After the invention of the plough and
harrow, man's inventive genius was tasked to produce
a reaping hook or sickle; and successively during the
many ages of the historic period has this plant called
into existence the scythe, the grain cradle, winnowing
machine, sowing machine, thrashing machine, and
within our own day and generation, the reaping machine. The prolificacy of this plant has brought into
existence the cart and the wagon in the earlier ages of
society, but in more recent ones it has demanded the
construction of turnpikes and macadamized roads
through the pathless wilderness; that canals be dug to ·

unite the waters which flow to the northward with those which flow to the equator; that boats be constructed, and ships with wide-spreading canvas were found to be indispensable; and lastly, the steamboat, steamship, railroad, and steam flouring-mill were as loudly and as earnestly demanded in our day as was the rude plough in the first days of civilization.

"There is not in the entire catalogue of plants another one which has been as instrumental in the development of mechanical ingenuity, and the intellectual faculties, as has been, and is, the wheat plant. It is true that fibre-producing plants, and prominently among these flax and cotton, have exercised considerable influence in the development of mechanical inventions; but upon strict examination it will be found that very many of the principles of mechanical structures and combinations of powers had already been called into requisition by the fibre produced by the sheep, and the thread produced by the silk-worm.

"In countries where the agricultural art, or rather the culture of the wheat plant, has fallen into disuse, there has civilization also retrograded; and were it not for commerce with enlightened and refined nations, several countries would speedily relapse into all the horrors of absolute barbarism. Were the wheat plant 'blotted out of existence,' society would of necessity revert to its original state. In vain would the miner delve in the bowels of the earth to bring forth the dark and heavy ore to make iron. No iron would be wrought because there would be no use for ploughs, and consequently, no use for the thousand mechanical contrivances for sowing, harvesting, thrashing, cleaning, transporting, and grinding wheat. Is it not astonishing to reflect on the number of persons engaged in the culture of the plant, the number engaged in constructing and improving machinery to gather and prepare the seed, the number engaged in transporting the grain from place to place, as well as the number engaged in the manufacture of flour, and the preparation of bread. Truly is not the wheat the plant, the corner-stone of civilization, and would not the destruction of it over-whelm society with darkness blacker than the storm-cloud at midnight! Does the extreme cold of winter destroy the germ of the stalk in the plant? have the rains been too frequent and too abundant, or has a pitiless and heartless hail-storm levelled it to the earth? Then how many are the thousands to whom is brought suffering and sorrow and hunger!

"While the hands of industry are busily employed in securing the product yielded by the wheat plant, every one is eagerly and earnestly shaping his demand for a *pro rata* of the results. This one has closeted himself, and buried himself in the study of law; that one has seized the pencil or the chisel; another has taken to the jack-plane; a fourth has mounted the fearful locomo-tive; a fifth has intrusted himself to the treacherous waves of the briny deep; a sixth has picked up the sledge, whose uses were taught to mankind by Vulcan, and from sun to sun strikes the patient anvil; all, all having a single and identical object in view, namely, *that of exchanging the fruits of their labors for the fruits of the wheat plant.* Thus is the action of society kept in a continual round of exchange, like a bark on a sluggish eddy, forever departing from the shore only to be forever arriving at it, and forever arriving only to be forever departing. The pearl-fisher dives fearlessly into

the fathomless deeps of the ocean for the animal product found among the rocky polyp-trees; the miner
excavates the subterranean shaft for gold; the artists
produce articles of the most exquisite workmanship,
and like a beast of burden, the porter tenders the services
of his physical strength in order to obtain a proportion
of the products of the wheat plant. All that we see or
hear, all that is done, all that is spoken, written, or
thought, is performed directly or indirectly on account
of the fruit of that plant, which introduced, developed,
and to-day maintains civilization."

Old Crevecœur's Speech.

When the aborigines of our country saw the refinement of character, the spirit of philanthropy, which
possessed the hearts of their white neighbors, their observing chieftain, Crevecœur, of the now extinct tribe
of the Mississais, is said to have addressed his people in
the following pathetic remarks:

" Do you not see the whites living upon seeds, while
we eat flesh? That flesh requires more than thirty
moons to grow up, and is then often scarce. Each
of the wonderful seeds they sow in the earth returns
them an hundred fold. The flesh on which we subsist
has four legs to escape from us, while we have but two
to pursue and capture it. The grain remains where the
white men sow it, and grows. With them winter is a
period of rest; while with us, it is the time of laborious
hunting. For these reasons they have so many children, and live longer than we do. I say, therefore, unto
every one that will hear me, that before the cedars of
our village shall have died down with age, and the

maple trees of the valley shall have ceased to give us
sugar, the race of the little corn (wheat) sowers will
have exterminated the race of the flesh-eaters, provided
their huntsmen do not resolve to become sowers."

Botanical Description of Wheat.

Although this portion of my treatise on wheat may be
quite uninteresting to men who are solely practical, still
I think every ambitious farmer will be interested in the
botanical description of a plant so eminently valuable
as wheat. Boys in particular, I think, will be ambitious
to learn the names of the various parts of the growing
plant.

That part of the wheat plant which farmers colloquially call the head or ear, is termed, botanically, a *spike*,
as 14, in the accompanying illustration. A subdivision
of a spike, or ear, is called a *spikelet*. In some sections
of the country, a spikelet is better understood if it is
spoken of as a breast of wheat. At A, in the illustration, a three flowered spikelet is represented. B B are
the beards or awns. The ear 14 is called beardless, awnless, or bald wheat. At the right hand, 1 represents the
rachis, or the centre of the ear, as it appears after the
grain and chaff are removed, either by thrashing,
or rubbing the ears in the hands. The spikelets are
placed on alternate sides of the rachis, so that the edges
of the florets, 5, 5, 10, in the spikelet, A, of the illustration, lie toward each other. At 4, the glumes are
represented. At 13, a kernel of grain is shown. B, 2.
represents a kernel of wheat enclosed in the chaff; or
such portions are spoken of as "*white caps.*"

Certain kinds of wheat are remarkable for white caps,

Previous to the invention of the thrashing-machines, when the wheat was thrashed with flails, or trod out with horses, white caps were a serious annoyance, when

FIG. 2.—Different parts of a wheat head.

grain was being prepared for market. But thrashing·machines remove the inner chaff, or the white caps. At

2

4, 5, 6, 7 an awned glume and kernel is represented, with the grain laid bare. Before thrashing-machines were invented, farmers considered it an important characteristic of wheat to thrash easily, and be free from white caps. The old bald wheat, and the Hutchinson wheat always thrashed easily. But the Whiteflint variety furnished white caps in untold numbers. But now some wheat-growers consider the Whiteflint variety the most desirable, as the kernels are enveloped closely in the inner chaff; consequently, the wheat midge is not so apt to injure the grain as if the chaff were more open.

How Kernels of Wheat Germinate.

"Lo! on each seed, within its slender rind,
Life's golden threads in endless circles wind;
Maze within maze the lucid webs are rolled,
And as they burst, the living flames unfold:
Grain within grain, successive harvests dwell,
And boundless forests slumber in a shell."

The germination of a kernel of grain, the manner of the growth of the roots of the young plant and their ramifications through the soil, the unfolding of plumule, or stem, and the full and perfect development of the ear and the full corn in the ear, all considered collectively, constitute a wonderful mystery! When we consider what a very minute and tender thing the germ of a kernel of wheat is; how easily a score of enemies may destroy it, or how quickly some adverse influence of cold or heat, or of both operating alternately, may destroy the vitality of the germ, it is really a wonder that farmers are ever able to produce a single bushel of wheat.

The accompanying illustration represents a kernel of

wheat with the groove downward. The part marked *a* represents the main part of the kernel which supplies nourishment to the growing plant.

By cutting a kernel of grain into thin slices with a sharp knife, the germ or embryo may be seen at *e*. At *b* the plumule, or stem, appears ; and *c* represents the radicle, while *h* and *d* show the first and second skin of the kernel. The true roots issue at the points of the kernel represented at *f* and *g*. J. H. Klippart states in his "Wheat Plant," that as soon as moisture has found its way through the canals in the husks or skins, *a*, *a*, *b*, *c*, and *d*, so as to be in contact with the

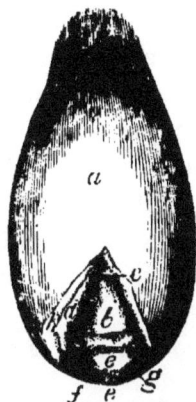

Fig. 8.—A kernel of wheat magnified.

starch cells, *e*, the moisture penetrates the cell-walls of the seed and its embryo, and there forms a strong solution. The seed has now the power of decomposing water. The oxygen in the water combines with some of the carbon of the seed, when the product is expelled as carbonic acid. The presence of moisture and oxygen induces putrefaction of a portion of the albuminous matter in the cells, which becomes an actual ferment, exhaling carbonic acid gas, generating heat, and converting the insoluble starch which is stored up in the kernel into soluble sugar.

The starchy substances deposited within the seed were undoubtedly designed to furnish food to the young plant until the roots and leaves have attained sufficient size to derive nourishment from the soil and the atmosphere. In wheat, starch is the most important ingredient of plant food.

The germination of a kernel of wheat is further illustrated by the figure herewith given, which represents
a grain of wheat highly magnified. B represents the
body of the kernel, composed of starch and gluten. A
is the cellular tissue, the original covering of the embryo
blade. C is the main root ; and D shows the hard cellular
matter which constitutes the base of growth of the root
and stem.   E, E, E are free cones of cells at the
points of roots.   F, F are lateral roots.   *a* is the future
stalk or plumule.   *d* is the course of bundle of dotted
fibre.   *e, e, e* are suckers ; and *f, i* represent the course
of spiral fibre.   *h, h, h* show the cellular tissue, or
covering of the blade.

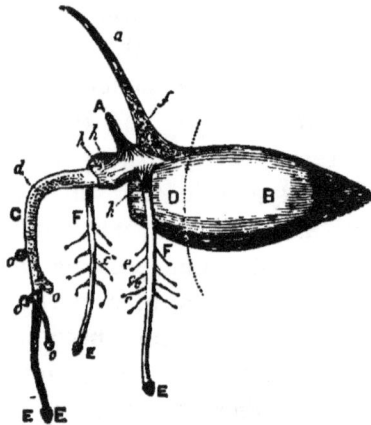

FIG. 4.

SPONGIOLES.

I have met with certain botanists who sneer at the
idea of there being spongioles at the ends of the roots
of wheat. Yet, all the most reliable authors of trea-
tises on botanical subjects speak of spongioles. And if

a person will examine the ends of roots of the wheat
plant, with a microscope, he will find a free cone, or
spongiole, at the ends of the roots E, E, Fig. 4; and
the same thing, highly magnified, is represented at
Fig. 5. The part represented by the letter *d* is the
root; and *c, b* is the lozenge-shaped cone. This free
capsule envelops the inner apex of the growing root;
but there is a space free from cells between the base of
the cone and the apex of the root which the cone covers.
Beneath this cellulated cone, or capsule, the growth of
the roots takes place, by the development of cells at the

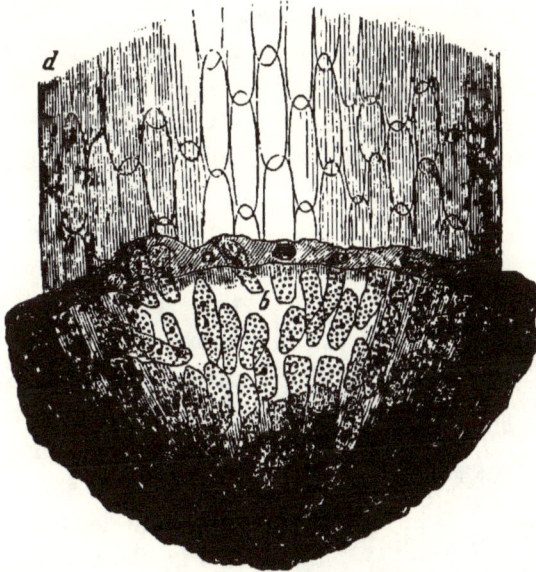

Fig. 5.—Spongiole highly magnified.

extremity of the inner apex of the roots. Soon after
the main roots are formed, suckers, or rootlets, *e, e, e,*
Fig. 4, are put forth, on the ends of which are minute

capsules, similar to the magnified spongiole represented by Fig. 5.

The grand practical point for farmers to consider is this: the capsules at the ends of the roots are thrust through the soil like the point of a plough; and the roots are formed behind them. This teaches us the eminent importance of assisting nature, by preparing a mellow seed-bed, through which the roots may spread with little difficulty.

The Stem, or Plumule.

The illustration herewith given represents the extremity of the stem of wheat, highly magnified, as the end appears when the wheat is coming up. Although this illustration resembles a stack of hay or straw, it exhibits the free capsule of cells and epidermic plasm, which are so nearly identical with those of the roots of the same growing wheat plant.

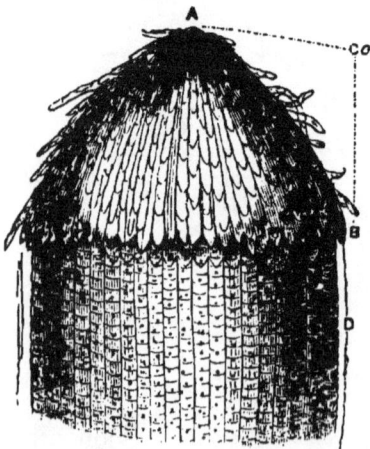

Fig. 6.—End of the plumule.

As soon as the plumule has forced its way through the soil, and appeared above the surface of the ground an inch or more —J. H. Klippart in his Wheat Plant states—that the stem gives birth to the first true leaves, as seen in Fig. 8 on a succeeding page, while the central bud is destined to become the future stalk. There can be no reasonable doubt that the cellular envelop, A, B, performs a similar function to the capsules of the roots, Fig. 4. In other words, the material in the envelop exerts a chemical influence on the soil which lies immediately above it, rendering the earth more yielding and pliable, so much so that the tender plumule can come up into the sunlight and air with little difficulty.

The plumule is of great importance to the existence of the wheat plant. By its existence we may readily demonstrate how dependent each organ of a plant is on the other, and how harmoniously every part performs its destined function in sublime silence. If the heart, or plumule, of the young wheat plant be pulled out from between the leaves, it will not be replaced by a new one. Yet, if the kernel or plant be not too much exhausted by a luxuriant growth, a new plumule will appear from the grain, or main root, directly below the surface of the soil.

The first effort of the growing plant toward more perfect development is to form a joint, or knot, immediately beneath the surface of the soil, and another a little above the surface. The upper one of these joints is the true commencement of the stalk. The joint beneath the surface marks the place from whence the coronal roots emanate, as has been already stated on a preceding page. These coronal roots are the chief laboratory for the preparation and distribution of the future nourishment of the growing plants.

THE ACTION OF ROOTS AND SPONGIOLES.

"There is no subject connected with vegetable physiology which more nearly concerns the practical cultivator, as well as the man of science, than the precise nature

of the *action of roots ;* for on them, more than on any
other organ of a plant, depends the health of crops of
every kind, without one single exception. That the
subject has not received more attention is one of the
curiosities of science. It is true there are many statements of variable character and value; yet even more
speculations respecting the manner in which roots be-
have—theories of excretion—assertions regarding the
chemical action roots are said to exercise on dead matter; but the quiet practical man who reads 'these beyond the atmosphere of science, is far from being
satisfied with what he finds in books.

"The question as to whether the roots of plants are
or not endowed with any special excretory functions is
one which has occupied the attention of many natural-
ists, as being one of considerable importance, as well to
the vegetable physiologist as to the agriculturist, in its
application to the principles of alternation of crops.
No absolute conclusion has as yet been come to, the
affirmative as well as the negative having been respectively maintained, either from general induction, or more
rarely from direct observation and experiment. The
opinion, however, that no such excretions take place, has
been the most generally adopted.

"The impossibility of closely following under the
microscope, in their natural circumstances, vegetable
phenomena which take place under ground, and consequently in the dark, and in an opaque medium, is obvious. As a nearest approach to it, Gasparrini has
caused the seeds of various plants to germinate under
glass, in water, or in well-washed sand, in the dark or
under diffused light, and thus examined their roots without disturbance in various stages and at various seasons.

He also raised plants for the purpose in vases of sand well pulverized and washed, so as to be able to free the roots for examination, at a more advanced period with the least possible injury. His numerous experiments appear to have been conducted with the most scrupulous care, for which, moreover, his well-known success in analogous researches offers a sufficient guarantee.

"It has long been known that roots absorb the nutriment necessary for the plant, by means of the young fibres which form the ultimate ramifications of the roots; that these fibres are terminated by a short portion of a loose and soft texture called by botanists the spongiole, Fig. 5; that this spongiole is the point of growth of the fibre, usually bearing at its extremity a kind of cap of a harder and drier texture, called the pileorhiza, a, Fig. 5, which is pushed forward by the fibre as it grows; and that, immediately below the spongiole, the fibre is usually more or less invested with a short down consisting of small spreading hairs. Gasparrini shows that the spongiole itself seldom takes any part in the absorption of the nutriment for the plant, but is nothing more than the young as yet imperfect part of the fibre, consisting of cellular tissue in the course of formation; that the pileorhiza is a portion of the epidermis or covering of the fibre, which, after a period of comparative rest, is torn from the remainder of the epidermis and pushed forward by the growth of the spongiole under it, and is ultimately cast off, to be reproduced by similar causes the following season; and that in the great majority of vascular plants the nutriment is either entirely or chiefly absorbed by the root hairs formed on the young fibres at the base of the spongiole, and which he on that account denominates suckers.

"Each of these root hairs or suckers consists of a sub-cuticular cellule of the epidermis, more or less length-ened out into a cylindrical hair-like form. It is at first uniformly smooth and straight, but at a later period either the extremity or the upper portion or sometimes nearly the whole length becomes variously deformed by club-shaped dilations, or irregular ramifications. The length of the suckers, and the shapes of these irregu-larities, are often more or less affected by the obstacles they meet with in the earth, but not entirely so; for when grown in water perfectly free from an impediment there is very great irregularity in both respects. In-ternally, however much ramified, the cell remains entire with one continuous cavity from the base to the extrem-ity of all its branches. Its walls also consist of a single membrane, no chemical reagent having disclosed any distinction between the walls of the cell and an external cuticle.

"These suckers appear to absorb the alimentary juices by endosmose over their whole surface. Like leaves on the young aërial shoots, they are formed on the young shoots of the roots; like leaves also they die and disap-pear after a longer or shorter season, leaving the old roots entirely without them.

"When fully formed, and before they decay, these suckers become more or less covered in their irregular branching portion (rarely in their basal cylindrical part), with viscous papillæ or adhesive globules, forming gran-ular masses, to which the surrounding earthy particles strongly adhere. Are these viscous masses excretions from the roots, or are they the residue of substances contained in the earth and chemically decomposed by the roots in the absorption of such elements only as

might be suited for the nutriment of the plant? It is
to the solution of this question that Gasparrini's experi
ments are chiefly directed, and he concludes that they
are entirely exuded from the suckers.

"In the first place he adduces several experiments in
refutation of those who believe that the tender fibres of
roots possess some chemically dissolvent properties, and
that it is by such means that they are enabled to penetrate into masses of hard substances, whether inorganic
or organic, such as the woody tissue of living plants.
In the case of the common mistletoe growing on a pear
tree, he followed the radical fibres of the parasite from
the woody tissue through the alburnum and the par-
enchyma of the bark sometimes to the length of half
an inch. They could be clearly traced their whole
length, although forming an intimate cohesion with the
tissue of the matrix, except the spongiole at the extremity, which was always free; but he never saw the slightest indication of any morbid alteration in the tissue
thus penetrated.

"In the case of the young plants of wheat, rye, barley, rape-seed, and others which had been caused to
germinate under glass, the process of excretion was
readily observed. Previous to the formation of the adhesive globules on the surface, the suckers were full of
a fluid in which floated a granular substance showing
clearly a circulation in two currents, the one ascending,
the other descending; after a time the suckers opened
at the extremity and discharged the greater part of the
granular substance they contained, the discharge being
preceded by a peculiar motion analogous to that of
pollen grains before they burst. The contact of a drop
of warm water accelerated the discharge; and if the

fibre was cut through at its base, the motion of the sucker was sudden and convulsive, and the contents discharged with considerable elasticity.

" In the roots grown naturally within the earth, the circulation of the fluid contents of the suckers, when observed, was slow and feeble. Those which yet retained the granular substance withinside, were as yet free from the external papillæ, while those covered with the viscous masses outside, were nearly empty internally. But in these cases the excretion appeared but rarely to have been affected by the bursting of the extremity, but usually by exudation, through the membrane forming the walls of the cavity, and that in a manner which could scarcely be explained by endosmose alone, but by some other force unknown to us, and which must be included in the mysteries of vital action.

" With regard to the effects produced by these exudations on the capabilities of the soil for the nutriment of other plants at the same time, or in succession, there is nothing to show that they possess any acid, caustic, or saline properties likely to act prejudicially on other roots. Whether the matter be compared to the fecal excretions or to the residue left by insensible perspiration on the skin of animals, it can well be imagined that it cannot serve for nutriment if reabsorbed by the same plants, nor probably if absorbed by others until decomposed; but owing to its extreme tenuity the decomposition takes place very readily; and as recent detritus of vegetable matter, its quantity is very small in comparison to that of the decayed sucker and pileorhizas, and of the numerous fibres which perish from natural or accidental causes. If in the relative effect of different plants on the impoverishment of the soil, the radical excretions have any effect, it can only be caused by the difference in the quality left in the soil by different species. Some of the plants known to exhaust the soil in the highest degree, such as flax and box, have few or no suckers to their roots and leave scarce any exudations. Rye and many other grasses deposit very little in comparison with crucifers and cichoraceæ. Hemp, on the other hand, which is a great exhauster, exudes a great deal by the roots; so do wheat and barley, but the exhausting effects of these plants may be traced to other causes. Thus, then, although from these experiments the fact of absorption and excretion from the surface of organs of temporary duration on the young shoots of roots is clearly demonstrated, we do not possess any data sufficient to affirm that the matter excreted produces any effect whatever on the capability of the soil to supply nutriment to other plants grown in it.

"One of the experiments made by Gasparrini is very instructive as to the noxious effects of vegetable manures in those first stages of decomposition which are so favorable to the development of moulds. In the month of January he sowed seeds of *Triticum spelta*, or as it is more commonly called *Spelts*, in a number of small garden-pots filled with well-washed Vesuvian sand. In one pot he placed a piece of young dead wood of Ailanthus glandulosus, in another a piece of bread, in another a portion of a green potato, in a fourth a portion of a radish root, in a fifth some parings of kid's hoofs and bits of nutshells, in the sixth nothing, for the sake of comparison. The pots were all watered with common drinking-water, exposed by day to diffused light, and in clear days for a few hours to the direct light of the sun, and placed under cover by night. At the end of a month each pot contained three plants, all, even those in the pot without any organic substance, equally healthy and luxuriant, about a span high, and with two leaves each.

"In the pot in which was the piece of bread, the roots of the spelt were much branched, the fibres almost all turned toward the sides of the pot; the numerous suckers were as yet scarcely modified, or had only slight gibbosities toward the extremity; no circulation was perceptible; the granular mucous substance inside was more or less abundant, and many were sprinkled externally toward the extremity with similar mucous granular masses. A few fibres approached within a certain distance of the bread, but none had penetrated within it. The bread had become a soft, putrid, spongy mass, covered externally with white branching filaments spreading from it into the sand in every direction, and already in many places having nearly reached the sides of the pot; and here and there a commencement of fructification seemed to show that these filaments belonged to a species of *Botrytis*. The spongy mass of the bread was also almost entirely occupied by a violet-colored mycelium which appeared to be that of a *Penicillium;* the filaments of this mycelium had also spread from the bread in various directions. Some had descended to the bottom of the pot, where they had attacked and produced a morbid alteration on one side of a bit of the rhizome of *Smilax aspera*, which had been placed over the hole of the pot. In another direction the mycelium of this *Penicillium*, together with a few filaments from the *Botrytis*, had reached a fibre of the *Triticum*, and had encircled it for the length of half an inch. The portion of fibre so attacked was soft, livid, and dead; and the extremity toward the spongiole was shrivelled and also dead. In the livid portion, the suckers were but little developed and mixed with the *Botrytis* filaments; but it was evident that the chief injury to the roots was produced by the *Penicillium*, whose filaments adhered firmly to their epidermis. In none of the other pots had the roots of the spelt come into contact with the organic substances deposited in the soil."

BLOSSOMING OF WHEAT.

In order to enable the beginner to understand more perfectly the character of the wheat plant, I shall endeavor to explain by the accompanying illustration, Fig. 7, the blossom of the growing wheat. This figure represents a glume of wheat in bloom, magnified twelve times. *a* represents a ruptured anther, which is that part of the wheat blossom that contains the pollen grains in which is found the male fecundating fluid, principle, or property of the blossom, by which two different kinds of grain growing in close proximity hybridize, or mix. That part marked *b* is termed the *filament*, or thread, from its thread-like form; and it connects the anther to the ovule or glume, as the case may be. The entire organ, *a, b*, is called a *stamen*. *a, c, c* repre-

FIG. 7.

sent the male portion of the wheat blossom; and *e, e* show the appearance of the female part of the flower. *d* represents the ovule, or unimpregnated seed, or part of the growing plant which is destined to become a seed, or the new grain. The pistils are always in the centre of the flower, and are attached to, or surmounted on the ovule, or ovary, to which they serve as ducts for the pollen grain, when brought in contact with each other.

It may be perceived by the illustration, that the anthers, *a*, have their exit at the upper portion of the glumes, so that the pollen may readily descend, by its own gravity, directly upon the pistils. The pistils and the pollen grain are covered with an exceedingly thin coat of mucilaginous matter, which causes them to ad- here, when they are brought in contact.

The grand practical consideration which I have had in view by recording these suggestions and facts, relative to the stamens, pistils, and pollen of the wheat blossoms, is to give practical farmers· a fair idea of the process of impregnation and hybridization. Very few farmers think of this fact. Thousands of practical men of fair intelligence know nothing about the means by which wheat mixes, and how varieties, when planted in a close proximity, mix and soon run out.

HYBRIDIZING WHEAT.

I pen elaborate suggestions under this head for the purpose of impressing upon the mind of every farmer the eminent importance of striving to keep his varieties of wheat from growing in close proximity, and conse- quently from hybridizing; and I could think of no more effectual way to accomplish the desired end, than by introducing to my readers the operation of hybridization.

D. J. Brown, in one of the Patent Office Reports, when alluding to the hybridizing of wheat, states that :

" The terms ' mule,' ' hybrid,' ' half-breed,' and ' crossbreed ' are vaguely and indiscriminately used by many writers ; but it is essential to accuracy, that more precise distinctions should be observed. The offspring of two animals of different species is a *mule*, and is seldom endowed with the procreative power, and still more rarely with a long-continued succession. The product of two plants of different species is a *hybrid ;* and although it is in general more prosperous than the mule of animals, it is still destined to yield at length to the beneficent law of Nature, which ordains that neither among animals nor vegetables shall the distinctions of species be obliterated. The permanent divisions among plants of the same species, often called ' varieties,' are properly *proles*, or races. The product of two individuals of the same species, but of different races, is a *variety*, as is every modification of this, effected by cross-fecundation with any other variety, or with any of the races of its species.

" Great advantages have been found to proceed from the practice of cross-fecundation, in the extraordinary improvement effected in the flowers, esculent vegetables, and fruits of almost every country. That the Cereals have only to a limited extent shared these advantages is a subject of just surprise to the curious inquirer; but, until very recently, it was doubted that much, if anything, could be accomplished in regard to them. Professor Gærtner, of Stuttgart, who has been said to have almost exhausted the subject in certain points of view; has declared the Cereals to be ' among the plants least favorable to cross-fecundation." In 1851, however, prize medals were awarded at the Industrial Exhibition, in London, to Mr. B. Maund, and to Mr. H. Raynbird, of the United Kingdom, for their respective collections of "hybrid Cereali." In their award, the jurors speak of the process, not as impracticable, but merely as being difficult, in consequence of the care requisite in removing the unexpanded anthers from one plant, and applying the pollen of another, and subsequently guarding them from the attacks of birds, insects, and other disturbing influences.

"Mr. Maund experimented with 'Cone' wheat, which contains much gluten, in the hope that by crossing it with a race containing more starch, he might obtain a whiter quality of equal value ; but it is not stated that he was wholly successful. Mr. Raynbird commenced his experiments in 1846, with the 'Hopetoun,' a white wheat, of long ear and straw, and fine grain, and 'Piper's Thickset,' a coarse red wheat, with thick, clustered ears, a stiff straw, and very prolific, but liable to mildew. Mr. Maund enumerates eight instances in which successful cross-fecundation had taken place, as follows :

"Mr. Maund found, as a general rule, in the cross-fecundation of wheat, that a strong male and a weak female produced a better result than a weak male and a strong female. This principle holds equally good in the animal kingdom as well as in the vegetable.

"The entire feasibleness of the production of new varieties of wheat by cross-fecundation, and its great desirableness, being thus established, it is not doubted that many intelligent agriculturists of the United States will be willing to institute further experiments for the purpose of developing improved varieties, or such as shall be found peculiarly adapted to the soil, climate, or demands of particular sections of the country; and, for their guidance, a few practical suggestions will here be given.

"New varieties thus produced resemble both parents, but seldom in an equal degree. In successful experiments, they are usually of earlier development than either parent, more prolific, and better adapted to withstand cold and drought. A late plant of an early, and an early plant of a late race, may be made to produce early, late, and intermediate varieties. Sometimes, when the first cross is not good, a mixture between it and one of the parent races, or even a second or third cross of this nature, may result in the desired quality. Two races, which do not cross freely, may also find a medium of union in a third. Again, a race that will not readily receive, will often freely impart impregnation.

"In every perfect head of wheat, there are, during the blooming season, both male and female organs of reproduction, three stamens and one pistil. The stamens, or male organs, shoot out beyond the chaff, or calyx, each having an anther suspended by a fine thread.

"The three males are designed to impregnate the stigma of the one female, or pistil, which is situated in the centre of the anthers. From these anthers, a powder, or pollen, is emitted, which adheres to, or is absorbed by, the stigma, and is conveyed by it down to the berry, or seed, at its base, and thus effects the work of fecundation. So decided is the preference of the pistil for the pollen of its own stamens, that it is often impossible to impregnate it with that of any other head,

while a particle of this is near. Impregnation takes
place best when the weather is dry and warm, as a peculiar warmth, and a certain electric state of the atmosphere, prepare the parts for this process, which always
occurs on a dry day. The opinion, indeed, has been expressed, that the pollen of the male conveys hydrogen
to the ovules of the female ; that oxygen is received from
the atmosphere, and carbon, in the form of carbonic
acid gas, from the roots ; and that, when the pollen is
destroyed by the rain, or from any other cause, the
carbon alone is found in the car; and this is the well-
known 'smut' in wheat. That pollen of the stamen is
essential to impregnation is at least certain ; and it is almost as certain, from what has been stated, that the total
destruction of the reproductive power of a particular
race of wheat must be effected, before the influence of
another can be felt. Two races being placed together,
therefore, a cross can only be certainly effected by clipping
the anthers from all the stamens of one variety, and leaving the work of impregnation to be effected by those of
the other exclusively. This may be done by any person
capable of distinguishing between the two races ; but,
perhaps, the safer guide to this distinction consists in
sowing the two in separate drills, very near each other,
say nine or ten inches apart ; and to render the work
still more sure, there should be no other growing wheat
within at least a quarter of a mile of that experimented
upon, the affinity between the pollen and the ovules
being of almost incredible force.

"As soon as the anthers show their first rudiments,
in a race upon which the cross is to be made, they
should be carefully removed, or clipped with a pair of
sharp scissors, leaving the female organs undisturbed.

Thus the races would be impregnated with the pollen
of one. When matured, the utmost care should be
taken to gather the seeds of the crossed race by
itself.

"Hybridization is an operation requiring dexterity,
a light and steady hand; and it has been frequently re-
marked that the operation is more uniformly successful
when performed by a female. Many singular facts with
regard to the structure of flowers have been discovered
through attempts to hybridize. In the common nettle,
the stamens have elastic filaments which are at first bent
down so as to be obscured by the calyx; but when the
pollen is ripe, the filaments jerk out, and thus scatter
the powder on the pistils which occupy separate flowers.
In the common barberry the lower part of the filament
is very irritable; and whenever it is touched the stamen
moves forward to the pistil. In the stylewort the stamens and pistils are united in a common column, which
projects from the flower. This column is very irritable
at the angle where it leaves the flower, and when
touched it passes with a sudden jerk from one side to the
other, and thus scatters the pollen."

KLIPPART'S SUGGESTIONS.

"When it is desired to obtain a hybrid from her-
maphrodite flowers, the first thing to be done is to remove the anthers; this is best performed early in the
morning, because the dew has swollen the anthers, and
prevents the opening of the little sac, which contains
the pollen. The simplest method of removing the
anthers is to use a pair of very small scissors or forceps.
Then at, or toward noon, carefully remove the anthers

from the flower with whose pollen we wish to impregnate, and shake them gently so that the pollen dust may
fall upon and adhere to the stigma of the flower from
which the anthers had been removed in the morning.
The heat of the day produces a dilatation of the pollen,
and thus facilitates its dispersion.

"In order, then, to hybridize, it is necessary to take
the heads of wheat which are intended to be the parents,
both male and female, when they have arrived at that
state of maturity indicated by Fig. 7, or *before* any of
the anthers have escaped from the glume. Suppose a
cross is intended to be consummated between the Genesee Flint, as male, and White Blue Stem, as female.
Then, on a dry and warm day—this state of weather
seems to be necessary, as at such times impregnation not
only more readily takes place, but appears to be more
successful—between 10 and 12 o'clock, hold the head of
the Blue Stem downward, and carefully open the glume;
then with a very sharp-pointed scissors, cut off the
anthers (*a, c, c,* Fig. 7), and let them fall to the ground.
Great care must be taken that no anther is permitted to
touch the pistil of the same head, either before or after
separation of the filaments (*b, b,* Fig. 7). This is perhaps
the most delicate part of the operation. After the
anthers have been removed, pollen grains from the
anthers of the Genesee Flint must be immediately applied to the pistil of the glumes from which the anthers
have been removed.

"In order to preserve the heads thus impregnated
from injury by insects or birds, they may be enveloped
in a hood of gauze, or Swiss muslin; but no caution
whatever is necessary to guard against accidental introduction of pollen grains."

CHARACTERISTICS OF A PERFECT VARIETY OF WHEAT.

As the growing wheat plants and ripening grain have so many enemies to encounter, and as variable climates and changing seasons greatly affect the quality of the grain and the yield per acre, it is eminently desirable that a variety should be selected for seed which will escape if possible, all the injuries incident to the wheat crop. I will mention the most desirable characteristics of a superior variety of winter wheat.

1. *Early maturity.* This characteristic must not be overlooked, as a period of only a few days in the maturity of the crop, will often decide whether the farmer is rewarded for his labors, or whether the wheat midge destroys most of the crop.

2. *Prolificacy.* By this I mean, that the variety shall be pure, having been cultivated with unusual care on a fertile soil, until the yield will be as large as it is possible for the soil to produce of any other variety of wheat.

3. *Midge-proof.* The glumes, or chaff, of certain varieties of wheat grow with an open chaff, which enables the wheat midge to commit its ravages with very little hindrance; while the chaff of other varieties grows close to the kernels, thus offering a very effectual preventive to the entrance of these pests of the wheat field. A variety that grows with a loose and open chaff should be rejected, and a kind of seed chosen that grows with the chaff close to the kernels.

4. *A thin skin, or bran.* Some varieties of wheat will yield several pounds more of flour than another variety. For this reason, that wheat which will yield the largest quantity of flour per bushel, is more profit-

able to cultivate, than a variety which affords a larger percentage of bran.

5. *Hardiness in winter.* Very few farmers in our country recognize this characteristic of wheat. Either they do not believe it, or they have not given the subject sufficient thought to satisfy their minds, that one kind of wheat may produce tender plants that the cold weather will destroy, while the plants of another variety, growing in the same soil, will not be injured by the cold weather. I consider this characteristic of wheat one of the most excellent features that can be named in any variety of winter grain.

Let me not be misunderstood on this point. I do not mean that the young plants of a hardy variety will not be lifted out by the freezing and thawing of wet ground, while the plants of a tender variety will be destroyed by the upheaval of the surface of the land. That is not my idea. No wheat plant can resist the action of the frost in heaving out the roots, when wet ground freezes and thaws. But, what I desire to be understood on this point is, that on dry land, which is naturally dry, or has been made so by under-draining, the plants of one variety of wheat will endure the rigors of winter without injury, while those which sprang from another variety of wheat sowed at the same period, will experience such serious injury by the *cold weather*—not by being lifted out by the frost—that the product of grain will not be half a crop.

A farmer can determine by observation whether a wheat plant has been lifted out of the soil by the frost, or whether the dead or injured stems and leaves remain as they grew. If wheat plants die without being lifted out by the frost, the evidence is conclusive that the variety is not so hardy as it should be. Every wheat-grower should take critical observations on this subject, with a purpose to reject a variety that will not endure the winter satisfactorily, and to improve those kinds that appear most hardy.

6. *Regularity of Rows of Grain.*—A perfect variety of wheat will produce regular and uniform rows of grain; and the kernels will all appear of a uniform shape and color. When the variety is not perfect, the heads will exhibit irregularities of form, like the Weeks Wheat on a succeeding page. The Andriolo shows a perfect wheat. The form of the heads, the color and shape of the kernels, may always be relied on, as a certain index to the purity of the variety.

7. *Stiffness of Straw.*—Some kinds of wheat will lodge, or fall flat to the ground, long before harvest time; while the stems of another kind will maintain an erect position until the grain is perfectly matured. The ears of grain will never swell out full and plump, filled with large kernels, if the stems are not kept in an erect position till harvest time. Grain that has a slender straw, therefore, should be rejected; and a variety should be chosen that produces stems which will not lodge, unless the growing crop is beaten down by protracted storms in connection with driving wind.

THE HABIT OF THE WHEAT PLANT.

By *habit* is understood the manner of growth and development of the stem, leaves, and roots. In order to be able to cultivate wheat with satisfactory success, a farmer should have a correct understanding and a lively appreciation of the habit of the growing plants, which will enable him to prepare the soil, put in the seed at

3

the proper depth, sow the most desirable quantity per
acre, and give the growing crop the proper cultivation.

In order to obtain a more correct idea of the habit
of the wheat plant, experiments should be made by
planting a few kernels of wheat.

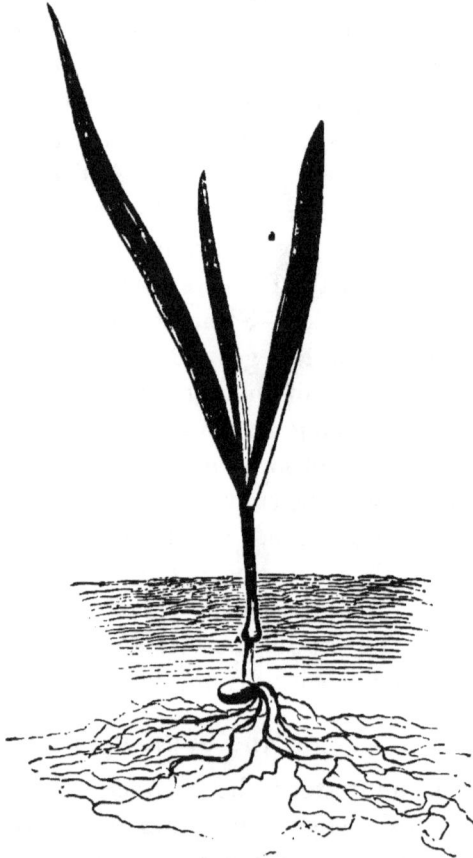

Fig. 8.—Wheat plant.

The accompanying illustration of a young wheat plant,
which sprang from a kernel planted by myself, will

serve to show something of the habit of wheat. Every
kernel sends out numerous long roots and rootlets, as
represented by the figure. The kernel was buried about
one inch deep. The longest leaf was about four inches
long when the sketch was made. The roots which
spring from the kernel are called the primary roots.
At A, a little below the surface of the soil, is a ring, or
bulb, in the stem, from whence the coronal, or secondary
roots spring, which all spread out horizontally; while the
primary roots strike downward as far as the soil has been
pulverized; and where the subsoil is not compact, the
roots frequently grow from one to four feet below the
stratum of soil moved by the plough.

Here is a point of eminently practical importance to
wheat-growers, which will be explained more fully under
the heading of the Advantages of Drilling in the Seed,
viz.: when the grain is deposited from one to two inches
deep, the primary roots, which issue from the kernel,
and the secondary roots springing from the joint A, are
so near each other that freezing and thawing of the soil
is not so liable to injure the plants during a mild winter
or late spring, as the numerous roots and fibres hold the
soil in a kind of mat, which prevents the frost from
heaving out the young plants.

The habit of the wheat plant is further illustrated by
the accompanying figure of a wheat plant which
sprang from a kernel planted six inches below the surface. The leaves, it will be perceived, appear slender
and not so strong and luxuriant as those of the preceding plant. There is a plausible and philosophical
reason for it. The substance which composes the kernel
is transformed into the primary roots and stem. If the
kernel is small, and is buried deep, there is sometimes

not enough nourishment in it to form a stem to reach the surface of the ground. When this is the case, both roots and stem cease to grow, and die before the young plant has come up. In five days after the kernel was planted, the first leaf appeared. In two days more the leaves were developed as here represented. The joint at A, insures the formation of a system of secondary roots, the office of which is to take up nourishment for the growth and fructification of the plant. At this point also the tillering of the plant takes place, and not where the primary roots unite with the stem at the base. The stem of this plant is represented as having been doubled.

Fig. 9.—A young wheat plant from a kernel planted deep.

TILLERING OF THE WHEAT PLANT.

As an effectual means of multiplying the young wheat plants, where the soil is sufficiently rich to sustain more than one stem, nature has provided for an increase of the stems, just in proportion to the amount of roots.

The illustration herewith given represents a stool of growing wheat which has sprung from a single kernel. If the soil is rich, so that large and strong roots are formed which afford more nourishment than one stem can appropriate to its growth and development; other plumules or stems will continue to appear until they can take up all the nourishment that the complete mat of roots supplies. See this subject more fully explained under the head of Thick and Thin Seeding.

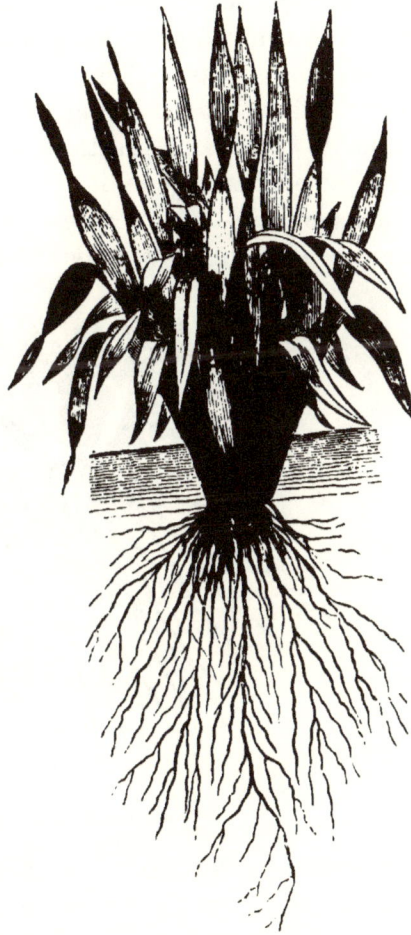

FIG. 10.—Stool of wheat.

The tillers always spring from the joint, knot, or bulb, just below the surface of the ground, when the seed is planted more than one inch deep. When the kernels are planted very shallow, it seems difficult to determine whether the new stems or tillers start from the grain, from the seminal, or primary roots, or from the coronal, or secondary roots. This a matter of little consequence. Yet the fact that the young wheat plant does tiller is a valuable one; and practical wheat-growers may take profitable advantage of it.

I have seen stools of wheat having forty-eight stems; and have had reliable accounts of stools of over seventy

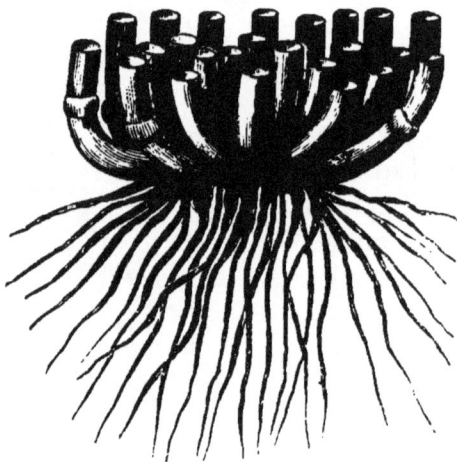

Fig. 11.—Stool of stubble.

stems with perfect heads. C. Miller planted a few kernels of wheat on the 2d day of June; and in August, one of the plants had tillered so much that he was enabled to divide it into eighteen distinct plants, all of which were transplanted. After a few weeks, these had tillered to such an extent, that the number of single plants put out before winter was sixty-seven. The next spring all these plants continued to tiller, until the number of growing stalks, from one kernel, amounted to five hundred. The soil was in an excellent state of fertility ; and the product of grain reported from a single kernel, was so large, that I cannot receive it with sufficient confidence to enable me to record the result in this place. What I have penned will be amply sufficient to show the practical farmer, when he has only one or a dozen kernels of wheat, how he may obtain more than a thousand-fold in one season. By understanding the habit of the wheat plant, when producing a new variety of grain, a farmer may accomplish in one year, more than he would be able to do in three seasons, if he be ignorant of this peculiar habit of the growing plant.

How the Stems are Formed.

Trees are exogenous plants ; but wheat and the other grains are endogenous. Trees and some other kinds of plants increase in height by the growth of the outside and the outer extremity of branches. But the stems of wheat increase in height by lengthening the cylindrical portions between the joints. The straw, or tubular stem, is formed nearly the way that lead pipe is made. The melted lead is forced out of an issue at the under side of a huge iron mould, by means of a piston fitting airtight, which is forced down upon the lead equal to a superincumbent pressure of one thousand tons ! The tube issues from the mould slowly, so that the metal has sufficient time to cool before it leaves the mould. Within a space of six inches in the mould, the lead pipe may be found in every stage of formation, from perfect liquidity to a solid. Perhaps an inch from the outside of the issue of the mould, the lead is in a semi-plastic state. A little farther up, the lead tube is in a semi-fluid condition. On the upper side of the joints of wheat straw, down in the sheaths, which fit the straw cylinders perfectly air-tight, the material which forms the straw is in a liquid state. The sheath is the mould, and the straw is the piston. By the vital expansion of the liquid above the joints, the length of the straw is increased between them, so that the upward growth of the plant takes place above every joint. If there be six joints in one straw, and the length of each is increased only one-eighth of an inch in twenty-four hours, the head of grain will be elevated above the roots three-fourths of an inch per day.

These facts in vegetable physiology will enable us to understand why the stalks of Indian corn often grow more than two inches in height in less than a day; and we perceive, also, something of the practical importance of having an abundant supply of nourishment for the roots of the growing wheat to take up and appropriate to the growth and development of the straw, at that critical period when portions of the straw are in a liquid state; as the wheat plant cannot lay up in store plant food to be employed in promoting the growth of the various parts at the time when the pabulum is needed most. The growth of wheat plants suggests many interesting thoughts to which I shall not allude, as the purpose of this treatise is primarily to bring out items of a practical character, without burdening the reader with interesting theories of no practical utility.

CLIMATOLOGY OF WHEAT.

For more than thirty years, I have taken observations on this subject, with a special reference to ascertaining what are the facts in the case with reference to the climatology of the wheat plant. My purpose has been, if possible, to lay down some reliable guide for beginners who may exist hereafter. But I regret to say, that I have been able to find nothing to corroborate the popular theory in relation to selecting wheat from different latitudes, with a view to secure a variety that will ripen as early as it possible for a crop of wheat to mature. (I may state, in parentheses, in this place, as the idea is quite irrelevant to the subject, that the ultimate object in procuring seed wheat from other climates is to get a variety of grain that will ripen before the wheat midge commences its ravages. Late-ripening wheat is far more liable to be destroyed by the wheat midge than if the grain matured ten to fourteen days earlier. See this subject elucidated under its appropriate heading—*Selecting Early Varieties.*)

Farmers have always said that, in order to obtain a variety of grain that will ripen earlier in the season, the seed must be obtained in a latitude farther to the north, except for wheat, which must be brought from a southern latitude. Numerous experiments have been recorded, showing that wheat brought from a latitude farther north, failed to mature as early in the season as the same variety had been accustomed to ripen where the seed grew; and when the seed was brought from the south, the same failure was observable.

I have, therefore, arrived at the following deliberate,

3*

and I think correct conclusion: that wheat is not different from Indian corn, and other grain, as it regards
climatology. I believe that seed wheat is governed by
the same laws that control other useful plants. The
seasons are so different that the same variety, cultivated
by the same farmer, and where soil and location are as
nearly alike as it is practicable to have them, will not
ripen at the same period in two, three, or four succeeding harvests. Consequently, when seed is brought from
the north, and it fails to produce a satisfactory crop, and
to ripen as soon as the same variety has been accustomed to mature, nothing definite is proved, in regard
to the climatology of the wheat plant; because the
field where the wheat was grown, may have been a
warm and quick soil, having a southern exposure ; and
the crop may have had the advantages of superior cultivation and a propitious season, and every circumstance
favoring a bountiful crop. On the contrary, the seed
may be sowed in a soil not so fertile as where it grew,
which would make a marked difference in the next crop.
Besides this, the soil may be cold, clammy, and late, the
cultivation inferior, the season unpropitious, and everything adverse to the production of a bountiful crop early
in the growing season.

This is the manner in which all our experiments have
been conducted. Consequently, the conclusions are incorrect. Because some farmers have obtained their seed
wheat at a few degrees south of their own locality, and
by superior cultivation and richer ground and propitious seasons have succeeded in raising better crops
than southern farmers, it is not safe and in accordance
with the laws of vegetable physiology to conclude that
we must secure seed wheat from a southern latitude in

order to have the crop ripen as early as practicable. There are many things that will exert a marked influence on the growth and fructification of wheat, which should not be overlooked when one is conducting an experiment to determine any·point touching the climatology of wheat, or of any other plant.

J. S. Lippincott, Haddonfield, N. J., writes on this subject:

"When importing seed wheat and any other seed of new or superior varieties of plants, attention should always be directed to the peculiarities of the soil and climate under which they originated, and those under which it is proposed to grow them. English varieties of spring wheat that are sown in February or early in March, have the benefit of early spring growth, and of a milder and moister summer than a spring-sown wheat can have in the eastern United States. The failure that has attended recent attempts to introduce English varieties of wheat is no new thing, such having been the almost universal result for many years past.

"If it be true that each variety of grain is adapted to a specific climate in which it grows perfectly, and where it does not degenerate when supplied with proper and sufficient nourishment, may not the consideration of the origin of each variety we propose to sow be of more importance than has yet been accorded to it in the selection of minor varieties, the product of our own country? The varieties of wheat that have originated apparently by accident (for there are no accidents in nature), or from peculiar culture, do not enjoy all the surroundings necessary for perfect continuous product. Causes yet unexplained are ever at work modifying the germ of the new growth, and the guardian care of man is needed to preserve unimpaired or to perfect the already improved sorts. In most soils we are aware that wheat degenerates rapidly if the seed be sown year after year where it was produced. Nor is it sufficient to prevent degeneration that the seed be taken from a different field; but that grown on a soil of different quality is to be preferred; and if from a different climate, but not widely diverse, it is found that the product is increased in quality and in quantity.

"English-grown seed when sown in Ireland generally comes to maturity ten days or two weeks earlier than the native-grown seed. In general, plants propagated from seed produced on a warm, sandy soil, will grow rapidly in whatever soil the seed is sown; and plants from seed produced in a stiff, cold soil are late in growing, even in a warmer soil. On limestone soils, which are often heavy, wheat seed, the product of sandstone regions, generally succeeds best. The experience of a Kentucky farmer shows that seed wheat obtained from a northern locality has failed with him, owing to late ripening and consequent injury from rust. The experiment was tried with three varieties of northern-grown seed, and with the same result in each case. When wheat from a southern locality was sown by the same experimenter, his crop ripened early, was free from rust and disease, and improved in sample over the original; while the main crop, in the same district, was ruined by rust and other diseases. This experience was corroborated by the result of four seasons of growth; and the southern-grown seed, because of its early ripening, is rapidly superseding all the later wheats in the district referred to. The kind of wheat introduced from the more southern region of Tennessee, or perhaps northern Alabama, is the 'Early May,' which, though small, possesses superior flouring qualities, and is now the ordinary wheat of some northern counties of Kentucky, where it does not deteriorate, but improves in quality. The controversy that was originated by the introduction of the Tennessee 'Early May' wheat into northern localities appears to have settled into the belief that the selection of southern-grown, early-ripening varieties is judicious where it is necessary that the grain should attain early maturity.

" The 'Mediterranean' is an early-ripening southern wheat, which it is said was introduced in 1819 from Genoa, Italy, by John Gordon, of Wilmington, Delaware. It is still an early-ripening and very valuable wheat, adapted to many districts where the more tender varieties, subject to the attacks of the Hessian fly, midge, or the rust, have rendered resort to this kind necessary. The introduction of the Mediterranean has proved an invaluable boon to many districts. Many other valuable kinds, noted for early maturity, etc., are of southern origin. The Rochester, or original White Flint, is said to have been of Spanish origin. The Turkish White Flint is not affected by fly, rust, or midge. The China or China Velvet wheat ripens at the same early date as does the 'Mediterranean,' as also does the Malta, or White Smooth Mediterranean. The 'Early Japan' wheat, from seed brought by Commodore Perry, is also from a warmer region than our own, and ripens early. So valuable has this variety been deemed by one grower, that he asserts that had Commodore Perry brought many bushels, it would ere . this have paid the expenses of the expedition from the increased productiveness through early ripening and adaptation to the wants of the country.

"All attempts to ripen wheat early by sending farther north for seed have signally failed, says a Kentucky farmer. The experiment of sowing Canada-grown wheat in Pennsylvania resulted in a ripening of the crop two weeks later than that grown from native seed. As to the cereals, which, as we have said, possess great flexibility, and are readily subject to the influences of soil and climate, we might naturally expect to find that wheat grown for a long time in southern Tennessee or northern Alabama, where the mean temperature of March equals, if it does not surpass, that of April in northern Kentucky and southern Ohio, would acquire a tendency to early vegetation, which it would retain when removed to more northern localities, and the plant be thus enabled by early maturity to escape the high heats of early summer, and insect enemies which appear at the period of the late ripening of northern-grown wheats. Though it may be advisable to use southern-grown wheat for seed, the rule, we fear, will not apply if such seed has grown more than two or three degrees farther south. All northern planters who have experimented with southern-grown seed-maize have learned that they cannot ripen the crop if the seed has been brought from a few degrees of lower latitude. This arises from the sudden decline of the temperature of September and October, and the early access of killing frosts, which shorten the period of growth to which the large and rank-growing southern kinds of corn have been accustomed, though the summer heats may have been the same as they had known in their native place. In the case of the southern wheats removed to a northern soil, the variety is not more rank or strong-growing, does not appear to require a longer season, but has had impressed upon it a proclivity to early vegetation by the influence of the early heats of March and April, which are not known in the north until April and May respectively."

DIFFERENCE BETWEEN WINTER WHEAT AND SPRING WHEAT.

It has been maintained by writers on wheat culture that the distinction between winter and spring wheat is one which arises entirely from the season in which the seed has usually been sown; and that they can readily be converted into each other by sowing earlier or later, and gradually accelerating or retarding their growths. If a winter variety is caused to germinate slightly, and then checked by exposure to a low temperature, or freezing, until it can be sown in spring, some writers have asserted that it may be converted into a spring wheat.

It requires a long time to change winter wheat into a spring crop. Still, it can be done, by persevering for half a dozen successive years. The usual way to change a winter wheat to spring variety is, to put in the seed a month later every season, until the period of vernal seed-time is reached. This makes it necessary to sow wheat during the winter months. But the desired object can be accomplished in a much more expeditious way than to sow seed in December, and the product of that crop, the next January, and the next season in February, the next in March, and the next in April.

The most expeditious way to change winter wheat to

spring grain is, to have the ground all ready for the seed in late autumn; and then, the day before the ground is frozen up solid, sow and harrow in, or drill in the seed. Unless the ground is covered with a deep snow, the grain will seldom germinate until the following spring. (Read the remarks on another page of this treatise, under the head of *Sowing Wheat in Winter*.) Should there be a heavy body of snow on the ground for two or three months, the wheat will sometimes vegetate, and get a fair start, before the growing season commences the next spring. As a general rule, wheat sowed at such a time does not succeed satisfactorily the first, nor the second season. But let the seed be selected with care for a few successive years, and sowed in the early part of the growing season; and after a few years, if the experiment has been conducted on a soil which is in an excellent state of fertility, a new variety of spring wheat will have been secured.

In attempting to produce a new variety of spring wheat from winter grain, seed of a very hardy and prolific variety should be selected, in preference to taking seed of some ordinary variety.

A writer inquired of the Editor of the "Germantown Telegraph": "What is Spring Wheat? Is it a distinct species of grain from winter wheat, and if so, where has it come from? If not, how was it produced from winter wheat? I have applied in many quarters for answers to these questions without success. A reply will oblige many besides myself." The Editor answered: "Spring wheat is a mere variety of winter wheat. Some of the oldest botanists made them distinct species; but winter wheat, sown early in spring, has ripened grain the same year; and other changes are produced in a similar way.

There are many varieties of wheat, of more or less permanence—produced by a difference of climate, or by successive sowings of selected grains, with some continued peculiarity observed. Even the compound heads of the Egyptian wheat (see *Egyptian Wheat*) produce single spikes after a while."

The author of the Farmer's Dictionary states that: "The distinction between the winter and summer wheats is one which arises entirely from the season in which they have been usually sown; for they can readily be converted into each other by sowing earlier or later, and gradually accelerating or retarding their growth. The difference in color between red and white wheats is owing chiefly to the soil; white wheats gradually become darker, and ultimately red in some stiff, wet soils, and the red wheats lose their color and become first yellow and then white on rich, light, and mellow soils. It is remarkable that the grain sooner changes color than the chaff and straw: hence we have red wheats with white chaff, and white wheats with red chaff, which on the foregoing principle is readily accounted for. The chaff retains the original color when the skin of the grain has already changed to another. We state this on our own experience."

J. II. Klippart, in his Wheat Plant, says: "To convert winter into spring wheat, nothing more is necessary than that the winter wheat should be allowed to germinate slightly in the fall or winter, but kept from vegetation by a low temperature or freezing, until it can be sown in the spring. This is usually done by soaking and sprouting the seed, and freezing it while in this state, and keeping it frozen until the season for spring sowing has arrived. Only two things seem requisite, germination and freezing. It is probable that winter wheat sown in the fall, so late as only to germinate in the earth, without coming up, would produce a grain which would be a spring wheat if sown in April instead of September. The experiment of converting winter wheat into spring wheat has met with great success. It retains many of its primitive winter-wheat qualities, and is inferior in no respect to the best varieties of spring wheat, and produces at the rate of twenty-eight bushels per acre."

THE FASTIDIOUSNESS OF GROWING WHEAT.

It has been stated by a certain writer, that "the wheat plant has no greater enemy than another wheat plant." But I cannot coincide with that assertion, as it is not in keeping with the habit of the wheat plant. If the wheat plant disliked the presence of another wheat plant, the original stool would not surely throw out numerous stems by its side, which should be attached to the same system of roots. But it is safe to say that the growing wheat dislikes the close proximity of grass or noxious weeds. And more than this, wheat has a capricious taste for its plant food, quite as much so as human beings, whose taste is so delicate that they can subsist on none but the most delicious and concentrated nourishment. Wheat must bear undisputed sway where the plants grow, or the stems, leaves, and grain will never be fully developed. Besides this, the growing wheat will not appropriate its nourishment from the rough material, as grass and clover do. Some plants will decompose stones, and hard atoms of the earth, and thus prepare plant food for its own use. But if a lib-

eral supply of pabulum has not been prepared by the vegetation and decay of other plants, the young wheat plant
fails to attain its wonted size, and to yield its accustomed amount of grain. Growing wheat must have its appropriate and chosen pabulum, or it will be folly to attempt to grow this kind of grain. Wheat, like the
grape, must and will have *mineral* food. The wheat
plant cannot produce fine grain out of coarse straw and
barren clods of earth.

Force in the Vegetation of Wheat.

The exercise of force in the production of the wheat
plant is an idea that is seldom thought of by farmers
of common intelligence. There is a vital force exercised when the kernel first sends out the germ and the
roots; and this force is constantly exercised, until every
plant is fully developed and the seed matured. It is
one of the fundamental laws of the universe, that where
there is motion there must be the exercise of some
force. When masons build a house, a force adequate to
the erection of the various parts of the edifice must be
exerted in fitting one part to another and bringing
everything to its proper place. There is a constant exercise of force against the force of gravitation, until the
house is finished. So it is in the growth of a wheat
plant: the roots must be formed, and the stem must be
produced by the vital force of the growing plant.
There is great force exercised by the plant in throwing
out numerous roots, sometimes as far downward, or in
a horizontal direction, as the plumule, or stem, grows
upward.

That man who has made holes in the ground with a

crowbar, understands something of the force required by plants to spread through the hard soil. In many localities a wooden staff can be thrust into the ground three or four feet deep, with a very little force. On the contrary, in most localities, it is exceedingly difficult to work a crowbar through the soil. What a powerful force must necessarily be exerted, then, by a plant, in pushing its roots through the hard soil. We frequently have ocular demonstration of the force exerted by small plants and trees. It is a common occurrence, where the soil is heavy, to see a crust of earth, that is formed over the growing stems, to be lifted up, so that the young stems appear above the surface of the ground, often throwing off a crust of earth more than ten times heavier than the entire plant would be, were both weighed in a balance. Then, there is the exercise of a constant force to keep the plant in an erect position. In many instances, the force of gravity on the growing plant exceeds the vital force exercised in developing the various parts and keeping the stem erect. When this is the case, stems fall to the ground before the grain has come to perfect maturity. We frequently see the effect of the operation of the vital force of a tree, the growing roots of which will lift heavy flag-stones of the sidewalk several inches above their level position ; and roots of trees growing near dwelling-houses frequently grow along the foundation wall and among the stones, and damage the foundation of the dwelling to such an extent, that repairs are required.

In the production of every plant, from the most delicate spear of grass to the towering oaks and rocking pines of the forest, there is a wonderful effort of nature to achieve a given result. The numerous fine rootlets and the tender blades are met by opposing f rces. If the intelligent husbandman will break up the hard soil, and reduce it to a fine and mellow tilth, a large share of the vital force of the plant that is used up in pushing the roots and stems through the soil, will be employed in developing the stem, leaves, and fruit.

The source of the force of the growing wheat plant, for example, is the substance in the kernel. If the kernel be small, of course the vital force must be very limited. For this reason, tender plants cannot flourish luxuriantly, when they first begin to live, if there be numerous lumps in the soil. Roots of tender plants, like wheat, seldom have sufficient force to enter hard lumps of earth. The roots will pass around and between them. But, as hard lumps furnish very little plant food until they are pulverized, wheat plants expend so large a proportion of the vital force in performing what implements of husbandry should do, that but little force is left to develop and mature the grain.

Stevens, in the Book of the Farm, states that the force of the vegetation of a single seed is so great as to be able to raise two hundred pounds, as has been proven by the process being made to split hollow balls of iron.

PROLIFICACY OF WHEAT.

The prolificacy of our cereals, and of wheat in particular, is a subject that has been seriously neglected for many years past, even by those who have a reputation for being excellent farmers. Seed wheat should be selected every successive season, with a direct reference to the prolificacy of the variety. In many instances, thirty bushels of grain might just as well be grown on one acre as fifteen, with the same cultivation and the same fertilization. When wheat is in the path of degeneracy, the best soil in the country, the most favorable season, and the most thorough and intelligent cultivation, will fail to produce a remunerative crop.

Intelligent breeders of swine select their seed animals with an especial reference to the prolificacy of the dam that will raise twelve or fourteen pigs. In some instances we see this principle neglected or entirely ignored. And what is the consequence? Why, instead of twelve or fourteen sleek, plump, and thrifty pigs, the sow drops only two or three at a litter. On the same principle, we often see short heads of wheat only half filled with small kernels of grain, when, if the seed had only been selected with a reference to its prolificacy, the yield would have been twice the amount realized.

It is not possible for any one to compute the pecuniary advantage that would accrue to our nation, were all the farmers of the country to make a proper selection of his seed wheat for only a few. successive years. There is a broad and inviting field open on this subject, for every ambitious farmer to exercise his skill in improving the productiveness of our wheat-growing fields by producing new varieties of wheat which will yield large heads and plump kernels of choice grain. The *prolificacy* of wheat may be improved to a wonderful extent by proper management; and if a prolific variety of wheat can be brought out, that will yield only a few bushels more per acre than the ordinary varieties, the advantage in the aggregate would be a consideration of no small magnitude. Dr. Vœlcker, in a recent letter, before the Royal Institution, London, stated that in the County of Norfolk the average produce of wheat was, in 1773, fifteen bushels per acre; in 1796, twenty-eight bushels per acre; in 1862, thirty-two to thirty-six bushels per acre —the increase being due to drainage, tillage, and to the growth of improved varieties.

On this subject, Hon. Isaac Newton, Commissioner of Agriculture, says: "A new variety of wheat introduced into a district has in some instances proved of very great value. It is said that the product of one quart of a variety brought from North Carolina in 1845 had in nine years benefited the farmers of Preble County, Ohio, alone, more than $100,000 by the gain over what would have accrued from the continued use of the old varieties."

The prolificacy of a variety can be determined only by experimenting with it, from year to year. The prolificacy of grain cannot be determined by the appearance of the kernels, any sooner than one can select a prolific hen, or sow, or a prolific rabbit.

LARGE WHEAT STORIES.

I have observed, for a few years past, that almost every agricultural journal will record now and then a fabulous account of the enormous yields of wheat per acre, which are published in good faith; but which are, in reality, in numerous instances, unmitigated falsehoods, originated for some selfish purpose. I regret to feel under obligation to record this fact, that I have perceived with astonishment that honest and truthful men, whose word is sacred and reliable in all the ordinary transactions between men and neighbors, will sometimes tell stories about their grain which are really untrue. They do not mean to lie; but the fact is, they *think* that a large yield of grain will sound well for their culture as skilful farmers, as well as for the productiveness of their ground. Therefore, they *think* and *guess* that there *may* possibly be so many bushels of grain per acre. By and by they look at their growing crops, and venture to speak of forty, or fifty, or seventy bushels per acre; and after thinking and talking about the matter for a few weeks, they make the confident assertion that their ground produced so many bushels per acre, when in truth the yield was very much less than the quantity mentioned. I will record a few facts on this subject that came under my own observation, which will go to show that honest and truthful men will sometimes talk at random.

I knew a farmer who secured the prize of a county agricultural society for reporting a yield of one hundred and eight bushels of shelled Indian corn per acre. The grain was measured thus: A bushel basket was filled with ears as neatly as they could be placed in the basket. Every interstice was filled with a part of an ear. The grain was then shelled off and weighed. Taking this basketful of ears as the basis, in pounds of shelled grain for every bushel of ears that was afterward thrown into the basket promiscuously, *without* shelling or weighing, the yield of grain was *computed* at the amount just stated. The laborer who husked the corn disclosed the manner of measuring and computing the amount of grain.

I have known other farmers to state, in the most positive language, that they raised sixty bushels of barley per acre, and sixty bushels of rye, or forty or fifty bushels of wheat per acre, when they had not measured a single bushel of the grain that grew on an acre; and this has been done, too, when *I knew* that their fields never produced more than about one-half the reported quantity. I have known farmers, who had gained a great reputation for raising excellent wheat, write to editors of their county papers or to certain agricultural journals that their crop would yield so many bushels of grain—an enormous product—when their neighbors knew that they did not raise a greater number of bush-els per acre than were produced on other farms.

I once purchased a quantity of seed rye of a distant neighbor, who published that his rye yielded sixty bush-els of superior grain per acre; and I learned the next season that, to all appearance, his yield of rye was no larger than my own, which was less than twenty-five bushels per acre. Only a few days ago, I read of a farmer who raised seventy-two bushels of excellent wheat per acre. But I never could credit the statement. Men sometimes count the heads of wheat that grew on one foot square of very fertile ground, weigh the grain, and make an estimate how many bushels will grow on one acre. But the true way is to harvest, thrash, and weigh the grain that actually grew on one acre.

It would seem, that if a farmer can raise a given quan-tity of wheat on one foot square, he could produce a yield proportionately large on one acre. But let us have the exact weight of grain that was actually produced on one acre. These airy estimates of a large yield, which are got up for some pecuniary effect, are not the true motive to induce farmers to cultivate their ground in a more thorough manner.

I have in mind a farmer, who stated positively and unqualifiedly, that he was raising cabbages on his farm at the rate of 10,890 per acre. He said he had less than

4

one acre; but what he *did* have "*was*"—not *were*—large enough to fill a half-bushel measure. As he was a man of truth, a person was sent to see his cabbages. He had one cabbage in his garden, and only one!! By an arithmetical calculation, it was found that, as there are $272\frac{1}{4}$ square feet in one square rod, if one large head would occupy only four square feet, 10,890 cabbages would stand on one acre. So the man could not be accused of stating an untruth.

Farmers who have seed wheat to sell will frequently state that their seed grain weighs so many pounds per bushel, or that so many bushels grew on one acre; all of which *may* be true. But measures often vary in size. Scales sometimes weigh too many pounds in a hundred. And, besides all this, if a variety of wheat does weigh 66 lbs. per sealed bushel, on John Smith's farm, his neighbor, near by, or remote, cannot expect to secure an equal yield, unless his soil and cultivation are both fully equal to John Smith's.

I make these suggestions that beginners need not expect to grow a heavy crop of grain on inferior land, when they have paid an enormous price for celebrated seed.

Hard, Soft, and Polish Wheats.

Some botanists have divided wheats into different species, from some marked peculiarity in their formation. Others, considering that they mostly form hybrids when mixed in the sowing, and that their peculiarities vary with the soil and climate, have looked upon all the cultivated wheats as mere varieties. There are, however, three principal varieties, so different in appearance that they claim peculiar attention. These are the hard or flint wheats, the soft wheats, and the Polish wheats. The hard wheats are the produce of warm climates, such as Italy, Sicily, and Barbary. The soft wheats grow in the northern parts of Europe. The Polish wheats grow in the country from which they derive their name, and are also hard wheats. It is from their external form that they are distinguished from other wheats. The hard wheats have a compact seed nearly transparent, which, when bitten through, breaks short, and shows a very white flour within. The soft wheats have an opaque coat or skin, and which, when first reaped, give way readily to the pressure of the finger and thumb. These wheats require to be well dried and hardened before they can be conveniently ground into flour. The Polish wheat has a chaff which is much longer than the seed, a large, oblong, hard seed, and an ear cylindrical in appearance. It is a delicate spring wheat, and not very productive; hence it has only been occasionally cultivated by way of experiment.

"The hard wheats contain much more *gluten*, a tough. viscid substance, which is very nutritious, and which, containing a portion of nitrogen, readily promotes that fermentation, or *rising*, as it is called, of the dough, which is essential to good, light bread. The soft wheats contain the greatest quantity of starch, which fits them for the vinous fermentation, by its conversion into sugar and alcohol. For brewing or distilling, therefore, the soft wheats are the best."

LIMIT OF THE WHEAT-PRODUCING REGION.

. A great deal has been written in regard to the climatic influences on the wheat crop; and I am sorry to

say that, for the most part, theories touching wheat
have been promulgated from year to year, by men who
never raised a bushel of wheat, and who were utterly
ignorant of the fundamental principles of agriculture.
On this subject, I herewith copy a few paragraphs from
a work written by J. Disturnell, on the Influence of
Climate, for the purpose of showing how common it is
for writers to reiterate, for well-established facts, certain theories that are palpable absurdities.   The writer
says:

"The limits of the culture of wheat and the common
cerealia are not so well defined in the United States, and
Canada and other portions of British America, owing to
the want of correct meteorological observations in the
different parts of this extensive and unexplored region.
It is safe, however, to say, that in Canada it extends
north as far as the 48th parallel of latitude, from the
Bay of Chaleurs to near the mouth of the Saguenay
River, and from thence to the Lake St. John, 48 deg.
30 min. north, including the valley of Lake Temiscaming
and all the head sources of the Ottawa River, extending
to Michicopoten Bay, situated on the north shore of Lake
Superior, 47 deg. 50 min. N. lat., having a mean *summer*
temperature of 59 deg. Fahr.

"To the west of Lake Superior it embraces the valley
of the Lake of the Woods, on the 49th parallel, running
northward and embracing the whole of the valley of
Lake Winnipeg, elevated 700 feet above the ocean ; and
the great valley of the Saskatchewan River, extending
still further northward to the 60th parallel of north
latitude, in the valley of Mackenzie's River.   To the
west of the Rocky Mountains, in the northern part of
British Columbia, and on the Island of Sitka, 57 deg.

north latitude, the culture of wheat and other cereals is prevented, owing to the low summer temperature which exists along the northwest coast of America.

"On the south, wheat can be raised profitably in the western portion of Texas and Arkansas, commencing at about the 30th parallel of latitude, excluding the Gulf Coast, where cotton flourishes to great perfection. Thus it appears evident that wheat can be raised to advantage from Texas to the British possessions on Mackenzie's River, running through about one-third of the distance from the Equator to the North Pole, and from the Atlantic to the Pacific Ocean.

"The harvesting of wheat through this extensive belt may be said to commence in the latter part of May, and continue until the latter part of August. 'It is said that the ripening of the "staff of life" will move steadily northward about twelve or fifteen miles per day, like a wave, until it sweeps up to the northern margin of the great wheat belt. A marching regiment in Texas, starting for the north, could barely keep before the ripening wave; and if they halted a day to rest, it would pass them. This wave stretches east and west across the Union, from the Atlantic to the confines of Kansas, and as it moves north it will grow longer and denser.' Minnesota, extending northward to the 49th parallel of latitude, is one of the finest wheat-growing regions on the continent. Indian corn also flourishes in the valley of the Red River of the North, which empties into Lake Winnipeg in about 50 deg. north latitude.

"The northern limit of wheat on the American continent may be said to be on the line of the isothermal or mean *summer temperature* of 58 deg. Fahr., where is found a fertile soil ; while Indian corn requires a mean

summer temperature of 66 deg. Fahr. and upward, embracing a still larger area of the earth's surface for its
growth than that of wheat.

"In Europe, on the coast of Norway, and in Finland,
wheat is raised as far north as 61 deg., in favored spots;
while the hardier cerealia, rye, oats, and barley, are cultivated as high as 68 deg. north latitude.

"The growth of grass or hay as an article of commerce
is less limited than wheat or the other cereals. It may
be said to flourish from the 38th to the 45th parallels of
latitude, although its limits in perfection are much less
extensive. The belt included within the parallels of 39
to 43 north, within the United States, having a mean
annual temperature from 47 deg. to 53 deg. Fahr., is its
most favorite region, where are produced the largest
quantities, and the best quality of butter and cheese.
South of 39 deg. north latitude, except in elevated regions, grass is of an inferior quality, and not much cultivated. In importance, as regards its value as an article
of commerce, it vies with the product of either wheat,
Indian corn, or cotton."

ABSURDITIES EXPOSED.

I have great respect for historians and literary characters, who have forgotten more than I ever expect to
know about certain things. But, when they write about
wheat, I happen to know when they assert facts that
can always be relied on, or whether their suggestions
are merely assertions which can never be shown to be
correct; and which are not in perfect coincidence with
the experience of practical wheat-growers.

When I was young, farmers were accustomed to state

that wheat could not be produced on the slopes of the lakes in Central New York. But now, experiments in raising wheat have shown that the clay loams of those localities yield the finest wheat. If there is any wheat in the country, fair crops, with good management, can always be found there.

Rye was the great staple in the line of cereal grain, in New England, so far as farmers were accustomed to raise grain. Consequently, if a farmer provided wheat bread for his family, he bought his flour, at an enormous price; because the impression was that wheat would not grow there. I have in mind large numbers of farmers, who purchase all their wheat flour, simply because they have imbibed the erroneous notion that wheat cannot be grown in Connecticut and other New England States.

Wheat will not grow, it is very true, where no seed has been sowed. Neither will apples grow in many of the Western States and Territories, where people affirm that they cannot raise apples. The true reason is, they fail to give apples a chance to grow. They do not plant trees, and give them suitable cultivation. And it is precisely so with wheat. It will not grow where the soil is not cultivated and kept in an excellent state of fertility. I have no confidence at all in the "climatology theory," that wheat will grow only in certain localities. As a general rule, where other grain and sheep succeed satisfactorily, fair crops of wheat can be raised, if the soil be enriched with the manure of fattening sheep, neat cattle, or fattening swine. Wheat can be raised on the drifting sands of New Jersey, in bountiful crops, if the soil be prepared properly for the seed.

INTRODUCTION OF ITALIAN WHEAT.

In the volume of Transactions of the New York State Agricultural Society for 1841, Jay Hatheway, Oneida County, New York, has recorded facts touching the introduction of this variety of wheat, from which the following extracts are taken : "The Italian spring wheat possesses a property which no other variety of this kind of grain can claim—that of growing well and yielding a fair crop of grain upon land so poor, that no other variety will succeed satisfactorily. On inferior land, twelve to fifteen bushels of good grain have been grown per acre. On good ground, thirty bushels per acre have been grown; and on the best wheat land the yield has reached from forty to fifty bushels per acre. The original seed weighed sixty-three pounds per bushel; and the first crop was sown in this country in 1832.

"This kind of wheat has a bright lemon-colored straw, which gives the entire crop a beautiful appearance when the wheat is growing. The kernels have a thin skin of a bright brown color; and from a given quantity of grain, more flour may be obtained than from any other kind of grain grown in this country. The flour makes excellent bread; and some have stated that flour made of this kind of wheat contains more gluten than other kinds of flour. It is said that in Italy the manufacturers of macaroni prefer this kind of wheat for making this article of food.

"This kind of wheat was first introduced into this country by a gentleman from Florence, in Italy, who, marrying contrary to the wishes of his father, was denounced and disinherited; and smarting under the severity and reproaches of an incensed parent, he resolved to emigrate to America, and to engage in agricultural pursuits. He brought with him a tierce of seed Italian wheat to the town of Florence, Oneida County, New York, where it was used for seed with excellent satisfaction for a few years; but in consequence of injudicious management in saving seed grain from year to year, this variety failed to yield satisfactory crops."

Some allowance must be made for an enthusiastic writer of the foregoing account of Italian wheat, as every skilful farmer knows that no variety of wheat that ever had an existence would yield forty or fifty bushels of grain on poor ground. This variety failed entirely in some parts of the country, from no other cause than the one alluded to—negligence in saving the seed from year to year. With injudicious management on the part of farmers in saving seed grain, the best variety of grain that was ever known would soon run out.

IMPROVEMENT OF WHEAT.

A good variety of wheat is capable of being greatly improved, provided the soil is of the right character, and very fertile in wheat-producing elements. When a man sows a small plot of wheat in his garden which has always been abundantly manured, so that the soil is well fattened with such fertilizing material as will make long heads and full and plump kernels, he is utterly surprised at the success of his experiment in a limited way. He concludes that his unprecedented success must be attributed to the *variety*, when almost everything is or was attributable to superior cultivation and fertilization of the soil. A vast deal depends on having a variety,

4*

the characteristics of which are well established. Yet, if the cultivation be inferior, the cultivator will most assuredly reap the bitter fruits of disappointment in his efforts to produce a large yield of grain.

I herewith condense an interesting account of experiments made in the Old World by Mr. Hallett, of Brighton. I will point out to young farmers—as well as to old ones—certain points in which this gentleman as well as all others will fail, as the premises are wrong.

Mr. Hallett's first idea was to increase the tillering power of wheat, so that less seed would be needed. That is all well enough, provided the soil is sufficiently rich to furnish an abundant supply of plant food for a large number of stems. If a plant of wheat be induced by any possible means to tiller largely, and the land be too poor to supply nourishment sufficient to develop such a large number of stems, the heads must be short and kernels of grain small. On this same principle, it will be found to be more profitable to grow only one large ear of Indian corn on a single stalk, where the land is not sufficiently rich to develop two, than to attempt to produce two ears, as they would necessarily be small. Yet, if the soil be so well fattened that there is sufficient pabulum to build up and to develop two large ears on a stalk, let that variety be planted. It will be folly to develop the habit of tillering in any kind of grain, unless the fertility of the soil be improved at the same time. Mr. Hallett proposed to improve the tillering characteristic by early seeding.

His next purpose was to increase the length of the ears and the number of kernels of grain in every head. This he proposed to accomplish by careful selection, and by what he has styled "careful breeding." How far he has been successful the result clearly shows.

As a starting point, in the fall of 1857 he selected two heads of "nursery wheat," coming as near as possible up to his standard of what a head of wheat *should* be. The grains of these two heads were kept separate and carefully dibbled in, one grain in a place, nine inches apart. Of one head the best grain produced ten stalks, with heads varying from seventy-nine to fifty-five grains, or a total of 688 grains. The *finest* ten ears, selected from the product of the other head, contained from seventy to fifty-one grains, and a total of 598 grains. Of the two original ears, one contained 43, and the other 44 grains, showing a gain of from 30 to 36 grains.

Next year the best head from the first-mentioned ear was planted as before. From this the best grain produced 21 heads, containing from 91 to 55 grains per head, or in all 1,190. The best *random* head of the other ear was also planted; but it was thrown out as being evidently inferior to the others.

From this, Hallett deduces the first proof of the correctness of his idea that careful breeding and cultivation was correct, and not the random selection of good specimens.

During the fall of 1859, the best head as above, containing 91 grains, and the worst, containing 65 grains, were separately planted. The best grain of the former produced 39 ears, containing 2,145 grains; but, owing to the extraordinary season of 1861, they were so injured by the wet that the two best ears, containing respectively 74 and 71 grains, were the only ones sufficiently uninjured to carry on the experiment; so that the head containing 74 grains was selected to carry on the experiment, not because of the number of its grains—for there was a falling off in this respect from the previous year—but because of the increased tillering power.

As before stated, in 1859, the worst grain from the best ear was planted. It yielded 15 ears, containing from 87 to 61 grains, or 1,086 in all. In 1860 the best ear of this sample was taken, and produced 1,909 grains from 24 heads, containing from 123 to 50 grains. This brings our account up to 1860; and as the original stock had been injured, Hallett started afresh from the last-mentioned head, the best grain of which produced 24 ears, the best one of which contained 123 grains. In 1861 the best grain produced 80 heads, the best one of which contained 132 grains.

Let us now note Hallett's improvement: In 1857 his shortest head was 4⅜ inches long, contained 44 grains, and gave 10 ears from the best stool. In 1862 his best ear was 9¼ inches long, contained 132 grains, and the best grain produced 90 heads or stalks on one stool. One peculiarity in his culture is the small amount of seed used. In his field culture, where the planting is necessarily done by machinery, he uses but four bushels on ten acres. In his large experimental plots he uses seed at the rate of but one bushel on ten acres, and plants by hand in squares of nine inches. He is a strong advocate of early seeding, and puts his field crops in, in September; 4 bushels on 8 acres, for the first half of the next month, and 4 bushels on 6 acres for the latter half; 4 bushels on 4 acres for the month after, and 4 bushels on 3 acres for the last month in the year. If used as a spring wheat, he advises that it should be put on at the rate of 4 bushels on 2¼ acres. These directions are for drill culture, and is much heavier seeding than he practises when planting by hand on his own estate.

His experiments clearly show the tillering power of not only his own wheat, but of any wheat, where space is allowed for it to accomplish this important part of its growth. One grain from the best ear of 1861 was planted by itself on well-prepared ground, so that its tillering powers should be unimpeded by competition. The result was that, after the produce of this single grain was removed, the stubble covered an area five feet in diameter, with 84 ears averaging $7\frac{1}{8}$ inches in length.

Great Yield of One Kernel.

"In order to show how soon the product of a single grain of wheat may be increased, I make the following extracts from Hallett's pen: 'From one grain planted September, 1859, I shall this year, September, 1861, drill forty acres. A whole ear in 1859 would have planted eighty times as much.'

"'I can show you a field of seven acres now up, which was in one grain two years ago, and one acre which was in one ear this day one year ago. In September last (1861) I drilled thirty acres with thirty pecks of seed. This is now, September 30th, well up, and the plants as thick as I could wish.'

"Inasmuch as Hallett's success in England is very different from a trial in this country, I will give the result of my own trial for three years past: In 1864, two weeks before the end of the year, I received my seed direct from Hallett's farm at Brighton. It should have arrived sooner, but owing to causes over which he had no control, it was delayed. The next day a thaw ensued, and I was enabled to stir up the mud in one corner of my garden to the depth of three inches, when I came to frost. A small portion of the wheat was put in, one grain in a place, six inches square. Of course it made no show until spring, when it came up early; but not very thickly, though it tillered out so that the number of stalks varied from eleven on the best, to five on the worst stool. It did not all grow, and future experiment demonstrated that about sixty-five per cent. was injured in its passage across the ocean. The remainder was planted in the fall of 1865, just before our regular seeding time; and one quarter of an acre planted came up in about the above proportion; that is, about thirty-five grains out of every hundred grew. This was truly a dull prospect, and was made more so from the fact that the midge injured the grain of what did grow. Early in the fall of 1866 we planted some of the best of our own seed as thinly as our drill would put it on—say one bushel to four acres; and having some of our imported seed left, we put a portion of it in, alongside of that of our own growth, at the same rate, without any allowance for injured grains in either case. At this time the difference is in favor of our own seed, it being quite as thick as our regular wheat on another part of the farm, while that from the imported seed makes but little show, nor should we reasonably expect much from wheat seeded at the rate of sixteen pounds per acre, and but thirty-five per cent. of this to grow. Those who have tried to acclimatize foreign wheat know that it cannot be done in one or two years. Thus far my experience confirms Hallett's idea that by 'breeders' he has fixed the peculiar type of his wheat; for under the unfavorable circumstances of our first trial the best head was 5¾ inches long, and in the second one 6 inches long."—*Cultivator*.

I cannot forbear to allude to the disappointment which scores of farmers have experienced after having purchased improved varieties of wheat, at fabulous prices, of those farmers who had made their ground as rich as it could consistently be rendered by rich manure. In this manner, by careful selection and judicious cultivation, they have accomplished wonders in respect to large and long heads and plump and a large number of kernels. On the contrary, slack farmers, who never half-cultivate their land, have sowed such choice grain, and produced wonders in the line of small ears and diminutive kernels.

Every farmer who has any idea of growing wheat should experiment, in a small way, with the seed in his garden, where the soil is very rich. I can record nothing that will be so effectual in accomplishing just what should be done, and what wheat really requires, as a few well-conducted experiments for improving the excellence of the seed.

The Nomenclature of Wheat.

Wheat hybridizes so readily, and varieties lose their identity in so short a period of time, that farmers are in doubt, whenever a given variety of wheat is spoken of, whether they really understand what kind of wheat they are talking or reading about, or not. I have observed that wheat, which is raised and said to be of a given variety in one section of the country, is so different from it in another State, that when compared, side by side, the grain is quite as different as two distinct varieties. The old "Bald Wheat," which was once— say about the year 1830—one of the finest varieties of wheat that was ever cultivated, lost its identity in a few years, by being allowed to hybridize with other varieties. The same is true of many other varieties. In some sections of the country, varieties of wheat that were originally awnless, have some awns or beards ; and certain varieties which were known as bearded or awned varieties, became partially bald. Under these circumstances, one feels like a man pursuing his course in an unknown, dubious, and uncertain way. If our Government possessed sufficient authority and influence to take hold of this subject in a proper manner, and establish a common standard of merit and an intelligible description of each variety, and keep every variety entirely distinct from year to year, farmers in different parts of the country would be supplied with some reliable guide in the selection of the various desirable varieties of wheat.

Now, why should farmers not have standard varieties of grain at Washington, by which to compare the varieties of grain produced on their own farms ? It appears to me that if our Government would establish some standard in relation to wheat, to which the farmers, north, south, east, and west, could look for reliable information, there would not be so much confusion in regard to the varieties of wheat which are worthy of cultivation.

For example: Some competent person should be authorized to collect several heads of all the improved and *approved* varieties, from numerous sections of the country; and then select a few ears of each variety, and place them in glass cases, where farmers could see them and compare their own grain with the standard samples at headquarters. Besides this, every variety should be neatly illustrated by an accurate engraving of one of the standard ears of grain; and accompanying each illustration should be an intelligible and plain description of every variety. Were I the authority in the United States, I would do the same thing in this treatise. But were I to attempt it, my efforts would only increase the confusion in regard to the varieties of wheat, as my illustrations and descriptions of certain varieties, which might be quite correct in a given locality, would not coincide with grain of those names in other sections of the country.

To illustrate still further the extreme difficulty of attempting to do anything correctly, by way of establishing the identity of any variety of grain, the reader must remember that the author of this treatise may give an illustration and description of numerous varieties of wheat, which are well known in some States, but which may be very unlike them all in other States. This difference should be settled by some authority which the whole country will respect and receive as correct.

NAMES OF VARIETIES.

I purposed, when I commenced writing this book, to record the name of every variety of wheat that I could hear of. But, when I met with the long list of names in the Report of the Superintendent of the Experimental Farm, Washington, in the Department of Agriculture, for 1865, I felt so thoroughly disgusted with names, that I at once abandoned the idea of presenting the reader with a list of the numerous varieties of wheat. I will give a few, simply to show what intolerable jaw-breakers some men will employ, when a monosyllable, that anybody could remember without difficulty, and which a child could speak, would be ten thousand times better in every respect. Here they are: Frumento Andriolo Esastico Rosso; Tauntondean; Flickling's Hallet's Genealogical; Schonermark's; Canadischer and Wiezacker!

There is another consideration touching the names of the different varieties of wheat which has induced me to omit names, which is this: Wheat bearing the same name, which has been produced on different kinds of soil, will frequently be as unlike as two distinct varieties, even when both samples grew in one field, only two or three years previous. The introduction, therefore, of a long list of names of wheat, which has never been tested, and which will never succeed, even if properly cultivated, would seem to be adding confusion and bewilderment, where the subject might otherwise be moderately clear and intelligible for all practical purpose.

The name of every variety of wheat should be significant of something, if possible; and always short, so that it may be remembered without difficulty.

THE PEDIGREE WHEAT.

This celebrated variety of wheat, which caused so much surprise among the farmers of America a few years ago, is a winter variety; and one of the heads is rep resented by the accompanying illustration, as the heads appeared before the variety had been improved by judicious selection of seed from year to year in connection with thorough cultivation on a rich soil adapted to this kind of grain. I have had one of the original heads engraved, for the purpose of showing how grain may be improved.

The heads are not smooth and beautiful, like many of our popular varieties; and there is nothing remarkable about the variety, any more than there would be in any of the choice varieties of winter wheat that are now raised in various parts of the United States.

This Pedigree Wheat was a very prolific variety; and had the samples which were sown been cultivated on rich wheat soil, this variety would, doubtless, have proved one of the choicest varieties of wheat that was ever cultivated in America. This variety was defective in one very important respect, namely, the grain was liable to shell out easily, when the crop was not harvested before the wheat was dead ripe. The grain made excellent flour, and there was a small percentage of bran.

FIG. 12.
Hallet's Pedigree wheat.

Fig. 13.—Improved Pedigree wheat.

The head of wheat on this page re presents the same variety as is shown on the preceding page. But this head is an exact representation of the Ped igree Wheat after the variety was improved by judicious management, with the exception that this cut is more than one inch shorter than the original head. The pages of this book are too short to receive an illustration of the full length of the im proved ears.

This variety of wheat had one radical defect, as a popular variety for cultivation, which is this: the chaff was very open and loose, so much so that the grain would shell readily, at harvest time, unless the crop were gathered before the kernels were fully ripe. Besides this, as the chaff was loose and open, the grain was much more liable to be infested with the wheat midge.

Large numbers of American farmers procured small quantities of seed of European wheat-growers, with the expectation that they would be able to raise forty bushels of choice wheat per acre, where they had heretofore grown only ten to twenty bushels. But, in almost every instance, they were wonderfully disappointed, as the heads grew but a trifle longer and larger than our improved varieties.

Most persons who received and cultivated this kind of wheat, being grievously disappointed in the growth of ears and yield of grain, denounced the variety as a notorious humbug. But the grand difficulty rested in their imperfect mode of cultivation. The soil where the originator of this variety cultivated his wheat was exceedingly rich in those elements of fertility which are essential to the growth of large heads and plump kernels of wheat. But the ground where American farmers attempted to grow this European variety was only in a common state of fertility, and by no means rich enough to develop ears of such enormous size. Before heads of giant size can be produced, there must be an abundance of wheat-producing pabulum in the soil available by the growing plants. Then there will be no difficulty in producing a bountiful crop of excellent grain.

I have had this Pedigree engraved for several specific reasons, one of which is to induce American farmers, if possible, to make an effort to produce such a variety of wheat as this Improved Pedigree is represented to have been. When an experiment of this kind is ever made, care should be exercised to have every characteristic of a perfect variety of wheat, developed as completely as practicable. (See the Characteristics of a Perfect Wheat, on a preceding page.)

Another idea is, do not go to England for wheat. Select the best heads of some improved American variety; and improve the seed, from year to year. Varieties of wheat brought from Europe to this country must first be acclimated; and more likely than not, after the wheat has been thoroughly acclimatized, there will be defects in it, just as there was in this noted Pedigree Wheat. But if the variety be improved on American soil, the crop will not fail, so long as the seed is selected with proper care from harvest to harvest.

RED CHAFF BALD WHEAT.

In the Transactions of the New York State Agricultural Society for 1842, Rawson Harmon writes thus about this kind of wheat:

"This variety was well adapted to the soil in the Genesee Valley of Western New York. In 1803, Peter Sheffer harvested forty acres of this kind of wheat on the Genesee Flats, that produced sixty and a half bushels of grain per acre. The same season, this variety, sown on the oak openings in this vicinity, was nearly destroyed by the Hessian fly. Its long and well-filled heads, the white and beautiful berries, gave it the preference over other varieties for more than twenty years; and some farmers in this vicinity [Western New York] continue its cultivation. The bran of the grain is thin; and it yields flour of superior quality. In 1833 I harvested sixty-seven bushels from one bushel of sowing, which grew on one acre and one-fourth of land."

I have copied this paragraph for the purpose of showing what a profitable and excellent variety of grain this "Bald Wheat" was, when the country was comparatively new; and before rust, the midge, and the fly injured the growing grain.

FIG. 14.
Bald wheat.

THE WHITE GENESEE WHEAT.

This variety, illustrated by the accompanying figure
of a head of wheat, represents what is sometimes called
the Canada Flint Wheat, which is an excellent variety, possessing all the external characteristics of the best varieties of winter
wheat. It is hardy, prolific, has a thin bran,
yields a large percentage of fine flour, and
resists the ravages of the midge much more
effectually than many other celebrated varieties. When the seed has been saved with
care, from year to year, and sowed on a fair
wheat soil, which is in an excellent state
of fertility, this variety ripens as early as
any kind that has been extensively introduced.

This variety is almost identical with the
White Flint described by Klippart, who says
that "this [the White Flint] is one of the
most valuable kinds in the Northern States.
The heads are not long but well filled, with
thirty to forty grains; the kernel is white and
flinty, large, and with thin bran. They are
firmly attached to the chaff, and do not shell
out, except when very ripe. The heads are
rather drooping, with but few awns, the straw
medium length, and very white and strong.

Fig. 15.
White Gene-
see.

The flour is very superior; the perfect wheat weighs
from sixty-three to sixty-seven pounds per bushel." This
would be an excellent variety to select a few heads from,
for producing an improved variety, as it possesses prolificacy, and is nearly midge proof.

THE RED BLUE-STEM WHEAT.

This is an old and very popular variety of wheat, which originated in Pennsylvania. It is one of the

FIG. 16.
Red blue-stem.

finest and most profitable varieties of red wheat. The growing grain withstands the ravages of the wheat midge better than many varieties, but not so well as some others. The chaff fits rather close to the kernels, but not so tight as the chaff of some other varieties. The Red Blue-stem Wheat is one of the most prolific varieties that has ever been cultivated; and the young plants endure the cold of winter with less injury than many other kinds of wheat. J. H. Klippart says, in the Transactions of the Ohio Board of Agriculture, that this variety makes as good a quality of flour as does any red wheat; the grain ripens three to six days later than the Mediterranean wheat; but no variety repays good cultivation so well, or yields so little when indifferently cultivated, as does this variety. Many of the more recent varieties of smooth, red wheats were derived from this old standard variety, which has been cultivated in many counties in Ohio for more than fifty years. The regularity of the rows of grain and the tightness of the chaff to the kernels show this to be a very desirable variety to cultivate. With proper selection of seed, and superior cultivation, the yield and quality may be wonderfully improved.

THE BULL WHEAT, OR OLD WHITE FLINT.

J. H. Klippart records the following suggestions of this variety. He writes: " This flint, Old White Flint, or Bull Wheat, appears to have had three distinct origins, so far as Ohio is concerned, viz.: in Trumbull and other north-eastern counties it was introduced from New York State some fifteen years ago—there it ripens with the Mediterranean; is not much subject to disease, and is considered a good variety. In Stark, Harrison, etc., it was introduced as much as thirty years ago from Pennsylvania, and is now almost literally ' *run out.*' But in Franklin and other more southern counties it was introduced from Kentucky, ripened about the 25th of July, and was in consequence soon abandoned entirely. Ten years ago Samuel Cole introduced it into Darke County, where it is doing well; at the same time it was introduced into Tuscarawas. This flint is of Spanish origin. The head is of medium length and well filled—straw white, clear and strong at the root, by which it is prevented from lodging; spikelets very adhesive to the rachis, and kernels very adhesive to the glumes. It succeeds best on loamy soils, and is rather susceptible to injury from frosts and insects. The berry is very hard from its silicious cuticle (hence its name), in consequence of which it is less injured by fall rains, and will stand in the shock a long time without sprouting."

Fig. 17.
Bull wheat.

5

THE INDIANA, OR GOLDEN STEM WHEAT.

This variety is a white winter variety; but does not possess the necessary characteristics of a perfect wheat. One of its defects is, the chaff is too loose, so much so that the wheat midge finds easy access to the kernels; and the grain shells out readily when the crop is being harvested. Another defect is, the straw does not usually grow sufficiently stiff to maintain an erect position till the time of perfect maturity. The cuticle of the grain is thin, and the percentage of fine flour is larger than the yield of some other varieties of wheat.

THE EARLY MAY WHEAT.

This variety was once one of the finest kinds of wheat that could be found in America; and in some localities it is still cultivated with excellent satisfaction. But as I have not, of late, come in personal contact with the Early May, and as there are so many conflicting opinions about the value of this variety, I feel in doubt as to what I ought to record about it. I have no doubt, however, that with careful cultivation, this would prove an excellent acquisition to the best varieties of the wheats now cultivated in this country. Whoever has this variety, *still pure*, should make an extra effort to improve it.

FIG. 18.
Golden stem.

The Genesee White-Flint Wheat.

The illustration herewith given represents the celebrated variety long known and cultivated as the Genesee White-Flint Wheat, which was a very hardy and prolific variety so long as the seed was kept distinct from other kinds of grain. But after it had been thrashed with other grain and allowed to hybridize with impure varieties, the White Flint character disappeared. The original grain was of a superior character, and yielded a large percentage of flour. But after the introduction of thrashing-machines, the purity of this variety became wonderfully adulterated, so that there seemed to be but little resemblance between the varieties raised in different parts of the country which were cultivated for the Genesee White-Flint Wheat.

J. H. Klippart says of this variety: "Perhaps the first of this variety introduced into Ohio was in Warren County, by Thomas Ireland, in 1842. From there it no doubt spread through the valleys of the Miami; in many of which it forms the main crop of the white wheats. It is best adapted to high and gravelly lands, and rarely if ever succeeds on a bottom soil. In Franklin County it is regarded as a much surer crop than when first introduced eight years ago."

FIG. 19.—Genesee wheat.

THE ALABAMA VARIETY.

This variety is sometimes known better by the White May Wheat. Before this variety had been injured by injudicious culture and defective management, it was one of the most perfect varieties of white wheat. ever cultivated. The ears and fine white grain closely resemble the celebrated White Flint Wheat. In many instances, this variety did not seem to endure the cold of winter as well as many other varieties. Before the Alabama Wheat had been mingled with other varieties of seed, with which the growing wheat was allowed to hybridize, a bushel of the grain would yield as large a percentage of superfine flour as any other known variety. But by perfunctory management in saving the seed, this valuable grain, in many localities, has lost its identity. The Alabama was nearly midge-proof so long as the purity of the variety was maintained. In some localities, this variety, at the present writing—November 1867—is cultivated with eminent satisfaction. Klippart says "it ripens about the same time the Mediterranean does, but is easily winter-killed, thus betraying its southern origin; yields eighteen to twenty bushels under ordinary circumstances; it comes highly recommended from Morgan County. Its general appearance is very like that of the White Blue-stem, with this difference, viz.: the head, when fully ripe, is a deeper yellow than the Blue-stem; the stem just below the head is

FIG. 20.
Alabama wheat.

a pale greenish-blue. There are from eight to twelve breasts on each side, with four grains in a breast."

BLACK SIX-ROWED ANDRIOLO WHEAT.

The ear of wheat here shown represents a mongrel, or hybrid variety of wheat, as may be readily perceived by the rough appearance of the glumes, the irregularity of the rows of kernels, and the destitution of awns at certain parts of the head. This variety has not been introduced sufficiently to warrant a recommendation. I simply give it a place to show the difference between a pure and well-established variety and a mongrel. This Black Six-rowed Andriolo Wheat is the product of a bald and bearded variety, the kernels of one of which were impregnated with the pollen of the other variety. Such varieties should always be discarded for seed, as the yield will always be less satisfactory than when good seed of a pure variety is selected and sowed from year to year.

FIG. 21.—Black Andriolo wheat

RED, HAIRY ANDRIOLO WHEAT.

I have given a sketch of this wheat, not for the purpose of recommending this variety, but to suggest to farmers not to attempt to grow it because the ears look so large, fair, and beautiful. This variety is a fair wheat, prolific, and possesses most of the characteristics of a superior variety of wheat. But the large awns and hairs with which the ears are covered are a serious objection to its general introduction. The variety came originally from Italy; but has not been introduced, except to a very limited extent. It is evidently a mongrel, or hybrid; and before it can be cultivated with satisfactory results, the grain needs to be acclimatized by selecting a few of the best heads and cultivating the grain on rich ground until a perfect American variety is brought out. This variety has *prolificacy*, for which reason, it would be a first-

FIG. 22.—Hairy Andriolo.

ıate grain to experiment with, for the purpose of improving its other characteristics.

THE KENTUCKY RED OR WHIG WHEAT.

This is an old variety, known in various localities by different names, among which are the Early Ripe Carolina, Kentucky Red, and the Whig Wheat. This kind of wheat was cultivated in several counties in Ohio, with eminent satisfaction, for a number of years. But, as the crop fell an easy prey to the wheat midge, this variety was discarded. I allude to this wheat for the purpose of teaching young farmers the transcendent importance of selecting those varieties of wheat for cultivation which are as nearly midge-proof as a wheat can be. Many farmers, by continuing to sow this variety, which *had previously* yielded fair crops, lost hundreds of dollars which they might have received without any more labor, if they had sowed some other variety of wheat.

Klippart says, that in Kentucky this variety is known as the "Early Ripe" wheat. The ears are of a great length, usually; the kernels of a light color; and sometimes the grain is shrunken. This variety has lost its identity in many localities, for which reason, it fails to yield a satisfactory crop. In some localities, however, the "Early Ripe" is still cultivated with the best of satisfaction; and few varieties excel it.

Fig. 23.
Kentucky red.

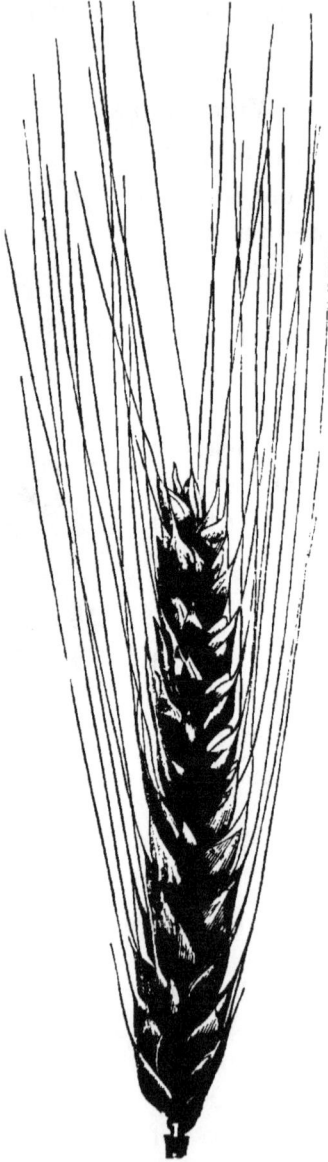

FIG. 24.—Four-rowed Andriolo.

THE FOUR-ROWED ANDRIOLO WHEAT.

The variety herewith represented is the Four-rowed White Andriolo variety, which was raised to some extent by the Hon. Isaac Newton, Commissioner of Agriculture, Washington. This is a beautiful variety, prolific, stands the winters tolerably well, and ripens early. The long awns, or rough beards, are an objection to it, as they are unpleasant to handle, and make so much chaff, which is a nuisance, when the straw is employed for feeding and littering sheep and horses. This variety has all the external characteristics of a perfect variety of grain; and were it properly cultivated, no doubt this would be one of the best varieties ever raised in America. The kernels of this variety are very uniform in appearance; and the variety is prolific.

THE DIEHL VARIETY.

The illustration on this page is an exact representation of the far-famed Diehl Wheat, which is familiar to almost every wheat-grower in the Northern and Western States. I know of no other variety of wheat, either spring grain or winter, that has been cultivated with more universal satisfaction than this wheat. It is a winter variety. This variety seems to come up as fully to the requirements of wheat-growers as it is practicable to have wheat. The grain is white and the crop ripens early in the season. It is hardy, prolific, and the plants endure the rigors of our northern winters quite as well as any other known variety. The ears are bald, or awnless, the kernels set very securely to the rachis, the chaff is close to the kernels, so that this variety may be truthfully denominated a "fly-proof" wheat. The grain does not shell out, when the crop is being harvested, as easily as the kernels of some other varieties. The straw is stiff; and thus far this variety has been exempt from injury by the rust.

"Colman's Rural World," published at Chicago, in a recent number, has the following remarks touching the Diehl wheat:

FIG. 25.
The Diehl wheat.

"This is the second year since the introduction of the Diehl wheat into this country. Its yield last year was considered above the average of other kinds of wheat

5*

sown here, and the consequence was, it was much sought
after to seed with last fall, and the whole crop was
bought up at $3 per bushel, at that time being from 50
to 75 cents per bushel above the market price of other
white wheat. In consequence of the high price asked
it went into the hands of many, and has been sown on
all the different soils of our country, from light sand
to heavy clay. The growth of straw has been good on
all, but it promises the best yield on the rich lands, and
where sown early. Where sown late, and on the same
day with the Treadwell, it was very much injured by
the midge, and the Treadwell was uninjured.

"We cannot say positively what its merits are when
compared with the other white wheats. Many think there
is nothing like it, while others are not ready to express
their opinions. There has been but little of it thrashed
yet. After it has been generally thrashed, it will assume its position.

"To sum up—with our present knowledge of the
Diehl wheat, if we had a good fallow, rich and clean,
we would sow the Diehl wheat, and sow early. If the
land was of moderate richness and to be sown late, we
would sow Treadwell. We think the Diehl requires a
dryer soil than the Treadwell. Persons wanting Diehl
wheat for seed this year should not pay fancy prices for
it, but should willingly pay for good, sound, clean seed
sufficient above the market price of wheat to recompense
for the labor of making it so."

Mr. John Johnston, the veteran farmer of Geneva, N.
Y., says in regard to the Diehl wheat: "My Diehl
wheat is pretty good. One field may yield about as
well as last year's; the other not. Cause: *not manured
for many years*. The variety has degenerated on the

one field, but not on the other!" Mr. J. adds: " If plenty of manure were applied, there would be less loss from midge. All that is needed to insure good crops is more and better manure. Diehl wheat is excellent for rich land, but not good for poor. This is not a popular doctrine, but it is true."

The head of wheat represented by this illustration was sketched from a head of this variety raised in Colorado, and deposited in the archives of the Agricultural Department at Washington. There is nothing remarkable about this variety, except the uncouth appear-

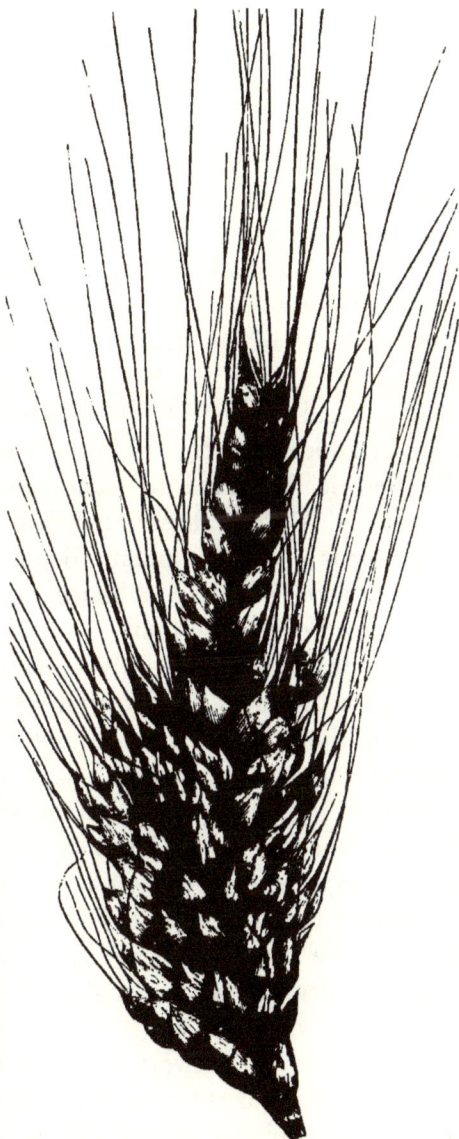

Fig. 26.—Egyptian club wheat.

ance of the ear. The variety is called the Seven-headed Egyptian Club Wheat. Mr. Klippart states that "this variety is known under the names of Egyptian, Syrian, Smyrna, Many-spiked, Reed, and Wild-goose Wheat. It derives its latter name from a story, which is current in the north, that four or five kernels, from which the American stock has proceeded, were found in the crop of a wild goose, which was shot on the west shore of Lake Champlain. It is called *Reed* Wheat, from the great strength of its straw, which serves to prevent its being prostrated in the field. It does not yield so much flour or meal as other kinds of wheat; and the flour is scarcely superior to that obtained from the finest barley. We find it described in some authorities as Mummy Wheat, or wheat three thousand years old. The following is a brief popular alleged history of it: It is said that some years ago a gentleman having occasion to unroll an Egyptian mummy, found enclosed with the body a few grains of wheat, which afterward, upon being sown with the modern Egyptian wheat, was found to be entirely dissimilar. The former contained nearly a hundred stalks, ranging in length from nearly five to upward of six feet, the leaves broader than usual, and fully an average as to length. The grain was in two rows or triplets, and on some, twenty triplets on a side, or forty on the ear. The ear contained a few barbs or awns on the upper end, and was open and distant between the grains. It flowered nearly a fortnight before any of the varieties sown at the same period. The modern Egyptian is dwarf, not more than four feet high, closely set and barbed in every part of the ear, and its general resemblance to its ancient progenitor is not greater than that of barley to wheat. Egyptian wheat, found in the tombs of the 18th dynasty—*i. e.*, from B. C. 1822 to B. C. 1476—has germinated when sown in Germany, and is frequently found in the tombs of Egypt. It has been grown by P. Poorman, in Stark County, O.

"This is an indifferent variety of wheat. The straw grows to the height of about five feet, is thick and pithy; the leaves are often ten inches long; the head, or rather panicle, is about four inches long, and nearly two wide and deep, and when ripe is of a reddish brown. The head consists of from five to twelve small heads densely compacted; the awns or beards are often four inches long, and of a very dark brown or blackish color. The lower part of the grain is inordinately swollen; it is very starchy, but not hard or flinty."

The Weeks Wheat.

Perhaps very few other varieties of wheat have been cultivated with more general satisfaction than this variety. (In numerous instances, this wheat has erroneously been bought and sold and advertised as the "*Wicks*" wheat.) But as I lived for many years within a few miles of the originator of this variety, at the time of his experiments with it, and am personally acquainted with him, I can correct any false impressions that have been promulgated concerning its identity, with the assurance that my statements are correct. There has been great confusion among farmers in regard to the identity of the Weeks wheat. In some instances, the heads were bald, while in others they were bearded, similar to the head herewith illustrated. Although the head of wheat from which this engraving was made was said to be the genuine Weeks wheat, still I know, from what

FIG. 27.   Weeks wheat.

I have often seen on my own farm and in the wheat fields of many of my neighbors, that the heads of the genuine Weeks wheat are not, as a general rule, so jagged and irregular as this illustration represents the variety to be. The heads of the true Weeks wheat, as I used to raise it, had four regular rows of kernels. In some instances, there were no beards, while other heads were covered with long awns. The originator of this variety communicated the following facts touching this variety of wheat, in response to my inquiries about its origin and other characteristics. He wrote under date of October 19, 1867, as follows:

"In answer to your inquiries, I would say that I found the head from which the Weeks wheat originated, in a crop of Mediterranean wheat. There were a few scattering heads of Hutchinson and Souls wheat mixed with the Mediterranean, among which this head grew. The product of the selected head was both bearded and bald wheat, nearly one-third being bald; and it continued to grow bald heads for three or four years, though such heads were carefully picked out every year. The midge worked in the bald heads very bad, whilst the *bearded was almost free* from their ravages. I therefore *rejected the bald, and grew the bearded.* I think the wheat is a cross between the Souls wheat and the Hutchinson.

"Respectfully yours,

"J. M. WEEKS.

"King's Ferry, Cayuga Co., N. Y."

E. A. King, of King's Ferry, Cayuga Co., N. Y., whose farm lies on the eastern shore of Cayuga Lake, and who has cultivated the Weeks wheat for a few years past, writes thus to the "Cultivator and Country

Gentleman ": "For many years the need of an early
and productive variety of wheat, and one free from the
'midge' or 'weevil' has been felt; and in the Weeks
wheat the farmer has such a variety. It is a choice
white wheat, making the very best of flour. Millers in
Ithaca and Auburn pay from two to four shillings more
for it per bushel than for any other kind. They say they
get more flour, and of a better quality, than from any
other kind. It is from eight to twelve days earlier than
any other kind which farmers have here, thus escaping
the weevil or midge. It has a good stiff straw, and
thereby escapes the Hessian fly. It is very productive
—twenty-five bushels not being a high average per acre,
and I have known it to yield as high as forty-five bushels per acre. It is no humbug, as scores of the best
farmers here will testify; and I actually believe that if
this variety alone was sown in the United States, the
crop would be doubled on the area over the present
crop. It need not be sown before the 15th or 20th of
September to do its best."

Golden-straw Wheat.

The straw of this variety is short and stiff, and is
consequently not liable to lodge. It does best on rich
sandy loams. The grain is not properly a red wheat;
but of nice amber color, somewhat resembling the
old-fashioned flint wheats. In Holmes County, Ohio,
it is rather of a yellowish cast. It ripens rather later
than the Mediterranean. It yields about twenty bushels
per acre; and improves under ordinary culture, and is
but little subject to injury by rust or fly. It is rapidly
growing into favor; and eventually may perhaps sup-
plant the Mediterranean.

The Red Andriolo
Wheat, represented by
the accompanying en-
graving, is similar to
the White Andriolo
Wheat, shown on an-
other page of this book.
This is a hardy varie-
ty, prolific, moderately
early, and possesses
most of the character-
istics of a superior va-
riety of winter wheat.
The long, rough awns
are an objection to its
cultivation, when the
straw is to be employed
for feeding stock or
littering their apart-
ments. Domestic ani-
mals dislike these
harsh, tasteless, and in-
nutritious beards, as
they are ruinous to fine
wool, liable to injure
the eyes of animals,
and when the chaff is employed
for bedding for horses, these
ugly, barbed awns are liable to
find their way into the sheath of
male horses, to their serious injury. Awns are of no advantage to wheat.

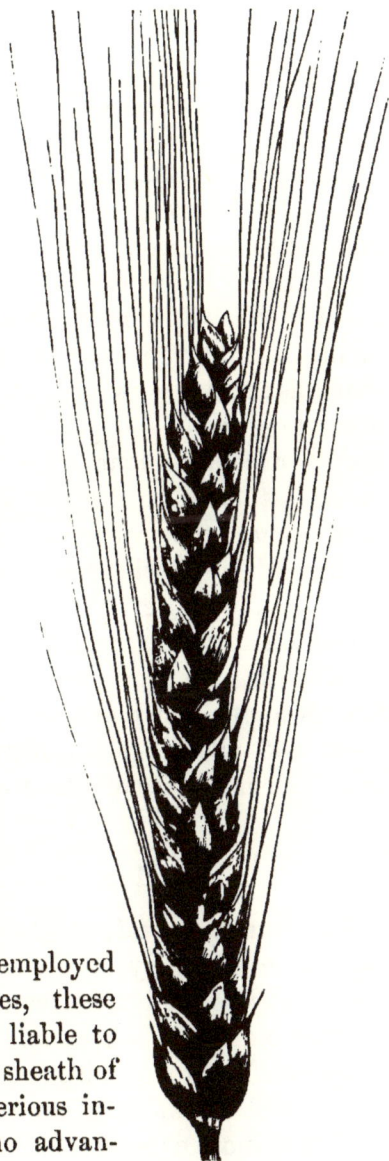

FIG. 28.—Red Andriolo.

THE TAPPAHANNOCK WHEAT.

This excellent variety of winter wheat has not been introduced to any considerable extent in the United States. Hon. Isaac Newton, Commissioner of Agriculture at Washington, experimented with this wheat; and the same season he died, 1867, he pronounced the Tappahannock the earliest and most promising of all the varieties of winter wheat with which he experimented on the government farm. Mr. Newton states that this variety does not seem to be so prolific as some other kinds; but the grain is of a fine quality, and it makes excellent flour. He thought this variety is much less liable to disease and the ravages of the fly than some other varieties. Farmers in other States besides Virginia, who have raised this kind of wheat, state that, as a general rule, the Tappahannock is extremely hardy and prolific, when the seed has been saved with care, from year to year; the yield of fine flour is large; the plants endure the winter extremely well; and all things considered, the Tappahannock is an excellent variety of wheat.

THE MEDITERRANEAN WHEAT.

This variety is said to have been introduced from Genoa, in 1819, by J. Gordon, of Wilmington, Delaware. It was cultivated for many years with eminent satisfaction, as the wheat midge injured the crop none to speak of. In many instances the straw was not sufficiently stiff to maintain an erect position till harvest. As it was more expensive harvesting lodged wheat, and as the yield was diminished by the falling down of the straw, and as the price per bushel was often twenty to thirty cents less in market than other wheat, this variety was almost discarded in many localities.

At present we have the Red Mediterranean and the White, both of which are cultivated with eminent satisfaction, where the seed has not been allowed to mix and to degenerate by injudicious management. Both the white and the red varieties yield bountiful crops; and resist the midge nearly as well as any other variety. The Mediterranean wheat matured ten to fifteen days before other varieties when first introduced. But, by slack management of the seed, the variety lost its early-maturing character. This wheat is known as a bearded and bald; and as white and red grain.

I have found so many different varieties which pass for the Mediterranean, that it will be utterly useless to attempt to pen such a description of the Mediterranean wheat as will prove of any service or satisfaction to even a small number of the readers of this book. Mr. Klippart, in his "Wheat Plant," speaks very favorably of the Mediterranean wheat; and my own experience is, that where the seed has not been allowed to degenerate by slack cultivation, this variety is one of the most profitable kinds that American farmers can cultivate.

When the Mediterranean Red variety was first introduced into the best wheat-growing regions of New York, many farmers refused to employ this variety for seed, simply because the straw was so slender that it would lodge, and frequently be tangled into a complete snarl, before harvest-time, thus diminishing the yield of grain, and greatly augmenting the labor of harvesting the crop.

The Black-Sea Spring Wheat.

This excellent variety of spring wheat was once one of the choicest kinds of spring grain that has ever been cultivated in the United States. But slip-shod farming soon brought the Black-Sea wheat into disfavor. Before it had been allowed to hybridize with other varieties, it was considered an earlier variety than the others; and it succeeded comparatively well, if sowed when it would be too late for other kinds to mature. It has been sown as late as the 20th of June in Eastern New York, and produced bright straw and a plump berry. This has been much liked, because it may be sown so late as to escape the wheat midge, and yet fill. As the wheat midge does not rage so much now as formerly, it is not so extensively cultivated.

S. Kieffer, of Jefferson County, N. Y., writes that the Black Sea wheat is not so valuable to manufacture into flour for exportation, because it is not so white and light, or soft to the touch of the finger, but makes good bread, of a rather yellowish color. It never has rusted or blasted with me, and I doubt if it has with anybody else when sown within the month of May. I have grown it upon interval land so rich that it lodged and lay flat upon the ground during the time it was filling until it was harvested; yet it was well filled, and yielded thirty-eight ($38\frac{1}{2}$) bushels per acre.

If this variety could have been kept pure, and the seed improved from year to year, according to the directions laid down in this treatise, farmers would have had a variety of wheat that would now be a great national blessing. It is a glaring reproach to American farmers, that they will allow choice varieties of wheat to deteriorate and run out, simply by perfunctory management.

THE RIO GRANDE.

This is a choice variety of spring wheat; but has not been introduced, except in a few localities. Wherever it has been cultivated for several successive seasons, with care, and the seed kept pure, the crops have given fair satisfaction. The straw is usually rather stiff, so that the growing grain is not prostrated by protracted storms. This variety has been grown quite extensively in some parts of Minnesota, and other Western States. Usually, farmers and millers have spoken well of the Rio Grande. I think that if the seed of this variety could be cultivated with the care alluded to under the head of Seed Wheat, the Rio Grande would be one of the choicest and most profitable varieties of spring wheat that has ever been cultivated in America. This wheat possesses all the characteristics of a perfect variety of cereal grain. But in numerous instances, the crop has been allowed to hybridize with other grain, so that, in some instances, it has lost its identity.

CHINA TEA WHEAT.

This is a spring wheat. The chaff is white; the heads are long and well filled with plump kernels, when the soil is moderately fertile. The kernels are large, and rather far apart. It is a bearded variety; and very prolific. On rich soil, the straw stands erect tolerably well. But some millers have complained of this variety that the bran is thick; and that the grain does not yield so much flour per bushel as the grain of some other varieties. The China Tea has been cultivated, in years past, quite extensively, in many parts of Western New York, with eminent satisfaction. In some of the middle counties of the State, where the seed has been allowed to hybridize, there has been not a little complaint about the unsatisfactory results of the China Tea variety. In some other States, this variety has been cultivated to a limited extent; and I have always found that slack farmers denounced it, while thorough-going cultivators of the soil speak well of the China Tea.

THE FIFE SPRING WHEAT.

The Fife Wheat and the Canada Club Wheat are said to be the same variety in certain sections of the country. But they are entirely distinct. They were both cultivated in Central New York, to a limited extent, for sevral successive years, when I resided in Tompkins County. The grain appears very much alike; but the straw, when growing, is quite unlike. I once grew both varieties on my farm; and I found that the Club wheat would mature a week earlier than the Fife. The straw of the Fife is short and stiff; and the variety is moderately prolific. The Fife wheat, with me, always resisted the midge satisfactorily; and the grain always made excellent flour.

SILVER STRAW WHEAT.

This is a variety of winter wheat full of encouraging promises to American farmers; but which has been cultivated only to a limited extent. It possesses all the

external characteristics of a perfect variety. The rows
of grain are very regular; the heads are large and well
filled with plump kernels; the grain is of a beautiful
amber color; the straw is stiff, and has a fine silver
lustre; the growing crop is nearly weevil proof; the
straw is seldom affected with rust; the young plants
endure the cold of winter, extremely well; and it is
one of the finest varieties of wheat that can be found
in New Jersey, where it is grown with eminent profit
and satisfaction.

UNDESCRIBED VARIETIES.

No doubt hundreds of my readers will wonder why
I did not describe certain varieties which have only a
local name, having been cultivated only in certain localities. I am aware that there are many, probably, excellent varieties of both winter and spring wheat, which
I have never heard of. I have heard of, and have seen
many varieties that I have made no allusion to in this
book; because I have not been able to learn anything
really reliable in regard to their characteristics. Where
I knew nothing of a certain kind of wheat, and was not
able to obtain reliable information touching its excellence, I have thought best to pen nothing about it.
There are many kinds of wheat in the Western States,
of which I failed to secure an intelligible description;
therefore, I have omitted the names.

CHAPTER II.

Soil, and its Preparation for Wheat.

> " But if your care to wheat alone extend,
> Let Maia, with her sisters, first descend;
> And the bright Gnossian diadem downward bend,
> Before you trust in earth the future hope;
> Or, else expect a listless, lazy crop."
>
> DRYDEN'S VIRGIL.

THE proper preparation and continued management
of the soil from year to year, lies at the very foundation
of successful wheat culture. A farmer may sow the
best and most prolific varieties the world ever knew, and
fail to raise a satisfactory crop of wheat, if the soil is not
just as it should be.

In preparing the soil for the production of a crop of
winter grain—wheat, rye, or winter barley—the aim
should always be to keep the vegetable matter and
the manurial portions as much on, or near the surface as
is practicable. The grand object of preparing the soil
in this way, is that the roots of the plants may spread out
horizontally, instead of striking in a more vertical direction. When they spread out horizontally, they form a
kind of mat in the soil, a few inches deep, which rises
and settles down bodily, when the soil freezes and thaws.
Therefore the soil may freeze and thaw a great number
of times, when the roots are matted together horizontally,
without throwing the plants out of the soil. Whereas,
when the vegetable matter is mingled with a good depth

of soil, so that the roots must necessarily strike deep before they can reach the necessary sustenance, they will be lifted out and broken by the frost after freezing only a few times.

Now, if we could invert only a few inches in depth of the soil—say three or four inches—and then pulverize the soil below this thin stratum of surface soil, thus keeping the largest proportion of humus and available fertilizers near the surface of the earth, there is no doubt but that we should see a very remarkable difference in more abundant crops of grain ; and at the same time it would be of a better quality, as its growth would not be stinted by the frosts of winter.

To show that this theory of cultivation is philosophical and practically correct, I will simply refer to the practice formerly in vogue, of sowing wheat on newly-cleared land, after the surface had been simply harrowed—or without ploughing any part of the ground. Winter-killing of wheat, when put in thus, was seldom complained of. As there was but little depth to the soil, all the roots spread out horizontally ; and it was almost impossible for the young plants to be injured by the freezing and thawing of the surface of the field.

Thousands of acres of the finest quality of wheat were cultivated, when the country was new, on ground that was simply harrowed over, having never been ploughed. The most abundant crops that the best wheat-fields of the country ever have produced, or ever will yield, grew where the timber had just been cut off; and where the logs and brush were burned to ashes, which were harrowed into the thin stratum of leaf mould that formed the seed-bed of the future crop. The land, in numerous instances, was so exceedingly rooty

6

and stumpy that it would have been an utter impracti-
cability to plough it. And yet, with all the deep
ploughing, thorough pulverization, and bountiful manuring, farmers find it difficult to produce as many
bushels of wheat per acre, on the same land, as they
were accustomed to grow, without any manure at all,
and without any preparation of the land, except a
superficial harrowing.

It is eminently important that farmers should understand that the manner of preparing land for winter
wheat, as practised by our ancestors, was compatible
with the habit of the wheat plant; and it was also the
scientific way of cultivation, with a view of avoiding
the injurious influences of freezing and thawing of the
soil, on the growing wheat plants. If the hard subsoil
beneath the thin stratum of mould could have been
broken up with a subsoil plough, without having been
turned above the rich seed-bed, the yield of grain would
have been much larger than the most bountiful crops
that grew where no implement of husbandry was ever
before used, except the common harrow. All the aged
wheat-growers of our country, who have a correct
understanding of the difficulties that are now met with
by wheat-growers, will appreciate these suggestions, as
they understand perfectly well how easy it was, when
they cultivated wheat according to the foregoing plan,
to produce a heavy crop.

There are other considerations which it is proper to
mention, that exerted a favorable influence towards the
production of a bountiful crop of grain, among which
may be mentioned the protection of the wheat plants in
the winter, by the extensive forests that shielded the
wheat-fields from the terrible winds that *now* remove

all the snow during the winter months; and also the liberal amount of excellent fertilizing material in the form of wood ashes. Allusion is made to these things more extensively in another part of this work. The main point to which I desire to direct the attention of wheat-growers is, the most favorable condition of the soil, and other circumstances, in order to produce a satisfactory crop of grain. Necessity required our ancestors to adopt the mode of cultivation to which allusion has been made. They might not have perceived at that time that those circumstances and conditions of seed-bed, and everything else, were more favorable than any other for the production of a bountiful crop of grain. But they see it now. The suggestion may never have occurred to them that it made any difference whether the best soil was kept at the surface or turned half a foot beneath it. But successful wheat-growers have learned that it *does* make all the difference in the world, whether the best soil is kept at the surface, when a crop of winter grain is to be raised. Read volume second, page 125, of Young Farmer's Manual.

Let this be the key-note, then, to successful wheat culture : to keep the best soil, or a thin, mellow stratum of rich soil, at the surface. Then make the subsoil as deep and porous by pulverization as practicable, by the use of the subsoil plough.

How Freezing and Thawing of the Soil affects Growing Wheat.

Practical farmers understand very well, how freezing and thawing of the surface of the soil affects the wheat plant. Doubtless every observing farmer who reads these pages, will recollect of having seen the surface of very wet and light ground lifted, so that the ice and a little earth would resemble a honeycomb. Every wheat-grower should have a correct understanding of the effect of freezing and thawing of the soil on the wheat plants, as the injury to the wheat plant arising from the freezing and thawing of the soil, is usually the most serious obstacle that farmers meet with in our wheat-growing regions. By the alternate freezing and thawing of the surface of the soil, the stools of wheat are lifted and separated from their hold upon the soil. The deep roots which penetrate below the reach of shallow frosts are broken off, and the earth is more or less loosened from the others. Here we perceive the disadvantage of depositing the seed too deep. The roots originating from the seed, being far below the surface of the ground, when the plant is lifted by the expansion of the soil, the stem will be likely to be separated somewhere between the surface of the ground and the roots. The plants then soon die. When the roots strike downward, their hold in the soil is loosened, when the frost lifts the soil; and as the wheat plants do not settle back to their original position when the ground thaws, the roots are soon worked upward, until they are raised almost clear of the soil, as if they had been pulled up by hand. Every practical wheat-grower is familiar with all these disadvantages in raising winter wheat. With spring grain, none of these things occur.

When the soil freezes, it is greatly expanded; and the expansion is all upward, because the unfrozen earth below, will not yield to the frozen stratum; and there is no vacant space to be filled by the lateral enlargement. For this reason, the *surface* of the soil is often elevated two, three, or more inches higher than it stands when the ground is not frozen.

If the position of shallow-rooted trees, where the ground freezes deeply, be compared with horizontal marks on a building that the frost does not lift, it will often be seen that they stand from one to two inches higher, when the soil is thus frozen, than when free from frost. As the roots of such trees lie nearly in a horizontal position, they rise and settle back with the lifting and settling of the soil. Thus it is with sod ground. The roots of the grass form such a tangled mat near the surface of the ground, that the entire layer of turf settles back in a body, keeping the roots in their true position.

I have in mind an instance which will illustrate the great expansion of the soil, even when beneath a heavy weight. In the basement of my workshop, there were two sticks of timber resting with their ends on the sills, and the middle of each stick was supported by posts set in the ground, where frost could not reach them. In very cold weather, the entire building would be raised by the freezing of the earth beneath the foundation, so that a plank, an inch and a half thick, could be put under the timbers, on the top of the posts.

With a perfect understanding of the foregoing suggestions, a farmer will be well prepared to do something to prevent in a great degree, or entirely, any injury to the wheat-plant from freezing and thawing of the soil. In order to prevent injury from this source, two things are essential. The first is, thorough drainage, where the soil is at all inclined to be too wet. Dry soils are affected but little by freezing. But when a soil is saturated with water, it often heaves several inches above its usual height. This process so disturbs the roots of

FIG. 29.

wheat, that they have no more hold on the soil than if just transplanted. Hence, they are apt soon to die.

The next consideration is shallow seeding, and cultivating the soil so as to keep the mould, or the richest part of the soil, at the surface.

I will endeavor to make this point more intelligible by an explanation of the accompanying illustration, which represents a young wheat-plant which has sprung from a kernel of wheat that was planted about six inches deep. The seminal or primary roots that have sprung from the kernel take such a firm hold of the soil, that when the surface is lifted the stem will be severed, as shown, at some point between the two systems of roots. Unless winter wheat is put in very early in autumn, the coronal, or secondary, or upper set of roots will not attain one-half the size herewith represented. I have shown a bulb just below the surface of the ground, much larger than it really grows, for the purpose of illustrating the principle on which the young wheat-plants grow. The upper set of roots seldom appear as large as they are here represented, until the plants have begun to grow luxuriantly the next spring after the seed is put in. We can perceive, at once, how easily the frost would heave out the growing plant, if there were only a few small roots issuing from the bulb, to hold it in the ground.

When seed wheat is ploughed in deep, if we examine the plants just before winter, we shall find that there are roots issuing from the kernel, as shown by the illustration, and none—or very few—at the bulb. After a period of freezing and thawing of the wheat field, in some wet place, let the stems be examined, and they will be found severed, as represented by the preceding cut.

Now, the great practical question again recurs—to which I have previously alluded—what can the husbandman do to avoid injury from freezing and thawing of the soil? I again repeat the answer which was hinted at under the Habit of the Wheat Plant, p. 49, that the seed must be planted shallow. If that kernel of grain shown in the last illustration, Fig. 29, had been deposited near the lower end of the bulb, all the seminal or primary roots, and all the coronal or secondary roots would be so close together that they would tend to form a mat of earth, like a sod, which would rise and fall with the expansion and contraction of the surface of the ground when it freezes and thaws. By this means, the injury arising from the heaving of the soil will be avoided, provided the best, the mellowest, and richest soil be kept at the surface of the ground.

The foregoing explanation of the management of wheat is applicable to winter grain—to rye as well as to growing wheat. In the culture of spring grain, we have no such difficulties to contend with. Let this section be read in connection with deep and shallow seeding on another page. I am fully satisfied, after thirty years' observation on this subject, that farmers must make themselves familiar with the principles of growth and of cultivation herein laid down, before they will be able to raise winter wheat with satisfactory success.

BEST QUALITY OF SOIL FOR WHEAT.

Many farmers have inquired, with much solicitude, why wheat will not grow on any soil that is fertile and mellow?—or, why a soil will not produce a good crop of wheat that produces fair crops of everything else?

But the correct answer is very obvious and brief. If a soil is destitute of wheat-producing material, it cannot produce a bountiful crop of that kind of grain. There are many soils that will produce fair crops of Indian corn, rye, barley, and oats, which will not yield a re-remunerating crop of wheat. And why? Simply because the roots of the wheat plant cannot find, in that soil, the right kind of material that is necessary to form the kernels. In one soil, the minute roots find an abundance of material, which they may take up, for the formation and perfect development of the kernels; while in another soil, the roots may send out their numerous little hungry mouths into every cubic inch of the soil, in search of material to produce the grain, and not find it. This is the great difficulty with a soil that will not produce wheat. And, until such materials are added to the soil, it may be cultivated and sowed in vain.

All farmers—or chemists—who know anything, practically, about raising good wheat, will admit that the best soil for raising good wheat contains a good proportion of clay. Wheat requires a firm soil. Therefore, a sandy soil is not a good one for wheat; neither is a mucky soil much better; because they are both deficient in those elements of fertility that are necessary to form the kernels, and also in that firmness which is so essential in a good soil for wheat. Yet I have seen fair crops of wheat produced on a sandy soil.

Our aluminous, heavy, slippery clay soils are by no means the best soils for the production of either winter or spring wheat; although they will yield good crops of wheat when well drained, and thoroughly pulverized and manured. Our country abounds in soils of a mixed character, which will produce a remunerating crop of

6*

wheat once in five or six years, while they cannot be set down as good wheat soils; and they cannot be very much improved for growing wheat, unless a vast amount of clay were thoroughly mingled with the soil.

Heavy, slippery clay soils abound in wheat-producing material. Therefore, such soils will not be exhausted of their fertility as soon as those will where there is but a small proportion of clay, or no clay at all.

On some soils, where sand predominates, wheat would not grow heavy enough to pay the expense of harvesting it. And the same is true of soils where alluvion constitutes the large proportion of the soil. A sandy soil will furnish silica enough to form a good, stiff straw, while a mucky soil will produce a slender and soft straw, which will fall down before the grain has matured.

The best soil for wheat is a soil in which the predominating characteristics are clay and loam, having neither too much of one nor too little of the other. The lighter loam soils, and such alluvions as have been brought from clayey localities, will often produce bountiful crops of excellent wheat; and sometimes a mucky soil will yield a fair crop of this kind of grain. But their fertility for wheat will soon be exhausted. Calcareous clays, gravelly clays, aluminous clays, as well as many soils that are a mixture of all these just named, with good management—cultivating, manuring, and draining — will, almost always, yield fair crops of wheat.

R. L. Allen, in the American Farmer's Book, says: "Wheat is partial to a well-prepared clay or a heavy loam; and this is improved when it contains, either naturally or artificially, a large proportion of lime. Many light, and all marly and calcareous soils, if in proper condition, will give a good yield of wheat."

In D. P. Gardner's Farmer's Dictionary, the author says: "Wheat thrives best on heavy soils."

The author of the Practical Farmer says: "Wheat succeeds best on stout loams."

In Stevens's Book of the Farm—an English work—the writer says: "Unless soil possesses a certain degree of firmness, that is, contains some clay, it is not considered adapted to the growth of wheat. At least, it is considered more profitable to sow barley upon it." (Read about Improving Soils for Wheat, in chapter on Soils, in the second volume of my Young Farmer's Manual.)

A practical farmer of Central New York wrote to one of the agricultural papers thus: "A firm, fertile, and dry soil is particularly adapted to wheat, and such soils as have been under-drained are more productive, and require much less manure. Wheat, whether winter or spring, does best in soils in which there is a good portion of clay. When the soil is composed for the most part of muck, as occurs in many places in New York, Canada, and some of the Western States, it requires much preparation before it will produce well; and such soils can only be made to yield heavy crops of wheat, with profit, when clay, in some form, can be supplied."

Wheat on Clay Loam.

The author penned the following article for the "Independent," soon after he assumed the editorial charge of the agricultural department of that paper:

Wheat, especially winter grain, requires a firm soil,

having in it a preponderance of clay. For this reason, our clayey loams are found to be better adapted to winter wheat than any other soil. A strong loam is better for winter wheat than a clay soil, although where clay is so abundant as to give a soil the character of a rich *stiff* clay, it will produce excellent wheat for a long succession of years. Still, when clay and sand are commingled in the right proportion to form a good loam, there is no other kind of soil that is better adapted to the production of winter wheat, that will make the whitest and best fine flour. A sandy soil is too porous for wheat, especially winter wheat. Spring wheat will succeed much better on sandy soil than winter. Mucky soils are quite objectionable for winter wheat, because they are too light. The freezing in winter expands them much more than compact loams, or clays, especially when they are not well drained. This great expansion disturbs the roots to such an extent that but few plants can survive the great injury from freezing and thawing. Clay gives firmness and solidity to a soil. Sand renders it sufficiently porous to drain off the superabundant moisture, which is the means of the great expansion when the soil freezes; and at the same time it renders the soil sufficiently porous for the roots to spread readily.

Another indispensable characteristic of a good soil for wheat is dryness. No soil, whatever may be its component parts, or however fertile it may be, can produce a large yield of winter wheat when there is an excess of water in it. What I wish to be understood by an *excess* of water is, more than the soil will retain by capillary attraction, or absorption. If a good clay soil, too wet for wheat, were rendered dry by under-drains three feet deep and not more than ten to twelve feet apart, its capacity for absorbing the surplus water would be greatly increased; and the wheat growing on it would be very little injured by freezing and thawing; and it would suffer less for want of moisture in a dry time.

Another important feature of a good wheat soil is a bountiful supply of nitrogenous matter and silica. When a soil is nearly destitute of these ingredients, the ears of wheat will always be short and light, and the kernels of grain quite small. In fertile loams, there is usually a pretty good supply of both substances. Where nitrogenous matter exists only in limited abundance, it may be supplied in good barn-yard manure, made by animals which subsist largely on coarse grain and oil-meal. Such manure will always produce great heads and large, plump kernels of grain. Silica is essential to produce a healthy, bright, and stiff straw. This may be supplied by spreading on a few hundred bushels of sand per acre, after the wheat is put in, and sowing eight to ten bushels of unleached ashes per acre, the next spring, or even during a dry time in winter, when ashes would not be washed away by high water. There are thousands of acres of inferior wheat soil in our country that might be made to yield remunerating crops of this kind of grain, by following the directions just given.

THE CULTURE OF WHEAT CHEMICALLY CONSIDERED.

At one of the meetings of the New York State Agricultural Society, Hon. D. Lee made the following remarks touching the culture of wheat, which, I think, will be read with no little interest. He said:

" By the aid of a little practical science, good wheat may be grown profitably in any county in the State.

"The wheat plant has been raised in a great variety of artificial soils, where each ingredient was carefully weighed, both before and after the plant was taken from the earth. By careful analysis, what the soil had lost, and what the plant had gained, was susceptible of demonstration. A very large portion of the elements of all cultivated plants comes from the atmosphere. The precise amount will depend alike on the composition of the soil and the nature of the particular plant upon which the experiment was made.

"I regard it as a fact of great practical importance, that wood ashes, even leached ashes, so abundant in the southern tier of counties of the State of New York, contain all the earthy elements of this invaluable bread-bearing plant.

"Our primitive forests have been for centuries draw ing the above earthy constituents of wheat from the soil. And instead of carefully preserving this indispensable *raw material* of good wheaten bread, thousands of bushels of leached ashes have been thrown away! Being but slowly decomposed by the vital action of plants, ashes are an enduring fertilizer, when compared with stable manure. Mixed with quicklime, their good effects are more speedily obtained. Lime will render alumina, either in the soil or in leached ashes, soluble in water, so that it can enter the minute pores of roots. Clay in the soil is always combined with a large portion of silica, and before it has been exhausted by continuous cropping it holds in combination considerable potash and soda. Lime, by combining with alumina, the basis of clay, liberates these alkalies and silica, which, uniting chemically, form soluble silicates of potash and soda. These also enter into the circulating nourishment of plants, and are decomposed in the stems of grasses and cereals. The silica goes to make vegetable bone, to keep the plant upright, while the potash and soda go back to the earth to dissolve as before."

Organic Elements of Wheat.

I come now to speak of the organic elements of the wheat plant, which form ninety-six or seven per cent. of its substance. Water and its constituents, oxygen and hydrogen, carbon and nitrogen, are the four elementary ingredients of all cultivated plants, beside their minerals. As there is no lack of water or of its elements, oxygen and hydrogen, our attention will be confined to obtaining a full supply of carbon and nitrogen. These are indispensable, and fortunately nature has provided an amount of carbon and nitrogen in the air, if not in the soil, more than equal to all the wants of vegetation. A large portion of the fertilizing elements of vegetable mould in a rich soil is carbon, and a small portion is nitrogen; both of which are usually combined with other substances. These important elements are often nearly exhausted in fields which have been unwisely cultivated; and I have paid much attention to the subject of cheap and practicable renovation.

By the aid of clover and buckwheat dressed with gypsum, ashes, lime, or manure, and ploughed in, when in blossom, much can be done in the way of augmenting the rich vegetable mould so desirable to a certain degree in all soils. Straw, corn-stalks, leaves of forest trees, and swamp muck made into compost with lime and ashes, are of great value. Charcoal, well pulverized and saturated with urine, I regard as the cheapest and most useful fertilizer that can be applied to a poor soil, for the production of wheat or almost any other crop.

The earths contained in charcoal, as the analysis of its ash demonstrates, are identical with the earths found in the wheat plant. Coal contains a very large portion of carbon, and will imbibe from the atmosphere a large quantity of nitrogen in the form of ammonia and its carbonates. Unlike stable manure, the salts of lime, potash, soda, and magnesia, it will not waste by premature solution nor by evaporation. On the contrary, it is of incalculable value to mix with the liquid and solid excretions of all animals, to absorb and fix in a tangible condition those volatile fertilizing elements which are so prone to escape beyond our reach.

When it is recollected that without nitrogen in some form, it is utterly impossible to grow one kernel of good wheat, and that a pint of human urine, or four quarts of that of the cow, or one quart of that of the horse fed on grain, contain nitrogen enough to supply sixty pounds of wheat, we may begin to understand something of the money value of this animal product. Additions cheaply made to even worn-out soils—supplying them with the comparatively small amount of ingredients essential to the production of grain, and without which wheat cannot be grown—would richly repay the farmer, and vastly enhance the wealth of the country. Analysis shows that a very small portion of the nutriment of wheat comes from the soil; but that portion must be restored in some form, as lime or otherwise, if we expect to make the earth yield profitable returns for our labor.

How the Kernels of Wheat are Formed.

In a few days after the blossoms of the wheat plant have fallen, the tender kernels appear enveloped in the chaff; and the material that forms the flour of the grain is in a liquid state, having been brought up from the fertile soil through the medium of the roots, stems, and leaves of the growing plants. At this period, the kernels are much larger and more plump than they will be after the grain is fully matured. If the kernels be crushed at this period in the growth of the wheat, a thick milky liquid will exude. After a few days, this fluid material changes to a plastic state.

The grain is then said to be in the "dough state." While the substance that forms the kernel is in a liquid condition, the grain is spoken of as being in the "milk state." All the exquisitely fine material that enters into the composition of the grain, is brought up to the ear in particles inconceivably small, having been picked up by the organs of the growing plant, and conveyed in the fluids of the stem and leaves to the kernels. It is exceedingly interesting to consider the untold number of living mouths attached to the numerous roots that pervade the entire soil, securing only a choice morsel here and there to be carried up to the head for the production of seed; and it is a most interesting fact to contemplate, that the roots of the wheat plant are so exceeding dainty, that they will reject entirely large quantities of the choicest kind of plant food, if it is not in exactly the right condition for making a choice article of wheaten milk. The consideration that all the choice wheat of commerce is the product of a milky substance which is formed of a material in the soil that is less abundant than the honey which the bees may gather from the opening flowers, teaches the cultivator of the soil the transcendent importance of fertilizing, pulverizing, and teasing the land by all the mechanical means in his power to bring it into that peculiar state of productiveness, which will supply the greatest amount of available material for the formation of wheat milk.

Domestic goats that roam about the streets of our populous cities, are ever ready to devour every sort of garbage, even to brown wrapping-paper; and their digestive organs are so powerful that milk is formed by these animals out of the roughest and poorest qualities of food. But the functions of the growing wheat plant are so delicate, that other plants which are stronger and more hardy than the wheat plant, must prepare pabulum for the roots of this plant to feed upon. For this purpose there is no other plant like clover for transforming the rough material in the soil into available plant-food, such as the organs of the wheat plant will appropriate to the production of "wheat milk." The hardy roots of clover will decompose and digest, so to speak, only a very small quantity of earthy matter which will form a wheaten milk, after the ground has been ploughed, and the clover roots have decayed. Yet, if the fine pabulum is in the soil, and if the land be prepared properly by thorough pulverization, the roots of the wheat plants will find the little atoms which are adapted to the peculiar requirements of those organs that produce the seeds.

The great practical point, therefore, for wheat-growers to consider is, fattening the soil with alumina, phosphorus, silica, and other fertilizing substances, which will afford an abundant supply of the right kind of pab-

ulum for producing "wheaten milk," without which a
bountiful crop of grain cannot be realized.

Alumina, being the base of all clay soils, furnishes
just what is required to produce large heads and plump
kernels of wheat. Although phosphorus, or phosphatic
material is the great manure for a turnip crop, it is eminently essential for wheat, if it can be applied to the
soil, say one year or more before the seed wheat is put
in. Silica must be furnished in liberal abundance, or
the straw of wheat will not possess sufficient stiffness
to maintain an erect position until the grain is harvested.

FATTENING THE SOIL FOR WHEAT.

After a wet soil has been thoroughly underdrained,
so that there are no apprehensions that the young
plants will be lifted out of the ground by freezing and
thawing; after the surface soil has been renovated with
clover and kept in an excellent state of fertility by a
judicious system of rotation of crops for several successive seasons; after the ground has been ploughed,
reploughed, and ploughed again, and again, and again,
and then harrowed, scarified, teased with the cultivator,
and fretted with the roller, and vexed with the clod-
crusher; and after every noxious weed has been exterminated, root and branch, and their leaves, stems, and
radicles have been changed into a fertile mould, the
hopes of the ambitious husbandman will not be realized
in beholding a bountiful crop of the full wheat in the
ear, unless he has *fattened* the soil. In this lies the
grand secret of raising wheat. Yet very few even of
our best farmers understand that this is the chief re-

quirement of the soil, after everything else to appearance has been done which is really essential.

Farmers often congratulate themselves, when they deposit the seed in a mellow seed-bed, that if any of their neighbors are so fortunate as to have a bountiful crop of wheat, they, most assuredly, will not fail to reap an abundant harvest. But they *do* fail, simply because the soil has not been *fattened*. A field often looks very mellow, at seedtime, the young plants attain a fair size before winter, and the growth of straw is luxuriant and heavy; but at harvest, the heads of grain are exceedingly short and the kernels small, because the ground was not properly fattened with those elements of fertility which are required to swell out the kernels like grain just removed from the steep-vat. The experience of every practical farmer will accord with these suggestions. We often see wheat, when it is cradled, as high as the laborers' heads; and the sheaves are very large, and numerous over the entire field. But the ears yield very little grain, because the soil has not been fattened.

Culture of Wheat on Prairie Soils.

Most farmers think that the prairie soil in which the plant food has been accumulating for untold ages, is all right for the production of a bountiful crop of wheat. Tillage, they think, is the chief desideratum on such soils. Thorough tillage is all that is required for a few years; but after a few crops have been removed, the yield of grain diminishes, for the simple reason that the soil has not been fattened with a direct reference to producing a crop of wheat. The sources of fertility must be husbanded—even in the rich prairie soils of the great West—in order to be able to raise bountiful crops of fair wheat. Straw is not what farmers desire. There is an inexhaustible supply of material for making a heavy burden of straw; but the material for swelling out large and plump kernels of fine wheat, is to be found only in limited quantities.

Those farmers who have attempted to grow wheat for several successive years on the prairies, experience the very difficulties that I have alluded to. This fact proves, most conclusively, that thorough culture is eminently essential to a bountiful crop of wheat; and it shows, also, that even the fertile prairie soils must be fattened or the wheat crop will be light.

The question then arises, How may such a task be performed? What to do and how to do it comes in, at this juncture, with wonderful pertinence. Well, what do we *desire* to do? Why, simply to maintain a high degree of fertility in the soil, so as to produce a bountiful yield of grain. Straw is not the object. A heavy dressing of straw applied to the soil only augments the crop of straw, which is, in some respects, more of a nuisance than an advantage. If all the grain be removed from the farm, and none of the refuse of the kernels be returned in the form of manure to fatten the soil, I reiterate what I have so often expressed, that the heads of grain will be short, and the kernels few and small.

It will not subserve the grand purpose under consideration, to remove the wheat and return the straw to the land, as many of the proprietors of the prairie farms have been accustomed to do. It is absolutely essential to adopt a judicious system of rotation of crops in connection with a system of mixed husbandry, in order to produce bountiful crops of wheat. Neat cattle, sheep, or swine must be raised in connection with wheat. And large crops of wheat cannot be grown where we see half-starved stock, as the manure made by lean animals, that are required to subsist on straw and hay only, will swell out the kernels of grain but little more than if the straw and hay were applied directly to the soil. Nothing will be added to straw and hay during its passage through stock into the manure heap and eventually to the field.   The grand object in feeding grain to domestic animals, is to secure a richer manure than can be made of straw and hay.

GANG PLOUGHS AND CULTIVATORS.

In many wheat-growing sections of the country, gang ploughs are employed for preparing the ground for a crop of winter wheat.   In other localities, "Ide's Wheel Cultivator," which is represented by the acccompanying illustration, is considered one of the most economical,

FIG. 30.—Ide's Wheel Cultivator.

convenient, and useful implements for a farmer.· This style is manufactured by Messrs. Tracy & Greenwood, Newark, Wayne Co., N. Y., in the midst of a famous wheat-growing region, where thousands of this kind of two-horse cultivator are employed instead of a plough. The teeth of this cultivator are made of steel, with the lower ends spread out so as to form a broad, flat edge, in such a form as to be self-sharpening. The excentrics gauge the depth at which the teeth are to enter the ground. By means of levers, the teeth can be elevated six inches above the surface of the ground, in a few seconds; or they can be adjusted to run at any desired depth, from one inch to six inches. It is an excellent implement for putting wheat ground in order; and there are numerous other instances where this cultivator may be used with eminent satisfaction and efficiency.

The wheels make it run very steadily, even on rough land. This style of cultivators is employed to a large extent in Central New York and in Canada, for cultivating summer fallows; and they save an immense amount of labor. In ten seconds the frame and all the teeth can be elevated several inches above the surface of the ground, so that the implement can be transported conveniently from place to place, while resting on the wheels. The teeth are strong, and with decent usage, such a cultivator will last a long time, and perform an untold amount of service. It is a very unusual occurrence to see such a cultivator clogged with sods and stubble.

ABOUT SUMMER FALLOWS.

The time has been when summer fallows were very much in vogue; and most of our best farmers thought, that, in order to raise a good crop of winter wheat, the land must be summer fallowed and ploughed, not less than three or four times ; and, sometimes, I have known farmers to plough summer fallows five times before the 1st of September. And those farmers that were most accustomed to summer-fallow their fields for a crop of wheat, cherished the idea that every ploughing increased the crop of grain sufficiently to remunerate for the labor performed.

Where land is infested with noxious weeds, or is filled with the seed of pernicious plants, it may be advisable to summer-fallow. But I think the better way is to cultivate a crop of Indian corn, instead of summer-fallowing the ground. If the field be overrun with elder bushes, Canada thistles, dock, daisies, or weeds of this character, apply a heavy dressing of manure, late in the spring, and grow a crop of Indian corn. By ploughing the ground late in the spring, the corn will get the start of the weeds, and maintain the ascendency, during the growing season, with but little hand labor. Read about Summer Fallows in the second volume of my Young Farmer's Manual.

ALDEN'S QUACK RAKE.

The illustration herewith given, represents an implement constructed with reference to the wants of farmers in localities where quack grass, or couch grass, has taken possession of the soil. This implement was invented by Alden & Co., Auburn, N. Y., in a region of country where this pernicious grass abounds to a great extent.

The teeth are made of iron, about three-eighths of an inch thick and eight inches long, each one having a nut on the upper end. The wood should be of the firmest kind of hard-wood timber, about five feet long and two by three inches square. The implement is guided by a pair of thills which are used to guide Alden's Horse Hoe, as shown in this illustration.

The manner of using this rake is as follows: After the grass sod has decayed, use the rake as a harrow is employed. About every three or four rods across the field, stop the horse, draw the rake back, and thus clear the teeth of the numerous roots which have been gathered by them in their passage through the soil. Let the ground be raked over and over, until every quack root

Fig. 31.—Alden's Quack-Grass Rake.

has been collected and dropped in a row on the surface of the ground. (See a cut and description of quack grass, and another quack rake, in my second volume of Young Farmer's Manual.)

WHEAT AFTER SPRING CROPS.

A farmer of Orleans County, N. Y., wrote to the " Cultivator " thus : " There appears to be great need of doing something to induce farmers generally to sow less

7

wheat after spring crops. Not but what good crops are sometimes grown in that way; but because the course pursued by a large portion of wheat-growers, makes it necessary to make a good summer-fallow, in order to be at all sure of raising a good crop of wheat—say of from 25 to 30 bushels to the acre. This necessity is very strongly shown by the large amount of poor wheat now on the ground, and that has been harvested during the last two or three years. Probably three-fourths of this wheat was sown after spring crops; and the principal part on land that, if well summer-fallowed, or sown on a good clover lea, would have given a good crop. But, by being put in rather hurriedly and late, as it almost always has to be, when sown after spring crops, and, as is more especially the case now, when labor is scarce and high, wheat does not generally get a sufficiently strong and vigorous start in the fall, to enable it to withstand all of the vicissitudes of a bad winter and spring, and bring it forward sufficiently early to escape the midge and rust. Not but good crops of wheat can be grown after spring crops, and be made very profitable, if sown on land sufficiently dry and rich; but because the principal part of the land thus sown is lacking in one or both of these important requisites. Consequently, while I do not wish to stop all farmers from sowing wheat after spring crops, for there is some very good wheat grown in this way, I would only have it sown where the land is sure to produce good crops; and I would be very glad to see all of our wheat land put in a condition to produce heavy crops without summer-fallowing. But we have to deal with circumstances as they actually exist, not as we would have them.

"Now, the real practical point for the farmer to consider, and that should control his decisions in regard to what crops to raise, is, that wheat has a good many enemies and adverse circumstances to overcome, to generally produce good crops ; and these can only be overcome and guarded against by a good strong growth in the fall ; and that the principal part of our wheat lands are not in a condition to give wheat such a start when sown after spring crops, though a good summer fallow, or a clean one, or two-year old clover lea, would give a heavy crop. And though it may seem like lost time to keep land in an unproductive state, while making a summer fallow, yet there are many reasons why a heavy crop on a summer fallow is better and more profitable than a light crop, or partial failures, after spring crops. Prominent among these is the fact that, in sowing after spring crops, the land has to be prepared twice in the same season, seed found for both the spring and fall crops, and the ground harvested over twice, while both crops may not be as valuable as one heavy crop of wheat, that may be grown on a summer fallow in the same time. Another advantage is, that a summer fallow gives a good chance to clean land that is foul. There are many pests to grain crops, like wire grass (*Poa compressa*) quack grass (*Triticum repens*), and Canada thistles (*Cirsium ar verose*), that seem to grow all the better for the cultivation usually given when wheat is sown after spring crops ; but which the thorough cultivation in making a good summer fallow, in the usually hot and dry months of July and August, will be very likely to subdue—at least to a sufficient extent to prevent their injuring the succeeding crop of wheat." If land is at all disposed to be wet, summer fallowing will not improve its productiveness.

Summer Fallowing for Wheat in Old Virginia. ·

J. W. Hoff, M.D., Wirt Court House, Va., writes: "Wheat is sowed on fallow ground, and after corn crops. The latter is put in with the old shovel-plough, and the former generally with the harrow. The varieties raised are the red chaff, the white wheat, and the Mediterranean. The Mediterranean is considered to be the surest crop; but the yield is not so great as, and the flour is inferior to, white wheat and red chaff. Guano is not used, nor any other manures, save, now and then, a few wagon-loads of barn-yard manure to the acre; so that it is hard to tell what our lands would do if properly manured and fertilized. Under the present mode of cultivation, the average yield per acre, of clean wheat, is about 8 bushels; although some land will bring from 20 to 30 bushels per acre; and I believe that the greater portion of our tillable land would, if properly fertilized and cultivated, bring, upon an average, 20 bushels per acre. The rust damages the wheat in this section of the country more or less every year. In 1850 it caused almost an entire failure of the wheat crops in all North-western Virginia. Early wheat suffers less from rust than late wheat. To avoid the rust, farmers should sow their wheat in the early part of September, when the season is favorable. Of the varieties of wheat mentioned, the Mediterranean is less liable to take the rust. Whether this is owing to any peculiarity in the growth of the wheat, its nature, or whether it be from its earlier growth and maturity, is not yet decided; but it is generally believed to be owing to its earlier maturity."

A farmer in New York wrote against the practice of summer-fallowing, and stated that land should be ploughed

but once for a crop of winter wheat; to which T. L.
Meinikheim, Surry County, Va., replied, in the " Cultivator," thus:

" In the summer of 1856, I had a ten-acre lot, which
was completely overrun with sorrel and wire grass.
The soil, a loose sand. I wished to seed to wheat in
autumn, but was told that the land was so full of acids,
that unless I limed it, I would get no wheat. Being unable to procure lime for less than ten cents per bushel,
and then be obliged to go *fifteen* miles for it, I concluded
to try to *expel*, instead of correcting the acids. When a
boy, I had heard an old Long Island farmer, when speaking of a drought, remark, that ' when the land becomes
thoroughly dried out, it becomes sweetened.' On the
strength of that, I started my plough, ploughing, harrowing, and replonghing from June until October. I was
told I was ' killing' my land ; but as land is cheap here, I
thought it ' wouldn't matter ;' at all events, it would kill
the grass too. One acre of the field I ploughed but twice ;
the other nine acres were ploughed *five* times, and harrowed ten times. In October I manured the whole field
with barn-yard manure, thirty cartloads per acre, ploughed
it down, and seeded to wheat and timothy, and har
rowed until the field had the appearance of a garden
seed-bed ; the one acre included.

" Now for the result. The nine acres yielded ten
bushels per acre of fine plump wheat, sold at $1.70 per
bushel, and netting me $4.25 per acre, besides the in-
creased facility of cultivation. I can now have it ploughed
at $1 per acre, when before it was hard work at $2 per
acre. The one acre ploughed but twice, yielded *three*
bushels of poor wheat, worth but $1 per bushel, costing
me $2.73 per bushel. Over the nine acres there was

quite a ' tolerable catch ' of timothy ; over the one acre
it never came up sufficiently to be visible. Instead of
the soil ' drying out,' it actually became more moist
after each ploughing."

REMARKS.—The reader must recollect that the soil
alluded to in the foregoing paragraph was a very light,
sandy soil, and in a poor state of fertility. By proper
cultivation, with a dressing of rich barn-yard manure and
red clover, the yield of wheat could be increased twofold, with less labor than was required to produce such
a light crop as the writer has reported.

THE OBJECT OF SUMMER FALLOWS.

J. J. Thomas, associate editor of the " Cultivator
and Country Gentleman," writes thus in relation to
summer fallows : " Of late years we see but few summer fallows—they seem to have ' gone out of fashion '
with the wheat crop ; still they have their uses, and we
will give a brief statement of the same.

" The object of summer fallowing is threefold—to
clean, to *deepen*, and to *mellow* the soil.

" 1. Clean culture is desirable; because weeds detract
from the perfection of the cultivated crops grown at
the same time on the same soil. The useless plants
take up the elements which would otherwise be taken
up by the useful—a trite statement, but one too little
heeded by the farmer. Hence the summer fallow is
employed to free the soil of weeds—(a *weed*, it should
be remembered, is ' any plant out of place ')—by the
destruction of their growth and of their seeds which
may be contained in the soil. A true fallow is *bare* of
all vegetable growth—it *rests* from the production of

plants of any kind. This character should always be given them as far as possible. The ploughing should be performed early—the sod carefully inverted—if sandy, turning flat—if clayey, lap furrows—and doing the work as regards moisture, when it will be most effective. Rolling will be beneficial on most soils—after this, the harrow thoroughly employed, and again the wheel-cultivator or gang-plough, so as to destroy the weeds which may appear, as well as to excite the germination of those which lie dormant in the soil, that they also may be destroyed.

" 2. Deep culture is beneficial because it enlarges the capacity of the soil to supply nourishment to plants. A deep, free soil will allow the fine rootlets of growing crops to extend through it at pleasure ; and such a soil is filled with their roots in a manner surprising to every one on a first examination. Numerous healthy roots insure a vigorous growth of that part of the plant above ground—such as is never observed on a hard and shal low soil. We believe deep ploughing has never failed to benefit well-drained soils (not naturally too porous and light already), unless the subsoil was of a very peculiar character. In such cases, deepening will prove beneficial if gradually performed—an inch or two may be brought to the surface at each ploughing without injury.

" 3. Fine culture—the thorough pulverization of the soil—is also necessary to its full productiveness. The ground should be open to the influences of air and moisture—should be free to the shooting of the most minute rootlets of the growing crop. The ameliorating effects of fallowing are in part due to the thorough disintegration of the soil by mechanical working and long exposure to atmospheric influences. Little addition of fertilizing elements may be made, but those lying inert, concealed in the debris of rocks, or waiting admixture to excite into action, are reduced or enlivened, and thus add to the power of the soil. A mellow soil attracts, as well as takes up, more moisture than a hard one. It is thus more likely to be in a state fitted for receiving benefit from the air, from its own ever-working forces, and from the mechanical stirring and manipulation it receives.

" *Thorough culture*, lastly, is the only profitable way of managing a summer fallow, or any part of the farm. To plough carelessly, with half-turned furrows and frequent balks ; to leave the field for weeks to grow up to grass and weeds ; to plough but four or six inches deep where one *owns* good soil much farther down, is some distance from the *right way*—from the true uses of the summer fallow."

ADVANTAGES OF SUMMER FALLOWING.

On this subject, " Colman's Rural World " says : ~

" It is well known that ploughing benefits land. This is especially the case with clay land, which is apt to have suffered from treatment, of which wet ploughing is a noted example. The sun and frost have an ameliorating influence. But the influence is confined mainly to the surface. Hence, frequent ploughing, in its course, exposes all the soil; and even the subsoil, which has never seen the light, can then with great benefit be brought up. That is the time to convert this raw clay soil or any under-soil, into mellow, useful ground.

" Land can be fallowed and lie idle one year with *profit*. The soil is so thoroughly improved, that in this respect alone it pays. The weeds are exterminated, which is another point scarcely second in importance, and in some farms is of the first importance. It gives a chance for *deeper tillage*, preparing the heretofore un-appropriated soil, which serves as so much addition, or manure, to the tillable ground. Further, fallowing the soil prepares it for a succession of crops without manure, equal to the benefit of a considerable quantity of ma-nure without this preparation. Besides, it gives a most excellent chance to dispose of manure. The rawest manure can be used in such a case to the best advan-tage, the soil acting upon the manure, and the manure upon the soil, by fermentation and mutual chemical effect. Lime can also be used with profit ; so can salt. In the fallow is the farmer's great advantage, when his farm ' is run out ' and has become weedy, as it general-ly will be after many years of cultivation. The labor, though it occupies time, is easy. Land requires rest once in a while to recruit its energies ; and stirring the soil is one of the most effective means of doing it, if done during the rains and heat of a whole season."

Summer Fallowing an Exhausting System.

Summer fallowing is an exhausting system of cultiva-tion. The entire soil is occupied more or less with roots of some kinds of plants, which, when the ground is ex-posed to the influences of a burning sun and summer showers, in connection with repeated ploughings and har-rowing, reduces everything that rain and sunshine can de-compose, to nourishment for plants. The soil that is being summer-fallowed does not dry out as soon as if there were a crop on it. If a strip a few rods wide have a

7*

crop growing on it, and another be summer-fallowed, the latter will be quite moist in hot weather, while the former feels dry to the touch. Consequently, the moisture, heat, and frequent stirring greatly facilitate the decomposition of such portions as contain mineral substances that enter largely into the composition of grain or grass. By this means, plant-food accumulates much faster than if the soil were shaded by a growing crop. Soda, lime, magnesia, potash, and silica, which are essential to produce a good crop of wheat, are rendered available to plants in greater abundance by summer fallowing. We know this is so from the fact that a summer fallow always produces a larger crop of grain. This is the result of summer fallowing for a few successive years. But, after three or four years have passed by, there will be a reaction. Summer fallowing will fail in its efficacy. This fact teaches us, that the fertility of the soil cannot be maintained long by naked fallows. It is better for all soils to be shaded. Their fertility can be maintained longer and at less expense by growing some kind of crops which shall be worked into manure, than by cultivating a naked fallow. See second volume of my Young Farmer's Manual.

Winter Fallowing for Wheat.

A practical wheat-grower wrote to the "Country Gentleman," that in America the climate is particularly well adapted for the making of good winter fallows. In fact, winter fallows may be made more serviceable than summer ones are in England; for, by commencing as soon as the crop is off, there are three months of better weather for killing weeds and sunning

the soil than any in that country. Of late years, summer fallows have been nearly discontinued in England,
rye and vetches being grown as a crop to be eaten on
the land by sheep, on the heavy clays, and turnips or
other roots on all friable farms. Formerly, the fallows
were worked chiefly in June, July, and August. But
here, they can be attended to better after a grain crop
is off, in August, September, and October; and if left
at the latter part of the last-mentioned month, so that
it is impossible for any water to lie soaking it, there will
be a splendid seed-bed in the spring, equal to any of
the beds so carefully prepared by the wealthy gentlemen's gardeners in Europe. The farmer having plenty
of stock, can haul the dung where it is required for
producing a crop of roots ; and thus, with such a long
period in the early part of fall and latter part of summer to prepare for everything, his ground will be far
ahead of the Englishman ; because, the latter cannot
harvest his grain till nearly two months later than the
American ; and consequently, is unable so effectually
to clean it, more especially as the sun is much weaker
there than here. Again, the frost, here, pulverizes much
more effectually than there. Yet, there are hundreds
of acres of winter fallowing there, to one here. They
have an average of ten dollars per acre per annum, rent,
to pay, which Americans know nothing of.

By adopting the system of preparing the soil for a
crop of wheat during autumn and winter, the grain
might always be put in quite early, leaving ample op-
portunity for cultivating roots.

Generally, the weather is very showery for some
weeks after the breaking up of winter, so that ploughing and harrowing are much delayed in consequence of

there being too much moisture to have the land work
well.   It may be fine and do admirably for a day or
two, when a wet day prevents going on with the job;
and a second day is lost, while the soil is drying.   A
great deal of delay might be avoided by preparing in
the autumn, and attending to the watercourses, if it is
low land, so that no water lies upon the soil; when it
will be found, after this winter fallowing, that oats, peas,
or any spring grain, will do much better drilled in at
once, the first day the land is dry, than if put in on
ground which is hurriedly cultivated, leaving the stones
and stumps to be in the way at harvest, or treading and
packing down the soil to its great injury.   Winter fallowing effectually and generally carried out, where the
soil is compact and heavy, would regenerate agriculture.
No business succeeds without forecast, and no class use
less forethought than the farmer.   Suppose a store-
keeper only paid attention to half his customers, and at
seasons of the year almost shut up shop, would he be
more unwise than the farmer who loses the whole of
the fall, and does not prepare his land for a crop of
spring grain?

A great deal of good judgment should be exercised
about winter-fallowing very light soils, which never bake
in hot weather.   When there is a large percentage of
alumina and lime in a soil, so that a furrow-slice rolls
over more like a huge slab of putty than the dirt of a
fertile soil, when the land is being ploughed, the fertility of the soil can be wonderfully improved by winter
fallowing.   Read about Fall Ploughing in my second
volume of Young Farmer's Manual.   Light soils are
sometimes injured more by winter fallowing than they
are benefited.   But, whatever may be the character of

the soil—whether light or heavy—water should never be allowed to stand, from day to day, on any portion, as standing water drowns the soil, and impairs its productiveness far more than most people are accustomed to suppose.

DEEP PLOUGHING FOR WHEAT.

In a late number of the American Farmer, Rochester, N. Y., the editor penned the following excellent suggestions in regard to deep ploughing for wheat, which coincide with my own views very well, except that the point with reference to keeping the best soil on the surface, is not made as clear as it should have been. Let the soil be pulverized as deep as practicable ; but let the mould—the best soil—be retained at the surface. The writer says : " The importance to the farmer of understanding the habits and peculiar characteristics of the plants he cultivates, as well as the nature and quality of his soil, is frequently illustrated. Let us take the wheat plant for instance, and we find, by almost common consent, it is best provided for in a shallow seed-bed. Very deep ploughing is thought to be not only unnecessary, but absolutely injurious. The young plant seems to need a firm under-stratum not far from the surface to imbed its roots in, and with this advantage they withstand the ' throwing out ' produced by alternate thawings and freezings, better than when the soil has been recently stirred to a very considerable depth.

" No one at this time of day can overlook, or be ignorant of the great advantages to the soil generally, of deep ploughing. 1st. It opens a much larger amount of soil to the range of roots, giving much more liberal pasturage than they could otherwise get.

" 2d. It increases very largely the supply of nutriment, by allowing the access of air, and by the process of weathering, acting upon the mineral elements of the soil.

" 3d. It preserves an equal quantity of moisture in the soil. We seldom have a rain so great as to produce an unhealthy stagnation of water about the roots of plants set in a soil seven or eight inches deep, and, on the contrary, we seldom have a drought of so long continuance as to extract all the moisture to that depth.

" These, and other known advantages from deep ploughing, we might dwell upon ; and apart from the well-known fact above alluded to, it would hardly be supposed that any crop, of whatever character, would be exempted from the good influences of the practice.

" We must make a proper distinction, however, between a natural subsoil, indurated and rendered impervious to the action of the air by centuries of rest—its original hardness and impenetrability aggravated by a long course of continuous treading, in ploughing the surface soil—and that firm, mellow body of earth, which is produced by deep cultivation.

" It is this firm, yet generous subsoil, which forms so valuable a matrix for the roots of the wheat plant, and enables them to resist the loosening effects of alternate frosts and thaws during winter. This important distinction, it will be observed, allows nothing to be detracted from the argument in favor of deep ploughing. It is only when the previous working has been, indeed, most thorough, that the wheat reaps a due advantage from the shallow ploughing. The understratum, though somewhat compacted in comparison with the loose surface soil, is so enlivened by the former breaking up, that the tender rootlets take firm hold and keep their place.

The advantage of this comparative firmness of the substratum is apparent in the practice, now so common, of seeding corn land to wheat, without any ploughing beyond what has been given to the corn. The action of the tines of the wheat drill, or any such scratching of the surface as will give the seeds a slight covering, is found to answer all necessary purposes even on tolerably tenacious clays. It is insisted, indeed, after much experience, that this is the most successful practice for corn-land seeding."

DEEP AND SHALLOW PLOUGHING FOR WINTER WHEAT.

On this subject, a writer in the "Cultivator and Country Gentleman" thus speaks of deep and shallow ploughing for wheat. He says:

"I have heard some farmers argue that winter wheat requires a deep, mellow soil; and to prove their theory, they would adduce instances in which the roots of wheat plants have been followed downward several feet deep. I have my mind on an instance where a well-digger traced the roots of a wheat plant over four feet into the earth. There appeared to have been in former years, in that place, a large hole or excavation, which had been filled up with surface soil, and had never become very compact; and the wheat struck its roots downward almost as far as the stems grew upward.

The theory of ploughing deep for winter wheat would be a good one, if we did not have the frosts of winter to contend with. The roots of the wheat plant are not elastic, like India-rubber. If they were, winter

wheat would not be very much injured by the freezing
and thawing of the soil.

"Every intelligent farmer knows that when the soil
freezes it is expanded; and as the expansion must
nearly all be *upward*, plants are sometimes lifted from
one to two inches, *i. e.*, the surface of the upper soil is
from one to two inches further above the subsoil than
it is when it is not frozen. Of course, this expansion
lifts the plants with it, and if the roots have struck
downward farther than three or four inches, they must
be severed between the frozen and unfrozen soil. But
in case most of the roots have shot out in nearly a horizontal direction, the plants and roots will all rise and
settle back bodily, as the soil freezes and thaws, and but
very few of the roots will be broken off.

"Now, when the soil is ploughed deep for winter
wheat, the roots must necessarily strike deep downward
in order to obtain sufficient nourishment, unless the
entire soil is filled with vegetable matter and manurial
substances for nourishing the young plants. But when
the large proportion of vegetable matter and manure
are near the surface, the roots all spread out nearly in a
horizontal direction, forming a kind of mat or tender
sod, which all rises in a body when the earth freezes,
without severing any of the roots, except those few that
have struck downward beyond the super-soil."

IMPORTANCE OF SUBSOILING.

The hard, impervious stratum beneath the fertile
mould needs to be thoroughly pulverized, so that the
roots of all kinds of cultivated plants may strike deep
and feed on the vast stores of mineral pabulum that

have been locked up for unknown ages. Almost all of our cultivable fields could be rendered vastly more productive by a thorough subsoiling. The deeper the soil the more productive it is likely to be, whatever may be the crop, except where the subsoil is already so porous and light that the roots of plants find little or no difficulty in striking as far downward as the tops extend upward. Almost all our wheat fields, when the soil rests on an impervious and calcareous substratum, should be subsoiled until a mellow seed-bed is prepared, sixteen or eighteen inches in depth. Subsoiling should always be performed with a suitable plough, and not with an implement that was made expressly for ploughing the surface soil. Some kinds of soil will be well-nigh ruined if turned upside down. Others will not be injured by deep trench ploughing. Every farmer or gardener should understand the character of his soils before he ploughs them.

A correspondent of the "Germantown Telegraph" makes some observations on subsoiling worthy of consideration: "We can readily see that the effect of subsoil ploughing and trenching will vary with the character of the subsoil; if the latter is hard and compact it will probably arrest the downward passage of the water containing the valuable portions of the surface soil, which upon being again brought to the surface will of course enrich the surface soil; but if, on the other hand, the subsoil is light and loose and of a texture not calculated to retain the saline constituents brought from above, they will pass through it, and when it is turned up it may for a time decrease the crops—for the only benefit gained seems to be that of deepening the surface soil, which even of itself is an important one. This may in a great measure account for the varied success which always attends subsoil ploughing, and a more careful attention to the difference may be the means of preventing much disappointment."

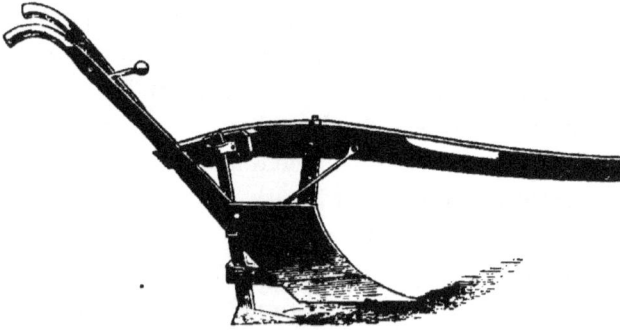

Fig. 82.– Gilbert's Subsoil Plough.

The accompanying illustration represents an improvement in ploughs, which is employed, with satisfactory results, in preparing the land for wheat, where the soil is of such a character as to require the subsoil to be kept beneath the thin layer of fertile mould on the surface of the ground. This plough has been introduced by the inventor, P. M. Gilbert, Kewanee, Illinois, in some of the wheat-growing sections of the United States; and farmers on our lake slopes, when the surface soil is thin, will find that it will be greatly to their advantage to use such a plough, rather than to turn all their mould below the subsoil.

It will be perceived that this plough has a subsoil attachment, which can be adjusted to run any desired depth in the bottom of the furrow made by the main plough.

In my second volume of the Young Farmer's Manual is an illustration of the usual style of subsoil ploughs, accompanied with suitable remarks about subsoiling different kinds of land. Consequently, my notes in this place are brief, on the subject of ploughing.

Remedy for the Lodging of Grain.

It has been assumed that the stiffness of the straw of cereal grain and the roughness and serrated edges of the leaves of all cereal plants, are due to the presence of the silica in the formation of the various parts of the plants just alluded to; and it has been shown by chemical analysis that the straw and leaves of plants that are rich in silica are exceedingly stiff and hard. Wheat straw generally, being much harder and harsher to handle with the bare hands than oats or barley straw, it has been assumed that the straw of this kind of grain contains a larger proportion of silica than the straw of oats or barley, which is always much softer when handled by those who are binding the grain in bundles. Pierri, a distinguished French chemist, has reported some interesting experiments touching the subject of applying preparations of silica in a soluble state to the soil where the plants are to be grown, for the purpose of furnishing material that would render the straw so rigid and stiff that it would maintain an erect position, and thus greatly enhance the yield of grain per acre. This chemist ascertained that the leaves of wheat contain seven or eight times as much silica as the joints of the same stalks to which both belonged, and the portions of the straw between the joints yielded nearly twice the amount of silica that was found in the joints. Arguing from these data, some writers have concluded that by applying silicated fertilizers, the leaves will be developed more in proportion than the stalks; and as large leaves will shade the lower parts of the stalks, instead of strengthening or stiffening the straw, a dressing of silica will exert an enervating influence; and the growing plants will maintain an erect position longer and better when no such silicated manure is applied. It has also been assumed that those grain stalks which bear the largest leaves are more liable to lodge than stalks having short and small leaves. This observation is a correct one; but the extraordinary size of the leaves of wheat is not attributable to an excess of silica in the soil, as silica, even when present in large quantities in the soil, does not produce unusually large leaves without rendering them correspondingly rough and stiff. It will be found, when grain lodges badly, that the leaves are large and much softer than the leaves of standing grain. Every practical farmer is familiar with this fact; and it shows conclusively that there is a deficiency of silica in the soil in proportion to the amount of other manurial material. If, for example, wheat be sowed on a light mucky soil where there is little or no sand or clay, the growing grain will be liable to fall down before the kernels are matured. There will be also an abundance of material to form large leaves and stalks; but as there is a deficiency of silica to impart stiffness to the straw, a driving storm of rain prostrates the growing plants so that they can never gain an erect position. The question then recurs: What may be done by way of cultivation or applying fertilizing material to stiffen the growing straw so as to keep it erect until the grain is fit to harvest? Throwing all chemical knowledge aside, and relying on

practical observations in the field, we learn that certain
causes produce certain effects, whether those effects are
attributable to silica or to the presence of some other
substance that enters into the formation of the straw
of cereal grain. The facts stand out with remarkable
prominence; and whether chemists are able to explain
the phenomena on principles strictly philosophical or
not, practical farmers may avail themselves of the observations and apply the knowledge to the augmenta-
tion of the crop of grain by cultivating and dressing
the soil so as to produce stiff straw that will maintain
an erect position till the grain is fully ripe. When
cereal grain is grown on a sandy soil where wood-ashes
have been scattered in liberal profusion, the straw is
always exceedingly stiff. Almost every practical farmer has observed how rank and stiff the straw of wheat
and oats will always grow where a brush heap or log
heap has been burned to ashes. On many wheat fields
in all parts of the country, the grain growing where a
coal-pit was formed, perhaps forty years ago, will stand
erect, the straw being very stiff, while the straw on every
side of the old coal-bed is too limber to maintain an
erect position. When wood-ashes have been spread
upon the soil in large quantities grain seldom lodges,
especially if there is only a small proportion of sand,
or gravel, or argillaceous or calcareous matter in the
soil. Where a ditch is cut through a mucky soil resting on a subsoil of clay or sandy loam, and only a
small quantity of this material is mingled with the surface soil, the growing grain will maintain an erect position much longer than the grain on either side where
there is no clay or sand mingled with the muck. With
these facts before our minds, a farmer who has only a

smattering of agricultural chemistry, understands what he may do with the assurance of success, by way of preventing his cereal grain from lodging. If the soil be light and filled with humus, attach a double or triple team to a strong plough, and turn up a new soil, which will furnish to the growing plants the desired material for making stiff straw. If the grain lodges on sandy land, let the ground be dressed with a liberal supply of marl or clay. Does the grain fall down where there is a preponderance of clay, apply a dressing of muck, sand, or peat. Whatever the soil may be, or whatever dressing may be applied, let it be borne in mind that wood-ashes, either leached or unleached, will make stiffer and brighter straw, and larger and heavier kernels of grain, than would have grown on the same ground had no wood-ashes been applied. These are incontrovertible facts which are not required to be established by agricultural chemistry. Those farmers, therefore, who sow their wood-ashes on their fields, where the growing grain is liable to fall down before it is ripe, will usually realize a larger profit per bushel than they are accustomed to receive when they sell their ashes for cash. Ashes may be sowed at almost any period after the growing season has commenced; but the effect will be more satisfactory if they be sowed soon after the seed grain is put in.

How to obtain Stronger Stems.

Prof. J. B. Lawes, of Rothhamsted, Eng., says that he has tried the experiment of sowing seed early—the last of August—and feeding with sheep during winter and spring, checking thereby the leaf and stem, and extending the roots, hoping thus to obtain a plant which would resist wind and rain, and have stiffer straw. The effort met with little success. "At one time," he says of other experiments, "I was in hopes that we might by some chemical compounds increase the strength of the straw; but I have been entirely unsuccessful, and do not anticipate there is much to be done by other experimenters." In regard to thin seeding for this purpose, he says that by keeping the plants further apart, so as to admit more light, a stronger stem may be obtained, but at the expense of increased labor in weeding, and, generally, a decrease in the quality of the grain.

What the Soil requires.

It is safe to assume, at the outset, that the atmosphere is all right. Our finite minds cannot conceive how any improvement may be made in the chemical constituents of the atmosphere, for the purposes of vegetation. With all our knowledge of chemistry, we are not able to effect any change in the atmosphere, that will be of any practical advantage, or injury, to growing crops. But we *can* modify the soil. By adding certain substances to it, the most barren earth and unproductive soil can be rendered exceedingly fertile and capable of producing beautiful crops. The inexhaustible quantity of plant food floating in the atmosphere is ever in an available condition for promoting the growth and development of plants. In respect to availability of plant food, there is a marked difference between the plant food in the air and the vegetable nutrition that is locked up in the soil. The plant food in the atmosphere is sure to nourish the growing plants, whenever the tender leaves open their ten thousand mouths to drink in the delicious morsels which are to aid in building up the stems and unfolding the various parts of the plant. The expanding leaves are always bountifully supplied with available nourishment. But it is not so with those parts of the plant that derive their nourishment from the soil. Growing plants may send their numerous rootlets into the earth for food, when the untold number of hungry mouths may be completely enveloped in atoms of just such substance as is required to promote the luxuriant growth of plants; and still those plants may famish, droop, and die, simply because the vegetable nutrition was not in an available condition to promote the growth of the plants. Human beings are sometimes cast away on the briny ocean, where they famish and die for want of a refreshing draught of water, when nothing but a vast sea is spread out before them.

Analytical chemists are capable of analyzing soil with such remarkable accuracy that they can detect a thousandth part of one grain of nitrogen, or phosphorus; and yet their analyses, when made with the utmost precision, may not always furnish any reliable data to aid the practical farmer in the cultivation of his fields.

CARBONACEOUS MATERIAL.

The vast quantities of suet stored about the kidneys of beef cattle, mutton sheep, and well-fattened swine, are composed largely of carbonaceous matter. The most excellent specimens of sugar are composed almost entirely of carbon. Charcoal is only a mass of almost pure carbon; and the costly, beautiful diamond, is composed chiefly of carbon. Let either of these substances pass through a chemist's hands, and he pronounces them carbon. But what will they accomplish towards building up the animal frame?

We feed our children with sugar, and the carbonaceous material in it nourishes them. The carbon in suet supplies large quantities of nourishment to carnivorous animals. But charcoal and the diamond, whether baked, or boiled, or fried, or broiled, or consumed without any preparation, will no more nourish the animal frame than salt water will quench thirst.

These illustrations will suffice to show what the soil requires in order to render it fertile and productive. In order to be productive, the soil must be well supplied with *available* plant food. This is one of the fundamental principles of vegetable physiology. If a soil be wanting in plant food, the first important thing to be done on the part of the husbandman, is to supply the deficiency. But if a soil contain plant food in abundance, and if the food be not *available*, the duty of the husbandman will be to adopt such a system of management as will unlock the sealed-up treasures, and thus enable the growing plants to appropriate the material beneath the surface to the production of necessary human food.

The question then returns with renewed emphasis— *what does the soil require to render it fertile and productive?*

Aside from the *mechanical* condition of the soil— which comprehends thorough pulverization—there must be a bountiful supply of nitrogenous matter and phosphoric acid in an available condition, where the numerous rootlets of growing plants can take up such substances.

In numerous instances, the chief element wanting to make a soil productive, is lime. But it is folly, and many times injurious to the soil, to apply a dressing of lime when lime is not the thing required. The only way in which a farmer can determine whether lime is required in a soil, is by numerous experiments on his own land.

Ashes are needed in almost every soil, on account of the amount of potash required to form a stiff, healthy straw. See my remarks about ashes in the latter part of this book, in the chapter on insects and diseases of wheat.

What a Barren Soil Lacks.

Daniel Lee, one of the most scientific writers of America on Agricultural Chemistry, writes:

"Every observing farmer knows that it is far easier to produce a large growth of *straw* than a great yield of *grain*. This comes from a lack of knowledge of the *things* which form the seeds of cereal plants. Phosphorus and ammonia, or available nitrogen and phosphoric acid—the things wanting in oat straw to make the seeds of this plant—are not very cheap nor abundant. Guano contains more of them than any other fertilizer now in the market. Bones also abound in these elements. Limestone that contains the remains of shells and animals, also possesses more or less phosphoric acid. But where a field is so badly worn that it will not bear over twenty bushels of oats, it had better be seeded with clover, and limed, salted, plastered, and ashed, as well as manured, to a moderate extent. This, with *subsoil* ploughing, will soon bring it up, while the crop of clover will pay all the expenses.

"Deep ploughing and clover, with its long tap-roots and numerous leaves, are admirably adapted to renovate a poor soil.

" In most of the wheat-growing districts, the rotation is limited to wheat and clover as a general rule—two seasons in clover and one in wheat. Sheep and horses eat most of the clover. In soils where lime and gypsum do not abound, they are applied, in greater or less quantities, to suit the particular case or views of the owner of the land. Mr. Elisha Harmon, of Wheatland, a large and excellent farmer, has one field that has borne a good crop of wheat every other year for fifteen years, without any diminution of the biennial yield. The alternating crop is clover. Wheatland, according to the late census, yields considerably more wheat per acre than any other town in the State. It is nearly covered with plaster beds, and its lime rock and soil abound in organic remains. These skeletons contain more or less of the elements necessary to form new plants and animals. There can be little doubt that if we should give to a field all the constituents of the crop we wished to grow, in a soluble form, and in due proportion, we might obtain a large yield every year of any plant. Where the elements of wheat are abundant, it is believed that they might be organized every year on one field, as well as every second or third year.

" The wheat plant contains lime, soda, and chlorine. Soda and chlorine form common salt, which, like the salts of lime and potash, are quite soluble, and liable to be washed out of cultivated soils. The frequent application, in small doses, of these constituents of wheat to wheat fields, must be advantageous, irrespective of rust. It is believed that the production of a *bright, hard,* and *glassy stem*, is a pretty sure preventive of this evil, whether it be a disease of the plant, or a parasite, or both. We infer that soluble silica, or such sand as forms glass, has much to do in making a bright, glassy straw, for the reason that the ashes of wheat straw yield, on analysis, from 67 to 81 per cent. of silica. As the sand in the soil that furnishes this silica is quite insoluble, unless combined chemically with potash, or soda, or both, we see the great value of salt to yield soda, and of wood-ashes to yield potash, not only for wheat, but for all grasses. By mixing salt with recently-slaked lime, in the proportion of two parts of the latter to one of the former (which should be moistened, and again mixed with muck or mold equal in bulk to the lime), the chlorine in the salt will leave the sodium or soda free, and unite with the lime, forming a soluble salt called chloride of calcium. Being soluble, this salt will supply wheat and other plants with whatever lime and chlorine they may need. In one hundred pounds of common salt there are forty pounds of soda, which, being set free by lime in a moist soil, or compost, will combine with silica (silicic acid), and form a soluble salt called silicate of soda. The soluble silicates of soda and potash are partly decomposed in the stems of grasses, leaving insoluble silicates. Leached ashes obtained from plants are made up in a good degree of insoluble silicates of potash, soda, lime, and iron, with a little carbonic, sulphuric, and phosphoric acids."

Different Kinds of Manure and Wheat.

Boussingault, a distinguished agricultural chemist, instituted several interesting experiments to ascertain

what effect fertilizers of different kinds would have on
the chemical composition of the grain, particularly in
the production of gluten; and he ascertained that certain kinds of fertilizing matter produced grain containing a large percentage more of gluten than other
specimens of the same kinds of grain, raised on soil
exactly alike, and which was in close proximity, but
fertilized with a different kind of manure. The large
proportion of gluten and starch in wheat, renders wheat
flour eminently superior to the meal of other cereal grain
for bread, cake, biscuit, and other articles of human food.
Indian corn affords a large percentage of superior starch;
but is deficient in gluten, for which reason Indian meal
will not make so light bread and biscuit as wheat flour.
The accompanying table will show the result of the experiment:

	BRAN, AND OTHER MATTER.	STARCH.	GLUTEN.
Human urine	25.6	39.3	25.6
Bullocks' blood	25.5	41.3	34.2
Night soil	25.5	41.4	31.1
Sheep's dung	24.3	42.8	32.9
Goat's dung.	24.7	42.4	32.9
Horse dung	24.7	61.6	13.7
Pigeon's dung	24.6	63.2	12.2
Cows' dung.	25.7	62.3	12.0
No manure	24.1	66.7	9.2

The variation appears to be almost solely between the
starch and gluten, as other portions differ but little.
The percentage of gluten in white wheat raised in the
United States, is stated to be 23 or 24 parts in every 100;
and the amount of starch, sugar, gum, and water, about
76 or 77. Wheat is valuable in proportion to the
amount of gluten it will yield in making bread and cake.

Certain kinds of wheat will yield much more than others; and the same grain, when grown for several successive seasons in a given climate, will yield more or less gluten, according as it is raised on a wheat soil—a soil containing a large proportion of clay—and manured with that kind of fertilizing material which tends to increase the quantity of gluten.

The table shows that ground fertilized with human urine produced wheat containing more gluten than the grain grown by the application of any other fertilizing matter. This suggests the great importance of saving all such liquid, and applying it to the soil, to increase the yield of this excellent grain, instead of allowing it to remain where it will be an offensive nuisance to the inmates of the dwelling-house. By having a few loads of muck, peat, finely-pulverized alluvial soil, sawdust, or some other good absorbent, where such fecal matter may be received, a large quantity of superior manure may be made during the year, for top-dressing wheat. Almost every kind of soil where wheat grows needs a small quantity of excellent manure.

HOME-MADE POUDRETTE FOR WHEAT.

Poudrette, when unadulterated and properly applied, is one of the most valuable manures for wheat that can be employed, because there is such an abundance of grain-producing material in the raw fertilizing matter of which poudrette is made. Very few families in America make any effort to utilize the large quantities of human excrement which are allowed to accumulate until the putrid mass becomes an offensive nuisance. With proper management, every family might accumulate a quantity of poudrette every year sufficient to produce all the wheat required for their daily bread through the entire year. It is true that the fecal mat ter of a single person amounts to only a small quantity per day. We will suppose the average accumulation will not exceed one pound. At this estimate, the quantity collected in one year would amount to three hundred and sixty-five pounds for each person, of superior fertilizing material, which will produce as much wheat as the same number of pounds of Peruvian guano, provided the former be properly composted. It seems quite unnecessary to enlarge, in this place, on the manurial value of human excrement and human urine, as every person of ordinary intelligence must know that such raw material abounds largely in just such substance as the growing wheat-plants must have in abundance, in order to develop a bountiful yield of grain.

The question then recurs, how may such offensive material be utilized in an advantageous manner so as to promote the growth of the wheat crop? I answer, by having the privy properly constructed, so as to save both the solid and the liquid portions, and render the mass inodorous, so that the compost may be easily applied to the soil. If the privy is properly constructed, there will be little difficulty in handling the fecal material with a shovel.

The accompanying cut, Fig. 33, will convey a fair idea of a convenient manner of making a privy for the purpose of saving the manure. The illustration hardly needs an explanation. It will be perceived that the building is supported on brick pillars. Stone, or durable wood posts, would subserve a satisfactory purpose. A water-tight box, with sides about a foot high, should be

placed beneath the building, and dry muck, or dry pulverized clay should be mingled with the daily accumu-
lations.   By allowing the box or sink to extend beyond
the side of the privy, it will not be found difficult to

FIG. 88.—Poudrette manufactory.

shovel over the compost in any part of the box.   A
water-tight lid should be placed over the box to exclude
rain and snow.   It is not necessary to place the box as
far under the building as it is represented in the figure.

Always keep an abundance of muck, dry clay, or
mellow earth on hand, so as to absorb all the manurial
properties that would readily escape into the air.   Keep
out ashes and lime, as these substances will injure the
manure.   A thin dressing of such compost will produce
a heavy growth of wheat.   Poudrette should always
be applied as a thin dressing on the surface, and covered
with soil.   (Read my remarks on this kind of manure
in the second volume of the Young Farmer's Manual.)

Why Nitrogenous Manures are required for Wheat.

Although an application of superphosphate of lime will grow a large crop of turnips with the aid of a very little organic manure, and red clover will grow luxuriantly on a medium-conditioned soil, with the aid of the same application, or a little plaster, yet no grain crop will reach the maximum on such a soil, no matter how rich you make it in all the mineral and inorganic elements, without a liberal application of nitrogenous, well-saved stall manure, or its equivalent in Peruvian guano or ammonia salts. J. B. Lawes, in his long series of experiments, ascertained conclusively that where every mineral element was in the soil necessary for a maximum crop of wheat, the yield of wheat on an acre was doubled by the aid of two hundred pounds of sulphate of ammonia alone; and Indian corn being a great feeder, it is in much greater need of more nitrogen (ammonia) than the more dainty wheat plant; in fact it may be truly said, the more ammonia the more corn, provided the soil is well drained and tilled. As neither the stalks nor grain of cereal plants contain nitrogen in anything like the proportion in which it is found in peas, beans, clover, and other leguminous plants, Mr. Lawes has come to the very reasonable conclusion that wheat, barley, rye, timothy, etc., destroy nitrogen during the process of their growth, or rather that nitrogenous compounds are used up and destroyed in making other matters in the soil into soluble plant food. Liebig says that quicklime applied to the soil, particularly to clay, dissolves the silicates into soluble plant food. If this is so, *auplus forte raison*,

8*

we should expect that the salts of ammonia would perform the same office to all the insoluble matters in the
soil necessary for the maximum growth of the plants it
supports.

The result of these experiments should teach grain-
growing farmers the great importance of also growing
red clover and other leguminous plants, which collect
most of their nitrogen from the dew, rain, and air, and
yet retain it in their tissues to twice the amount that it
is found in the cereal grasses. Thus, clover, peas, beans,
etc., whether ploughed under in the green state or fed
to animals and the manure applied to the soil, are nearly
thrice the value of manure made from the cereal grasses.

On the light, sandy soils of Georgia, the cow pea is
grown as a manuring plant, and ploughed in green ; as
peas and beans contain three times as much nitrogen
as wheat or other cereals, the Georgia planter proves
the truth of chemical analysis in his own success. The
clover plant being of the same order as the cow pea
(leguminous), consuming little, but affording a great deal
of nitrogen, so necessary to all cereal crops, every farmer
who grows grain, or even timothy and other narrow-
leaved grasses, should also grow clover without stint.
But while the cereals require a soil richer in nitrogen
than in the mineral elements of plant food, yet a liberal
supply of superphosphate of lime will also add to the
incipient growth of cereals, and to the stalks but not to
the grain of Indian corn, and to turnips and all leguminous plants the minerals are especially beneficial.
Mr. Lawes wrote to a farmer thus : " When the alkalies
and phosphates alone are used, the pasture is a mass of
clover and trefoil ; but when ammonia is used, is all
grass." (See " Maine Farmer " on this subject.)

MANURING WHEAT, BY JOHN JOHNSTON.

John Johnston, of Seneca County, New York, whose
authority on wheat-growing has ever been considered
unquestionable, wrote to Colonel Johnson thus : "What
success I have had in raising wheat is *mainly* from manuring. Before I ever thought of draining, by manuring my driest land, I raised excellent wheat crops. Now,
by having all my land dry, a great deal *less manure will
answer*. On dry land manured, the wheat, or at least
the greater part of it, gets forward in spring, so as to
escape the midge ; at least in common seasons. It does
so with me ; and I am more and more convinced, that
where a farmer has a good crop of straw, it will pay
him well to feed all the sheep he can, even if he feed
them each one dollar's worth of oil cake meal, and get
the pay only *in the manure*. But it is scarcely possible
that the sheep will not pay it. If he shears them, they
will at least give him two pounds of wool more per
head ; and then, the carcass, for either keeping over, or
for wintering another season, is, I firmly believe, worth
a dollar. I have often fed merino lambs not over seventy cents' worth of oil meal during winter, and good hay ;
and sold them in spring, say April and May, at five dollars each, when, if they had been fed in the common
way of feeding, they would not have been worth more
than two dollars, if that.

"Then, only think of the difference in the value
of the manure ! I tell you, sir, if your society (The
New York State Agricultural Society) can only induce the farmers of the State of New York to feed
their stock plentifully of grain, or oil cake, and make
their land dry by under-draining when it is wet,

we shall make better crops of wheat than the average yield was, at any time, since I was a resident of the State. There is no guess-work about this, for with me, it has proved true; and it cannot fail to be so with others. It is true that we must expect some failures. But if farmers will do their duty to the land, their failures will be fewer and farther between than ever heretofore. I have seldom seen a failing crop of wheat when it got a good root in autumn. I had a small piece of land, say not quite two acres, that never was manured. In 1856, the wheat on that part of the field was quite light, and the other part of the field (twenty-six acres) excellent; and on the first of October, 1856, I gave one-half of the piece a light manuring of rotten manure from the cattle-yards, say at the rate of about ten common two-horse wagon loads to the acre—the manure showed immediately on young clover. I summer-fallowed the field; and sowed with wheat early in September. The wheat was no sooner up, than that part manured showed plainly, from the part that was never manured. Some may say, why did he not manure the whole of the piece when he was about it? I answer, that I left a part of it to convince my tenant (as I don't work much of my farm myself, now), and others who may see it, the necessity of making and saving all the manure possible. (Nothing will make people believe like seeing.)"

MANURING WITH GUANO.

R. T. Hubbard, of Buckingham County, Virginia, writes, in relation to the practice of applying guano to the soil for wheat, as follows: "Within the last five years, several farmers in this and the adjacent counties

have sown guano upon their wheat land; and, while I
have heard of some disappointment, the testimony pre-
ponderates in favor of guano as a valuable fertilizer. This
manure condenses great power in a small bulk; and
hence its *portability* gives it a great recommendation
with all who properly appreciate the value of labor and
time. The quantity generally sown upon wheat land
is 200 pounds to the acre. I believe that most of those
who use guano in Virginia have acted upon the plan—
strongly enforced a few years ago—of *ploughing* in the
guano *deep*, then sowing the wheat, and covering it by
the harrow or one-horse ploughs. The reason assigned
in favor of burying the guano deep, is the tendency of
its ammonia to escape rapidly. To guard against this
tendency, plaster may be mixed with guano in proportion of one-fourth of the former to three-fourths of the
latter; thus combined, the sulphuric acid of the plaster
will unite with the ammonia of the guano, and retain it
for the gradual nourishment and progressive development of the growing crop. So far as my limited experience has enabled me to judge, I am opposed to ploughing in guano very deep. Instead of ploughing it under
to the depth of eight or ten inches, with ploughs drawn
by two or three horses, I prefer to plough it in with one-
horse ploughs, and to cover the guano only three or four
inches. In this way I believe the guano becomes more
speedily and more thoroughly incorporated with the soil
than at a lower depth, and that the effect upon the
wheat crop is more beneficial. I am aware that this
method has been objected to upon the ground that, although the effect of guano may be very apparent and
very salutary when thus applied, it is more evanescent
than when covered deep. On the contrary, I think that

the effect of guano is not only more decided and bene
ficial when it is ploughed in superficially, but that its
effects are equally, if not more, permanent. Ammonia
is one of the most valuable constituents of stable manure;
yet the almost invariable practice—a practice sanctioned
equally by experience and observation—is to plough in
this kind of manure superficially. I have heard of no
one in Virginia whose success in the use of guano has
been more encouraging than that of Mr. Willoughby
Newton, of Westmoreland, who has been convinced by
experience that guano exerts a more powerful influence
when ploughed in superficially than when ploughed in
deep, as recommended by others. This manure augments the crop of wheat, and insures a good stand of
clover; but in our country its effect is not supposed to
continue more than twelve or eighteen months beyond
the period of application."

FURTHER TESTIMONY ABOUT GUANO.

E. G. Booth, Nottaway County, Virginia, writes thus:
" Guano and other fertilizers are so generally used now,
and so much more attention bestowed on improvement
of land, that the product has been greatly increased
within the last few years. I have not used *guano* ex·
tensively, but sufficiently so to express the confident
conviction that it would quadruple the product on poor
land. The proportion of increase is not so great on rich
land. The plan generally adopted in this section is to
turn it under with a two-horse plough. Intelligent
practical farmers are now preparing to harrow it in with
the wheat. I consider it such a powerful stimulant that
it will act well when applied in most any way, except
top-dressing. It is too volatile for that."

Burying Manure Deep or Shallow for Wheat.

Notwithstanding all that has been written on the subject of burying manure shallow, in preference to covering it deep, there are still some farmers who will contend that it is preferable to scatter the manure in a deep furrow, to simply covering it with a thin stratum of earth. It is far better to cover manure only two inches deep, for winter wheat, than to bury it in a furrow six inches in depth. I may repeat what I have stated in another part of this book: that manure for *winter* grain should always be kept near the surface of the ground, so that the coronal roots of the wheat plant (or the winter rye, or winter barley plants) may spread out horizontally, rather than strike downward nearly in a vertical direction, as horizontal roots will keep the young plants from being lifted out by the freezing of the soil. (See the chapter on Manures, in the second volume of my Young Farmer's Manual.)

For the purpose of testing the advantage of burying manure shallow, some farmers in Pennsylvania tried an experiment in applying manure to their wheat ground. One farmer contended that manure should be turned under deep with the first ploughing; and the other that it should be buried shallow, with the second ploughing. To settle the point as near as possible, these two agreed to try one-half of each of their fields each way, and let the the rest judge by vote which was best. In both cases one-half of the manure was hauled out as soon as the oats were off, and ploughed under deep; then the remainder of the field was ploughed to the same depth, well harrowed and rolled; the balance of the manure was then hauled out, spread, and a portion (about one-fourth) of each field ploughed in shallow (six inches deep), and the remainder of the manure was allowed to remain on the surface till near seeding time, when it was also turned under shallow.

The two fields were visited by a committee, and a report of each visit prepared. The whole of the reports summed up is about this: that throughout that portion where the manure was turned under by the second ploughing as soon as spread, the wheat was always the best in appearance; the straw is better, and the grain is heavier and plumper. The decision was, that the manure should be turned under about six inches deep with the second ploughing, and *as soon as spread, or as soon after it is spread as practicable.*

REMARKS.—If a farmer will reflect for a moment, common sense will convince him, that the fertilizing material should be deposited, as nearly as practicable, on a horizontal line with the seed, so that the young roots may derive nourishment from it, soon after the plants begin to grow. When manure is spread on a grass sod, or clover sod, whether wheat is to be raised or any other grain, the land should be ploughed shallow, for the purpose of keeping the manure as near the surface as practicable.

SHALLOW PLOUGHING FOR WHEAT.

The Editor of the " Genesee Farmer " recorded the following remarks, in relation to the culture of wheat. But the reader must bear in mind that he has reference to wheat on *light* soils. Every intelligent farmer knows that it would not improve the productiveness of heavy, clay soils to roll the surface, or tread it with sheep. The allusion made by the writer to ploughing clover sod shallow for wheat, corroborates what I have advocated in this book—that a shallow stratum of mould should be prepared on the surface of the land to induce the roots to spread horizontally as much as possible, for the purpose of resisting the action of frost in heaving out the young plants. The writer says:

" A wheat soil must be compact. If it is not so natur ally, mechanical means should be employed to compress it. Treading light wheat land in the fall or early in the spring with sheep, is frequently beneficial, and a good heavy roller is decidedly advantageous. Crosskill's Clod Crusher, compressing land, as it does, similarly to the treading of sheep, is found very useful on sandy wheat fields in England. We are earnest advocates of deep ploughing and thorough pulverization of the soil, but these must not be carried to excess in wheat culture. It is easy to make the light land too fine and loose for wheat. When wheat is sown on a clover sod after one ploughing, it is not advisable to plough it too deep; if the sod is all covered and a good 'seed-bed' obtained, that is enough. Subsoil and plough deep for corn and root crops; and, if the ground be summer-fallowed, let it be subsoiled for wheat also; but if wheat is sown at one furrow on a clover sod turned under immediately before seeding, we should seldom go more than six inches deep. The best large field of wheat we ever saw in England, was on a calcareous loam that had been two years in red clover, grazed with sheep, which, a considerable portion of the time, were allowed a pound of oil-cake per day. It was ploughed about three inches deep, just before sowing, and a bushel and a half of seed drilled in per acre, one foot apart in the drills. The yield was fifty-five bushels per acre."

WHEAT AFTER POTATOES.

From a letter penned by J. W. Hutchins, a practical farmer of Templeton, Mass., the following extracts are taken on this subject, which will corroborate the point that has been repeated and again reiterated, that in order to raise wheat successfully the ground must be thoroughly fertilized with rich manure at least one or two seasons previous to the time of putting in the seed. The writer says : "In some parts of New England there is considerable prejudice among farmers in regard to the culture of wheat. Many having tried once or twice to raise this kind of grain and failing, declare that wheat cannot be grown successfully except on certain farms. I, however, believe that wheat can be cultivated with profit by most farmers in New England, although it requires some experience to raise a good crop. In saying this, I do not wish to be understood that wheat can be raised with satisfactory profit on all kinds of soil, for it cannot. Still, I do believe that most farmers in the New England States can, by judicious management, and they ought, to raise wheat for their own families. Wheat ought to be grown because it is an excellent article of food ; and when successfully cultivated, it is more profitable than any other grain. Moreover, a crop of wheat exhausts the soil where it grows, less than a crop of oats or barley ; and grass seed when sowed for stocking down the land, will germinate and grow better than when sowed where other cereals are growing. Having had considerable. experience and good success in raising wheat and other crops, perhaps it may not be amiss to record some of my observations and practice, for the benefit of my brother farmers ; although I feel that I am just a *beginner*, and by no means master of the science of agriculture, which is the greatest of all sciences. And as every science is developed by small beginnings, why may I not add my mite of knowledge to aid those who may be inquiring after truth?

"The seasons, of course, will exert more or less influence on all kinds of crops. Still, in order to raise bountiful crops of any kind, farmers have duties to perform; and if they expect to succeed and thrive, it behooves them to ascertain what these duties are. I seldom fail to raise a bountiful crop of wheat, and hardly ever realize less than twenty bushels per acre; and I have raised as many as thirty-five bushels per acre. Last season I raised, on two and a half acres, and from four and a half bushels of seed, seventy-five and a half bushels of grain by weight. My mode of procedure is as follows: I usually raise a crop of wheat after potatoes. When I first break up a piece of land, I almost invariably plant Indian corn and manure in the hill with wood ashes, etc. The next season the land is heavily manured with barn-yard manure, and planted with potatoes. No manure is applied in the hill, except gypsum. I have raised but two poor crops in eleven years; and some seasons my ground has produced four hundred bushels of potatoes per acre. Land thus managed, has been planted two successive seasons. By the numerous operations of ploughing, hoeing, and digging the potatoes, the manure is thoroughly rotted, and mingled with the soil, instead of being left in large lumps to evaporate and thus lose its strength. By this management my land has been enriched and the fertility equalized, and is thus in an excellent condition to produce both straw and grain. In conclusion, I would say to farmers, if you have ma-

nured your land bountifully, plough deep and put in your
grain early; and do not be afraid of planting the seed
too deep.   Keep your old-fashioned, iron-toothed harrows off the land where seed wheat has been sowed;
because this style of harrow does not work the grain
into the soil as deep as the seed should be buried.   And
more than this, the more you harrow mellow ground
with such a harrow, the harder it becomes.   Procure a
good cultivator harrow, as such implements work like a
charm, leaving the ground light, and bury the seed as
deep as it should be covered.   I sow spring wheat of
the French Tea variety."

GROWING WHEAT AND TURNIPS.

> " No bone-dust, no turnips ; no turnips no wheat ;
> No wheat and no turnips, no cattle no meat ;
> No turnips, no cattle, nor manure in the yard,
> Makes bills for the doctors, and farming go hard."

If there is any one practice among American farmers,
for which they deserve sharp rebuke, it is for permitting
such immense quantities of bones to be exported for the
improvement of the agriculture of foreign nations.
Thousands of tons of bones are collected annually in
Chicago, Buffalo, New York, and other populous cities,
and shipped to European countries to fertilize the land
for raising turnips, wheat, fat cattle, and sheep.   And
yet, American farmers, in stupid quietude, look on and
say: "It don't pay to collect bones, and apply them to
the soil."

It will pay.   They have not tested the application of
ground bone.   There is not a meadow nor a pasture in
the land—with very few exceptions—that will not be

greatly benefited by a dressing of ground raw bone. Thousands of acres of the best farming land in New England are in a low state of impoverishment for the want of a liberal dressing of raw ground bone. Such fertilizing matter is the very life of the soil. European farmers understand and appreciate this fact. They know it pays to ship bones from America to enrich their farms. The value of every ship-load of bones that is picked from our land cannot readily be computed in dollars and cents to the agriculture of our country. England delights in her own fatness produced on the choice cheese of American dairies, while we mutter and grumble over a pot of the whey. Europeans rejoice over the rich, sweet American butter, while we are so unaccountably stupid as to be satisfied with the butter-milk. Our farmers dig and delve, and rake and scrape their grain-fields, meadows, and pastures to get phosphatic fertilizers to send to Europe to produce big crops of turnips, and then grumble and denounce their own land as good for nothing, because their turnips refuse to grow as they do in Eastern countries. The truth on this point is, American farmers must save and apply more manure to their impoverished land: especially must they save bones for growing a crop of turnips. As soon as we can produce a bountiful crop of turnips we can grow wheat. Wheat and turnips in England go hand in hand. And when the wheat soils of America are rendered sufficiently fertile to produce a crop of turnips, we may have the eminent satisfaction of seeing bountiful crops of choice wheat, where now the yield will scarcely defray the expenses of harvesting and thrashing the crop. Sometimes a farmer will have to cultivate for several years before he can produce wheat.

WHEAT AFTER PEAS.

A crop of peas is one of the most advantageous crops to precede winter wheat. In many sections of the country, where winter wheat is cultivated to considerable extent, a crop of early peas is preferred, as a preparatory crop, where winter wheat is to grow. But, a thin dressing of well-rotted barn-yard manure is usually prepared during the summer, and ploughed in, after the peas are harvested. In some instances the manure is hauled to the field as soon as the peas have been removed, and is ploughed under, and the wheat put in as soon as it is practicable to do it, after the first of September.

Another mode, which is preferred by some good farmers, is to remove the peas as early in August as practicable, and plough the ground from six to eight inches deep; and then, about the first of September, spread the manure, very evenly and thin, over the entire soil; and then plough it under with a gang-plough, or with such a cultivator as is illustrated on page 142 of this book, adjusted to run about four inches deep, after which the wheat is drilled in.

The preparation which the barn-yard manure receives, when it is applied for wheat, after a crop of peas, is, to haul the manure from the barn-yard in the former part of the season, and pile it up in the field during the summer, forking it over sometimes, in order to have it well rotted and finely pulverized; and after the ground has been ploughed once with the common plough, and sometimes crossed with the gang-ploughs, the manure is neatly spread on the surface, and the ground thoroughly harrowed, by which the manure is about all covered with more or less earth near the surface of the ground. This system of management usually insures a fair crop of wheat. But, on certain kinds of soil, the preparation is not as it should be for a crop of winter grain. Where the surface soil is thin—where there is only a thin stratum of vegetable mould, special care should be exercised to keep the mould at the surface, and not turn it all seven or eight inches beneath a cold and unfertile subsoil. I have observed, that some farmers have failed entirely to produce a fair crop of wheat after peas, because they did not observe this precaution, to keep their best soil at the surface. There was only a thin stratum of mould resting on a heavy, calcareous clay, which was turned up to the surface; while all the manure and fertile mould were buried beyond the immediate reach of the young plants.

The ground, in such localities, should always be ploughed shallow; and the seed-bed should be deepened by a regular subsoil plough, or with such an one as I have illustrated on page 162. The best soil should be kept near the surface; and the fine manure should be covered as lightly as practicable, for the reason which has been assigned in the former part of this chapter. (Read also the remarks under the Habit of the Wheat Plant; and How Freezing and Thawing Injures Growing Wheat, on page 126.)

As a crop of early peas will mature in a short period of time; as the vines grow rapidly, and thus get the start of weeds; and as the crop takes up only a small quantity of the wheat-producing material in the soil, this crop can be raised with more profit than a crop of oats, barley, or Indian corn, in some instances. A crop of growing peas, when there is not an excess of moisture in the soil, will often render a compact and lumpy soil as mellow and lively as a friable loam. When the peas are fed out to fattening stock, and the manure of the animals saved with care, and returned to the soil where the peas grew, the pea crop will always be found an excellent ameliorator of a heavy and poor soil. A crop of green peas will always be found fully equal to a crop of red clover to turn under with the plough as a renovator of a poor soil. Yet I would prefer a crop of Indian corn for such a purpose, as the stalks will furnish more vegetable matter than a crop of peas. (Read the chapter on Manures in my second volume of the Young Farmer's Manual.)

Peas are a very exhausting crop, when everything is removed from the field and nothing returned to the soil as an equivalent for the crop. But when the peas are all fed out to stock, and their manure saved and applied to the land, peas are an excellent renovator; and where the soil is heavy, a crop of peas should constitute a prominent one in the rotation system, especially where winter wheat is cultivated.

Joseph Harris, who resides in one of the finest wheat-growing counties of New York, writes: "In preparing heavy land for wheat, it is still necessary, in many cases, to resort to summer fallows. On the light soils we may take a crop of beans, planted in rows and thoroughly horse-hoed, and sow wheat afterward. On heavier soils I have seen an excellent crop of wheat follow a crop of peas, which had been sown instead of fallowing. The great drawback to the peas is that they are affected by the bug. But if fed out early to hogs, the bugs do not injure them materially, while they are very fattening and make rich manure. You can com-

mence feeding them to hogs on the land, while the peas
are still green."

Sheep in Connection with Wheat.

Although bountiful crops of wheat may be produced
by the application of commercial fertilizers to the soil,
still the true way to grow wheat successfully is to keep
sheep and make mutton, and at the same time employ
their manure to maintain the fertility of the soil.
Bountiful crops of wheat can be grown in connection
with fatting neat cattle and hogs, or horses, provided
the animals get a liberal supply of coarse grain ; and
providing also their manure be saved with care and applied to the soil. Farmers may set it down as an incon
trovertible fact, that they cannot grow wheat of any
kind successfully, without applying to the soil some kind
of fertilizing material that will supply an abundance of
grain-producing pabulum in the soil for the development of the wheat kernels. I will reiterate what will
bear repeating again and again, that if the land be manured with strawy manure, the crops of wheat will be
mostly straw, with a small yield of grain. We cannot
cheat any soil by manuring with haulm, and think to
get a heavy yield of grain. If the ground be enriched
with grain-producing material, a farmer can hardly fail
to realize a fair crop. One of the most efficacious ways
to secure a bountiful yield of wheat would be to sow
wheat flour, or drill it in with the seed grain.

If I desired to produce the largest crop of wheat that
had ever been grown, after enriching the soil with a
liberal dressing of the best manure, I would sow thirty
or forty bushels of wheat flour per acre, drilling it in

with the seed grain. Such a dressing would operate like magic in the production of a heavy crop of wheat. I would not recommend the practice of sowing wheat flour, for the purpose of producing an enormous crop of grain; I simply allude to this suggestion of fertilizing the soil with wheat flour, for the purpose of showing that in order to raise wheat there must be some material in the soil that the wheat plants will take up and appropriate to the development of the new grain. These thoughts will show the young farmer what the soil requires.

Now, the question arises, how can a farmer employ his grain as a fertilizer, and at the same time avail himself of its cash value besides? I answer, by making mutton, and applying the valuable manure of his fat sheep to his soil. When grain or meal is fed to fattening stock, only a small part of it is appropriated to the growth and development of the animal, while a large proportion is cast out into the manure heap. This is the material for producing a large yield of grain. Manure that is made by fattening sheep will furnish large supplies of just such materials as the wheat plants must have, to yield a bountiful crop of grain. Consequently, if a farmer will combine sheep-fattening with wheat-growing, he can scarcely fail to bring an ordinary soil into such a state of fertility, in a few years, that he can reap bountiful crops of wheat of a choice quality. But sheep-raising and wheat-growing will not succeed at all satisfactorily, unless sheep are kept in a growing and thrifty condition by feeding large quantities of coarse grain, and oil meal and turnips, or roots of some kind. A farmer may just as well take the products of his land and pitch them into the mill-pond, and think to improve the productiveness of his land, as to attempt to feed and fatten sheep without first selecting animals that will fatten readily. Another consideration is, proper protection of sheep. Wet and cold weather is exceedingly detrimental to sheep of any kind. Water dripping through leaky sheds is very disagreeable and injurious to sheep. They always hate a wet and cold place, as much so as a neat cat hates a wet floor.

The leading idea in fattening sheep should be, to prepare a large supply of rich manure, especially when a crop of wheat is desired. A flock of sheep will reduce a large stack of straw to manure more readily than it can be done with a lot of neat cattle. But the sheep must have grain, and some oil meal mingled with the grain, or with the grain meal. If sheep are young, and have excellent teeth, and a grist mill is not conveniently near, it will not pay to grind grain before feeding it to sheep, as they masticate their feed remarkably fine. It is a rare occurrence that any kind of grain or seeds of noxious weeds pass through sheep without having the vitality of the germs destroyed. For this reason whole grain may be fed to sheep with satisfactory profit, when the same grain could not be fed to neat cattle with desirable results. I think farmers will understand my idea of feeding sheep on coarse grain with a view to renovating the soil for the production of wheat. There is no other feasible and practicable manner of maintaining the perpetual fertility of the wheat fields of America than by growing red clover, fattening sheep, hogs, or neat cattle, and raising a bountiful supply of turnips for stock during the foddering season. By feeding coarse grain, turnips, oil meal, red clover, and wheat straw to sheep, and by applying their manure judiciously

to the land, after a few years of skilful management the
productiveness of poor farms may be greatly improved,
and good land can be rendered much more productive.
Oil meal and coarse grain fed to sheep in connection
with some hay, cornstalks, and wheat straw, will make
a quality of manure that will produce wheat on almost
any kind of soil, whether it is light or heavy.

WHEAT AND CATTLE.

In the second volume of my Young Farmer's Manual
I penned some suggestions touching the importance of
adopting a mixed husbandry.   That is the true way to
maintain the fertility of the soil, especially where raising wheat constitutes a part of the products of the
farm.   Intimately connected with the subject under
consideration are the remarks of the Editor of the
" Western Rural," who writes :

" Michigan farmers have a mania for growing wheat,
while they too much neglect other important and profitable farm products.   In 1860, Michigan produced
8,313,185 bushels of wheat—a little more than one-
twentieth of the whole amount grown in the United
States.   Of cheese in the same year it produced only
2,009,064 pounds.   The little State of Vermont, with
an area about two-elevenths as great, produced 8,077,089
pounds of cheese, but only 431,127 bushels of wheat.
That Vermont did not grow so little wheat because her
soil is not adapted to wheat culture, is shown from the
fact that the average yield of wheat per acre in Vermont, in the year 1864, as shown by the Report of the
Department of Agriculture for January, 1865, was fourteen bushels per acre, while in Michigan the average

yield per acre for the same year was but twelve bushels. Thus it is seen that although the farmers of Vermont can grow fourteen bushels of wheat on the amount of land from which Michigan farmers get twelve bushels, yet the Vermont farmers prefer to give attention to dairy products to the almost entire neglect of wheat. Why is this? Evidently because they find dairy farming the most profitable.

"Michigan farmers do not manufacture cheese enough to supply the home market, but give their labor and land to the production of but twelve bushels of wheat per acre. In the early days of the State, when wheat was almost the only article that brought the farmer ready money, when it was a sure crop, when the soil was a virgin one, and when most farmers possessed but little capital, there were doubtless good reasons why wheat should be grown almost exclusively; but we are convinced that those reasons are not now so strongly in force, and that there are other and strong reasons why our farmers should give greater attention to dairy products and stock.

"We do not object to the growing of wheat *per se*. It is one of our most valuable crops. When a proper rotation is pursued it can scarcely be dispensed with. What we do object to, is the great attention given to wheat-growing to the exclusion of other branches of farming which are as profitable as wheat-growing, or more so. As we said above, our farmers have a mania for growing wheat, a mania which they pursue to such an extent that their lands grow less and less fertile from year to year. Growing wheat as most Western farmers grow it, is a continual draught on the resources of the soil with no adequate return; and however rich a soil

may be at first, it will in time deteriorate under such
usage.   Clover and plaster are the principal fertilizers
on most wheat farms.   When their use is continued for
a series of years, the farmers begin to complain that
their land is 'clover-sick' or 'plaster-sick;' that it
will not give profitable returns.   Land so treated will
inevitably give out.   It is every year deprived of many
of its most valuable constituents in the crops of wheat
which are taken off—constituents which are by no means
fully returned in the fertilizers, clover and plaster.
That our lands are losing their fertility, we see in the fact
that they now produce less per acre than the naturally
poorer soil of the Eastern States; for in those States
such an exhausting system of cropping is not pursued.

" Now by giving to wheat no more than its due share
of attention, by keeping a large portion of land in
meadow, and pasture, and root crops, and feeding the produce to animals either for the dairy or the shambles, farmers will surely reap as large immediate returns as when
wheat is the main crop—and we believe much larger—
and can, by aid of the large amount of manure which
they will manufacture, keep their land in excellent condition."

This is the key note to successful wheat-growing all
over the world—raising stock, making beef, mutton, or
pork, and applying rich manure to the soil.   The sooner
farmers become so thoroughly convinced of this fact,
the better it will be for their pockets, for the land, and
for the whole country.   It is exceedingly unfortunate to
our country, that our valuable wheat fields, all over the
land, are depleted and almost ruined by a bad system
of farm management.   Our successors will feel this slack
cultivation.

Fink's Iron Cultivator.

The accompanying figure represents an excellent cultivator, recently invented by J. Fink, Baldwinsville, Onondaga County, N. Y., which possesses many points of superior merit. The frame is made of iron, and the teeth are of superior steel. The implement possesses a

Fig. 83.—Fink's Iron Cultivator.

combination of desirable points, which constitute an efficient · and convenient implement for cultivating summer fallows, winter fallows, for scarifying stubble ground, and dressing out crops in rows; and besides this, many farmers think it the most effective implement for digging potatoes that is now in use. Where there are more or less stumps, stubs, or rocks, to cultivate around and among, a cultivator having handles will be found more convenient than one without handles.

The wings are so arranged, that the teeth can be made to cut a wide trough; or they may be contracted so as to cut only a narrow strip, either deep or shallow. As the cut affords such an excellent idea of the implement, the foregoing verbal description will be sufficient to convey a fair understanding of its construction and operation.

CULTIVATING GROWING WHEAT.

It has been often suggested, that wheat would yield a much more abundant crop of grain, were the growing plants cultivated with a horse-hoe and hand-tools. We have, however, no experiments to establish this point. On the contrary, judging from the habit of the wheat plant, I think that the less the soil is stirred after the wheat is put in, the better it will be for the growing crop. I will tell why. Every wheat plant sends out numerous roots near the surface of the ground. If we examine a stool of growing wheat on new land, when the surface is covered with a fine, vegetable mould, we shall find that there are more roots near the surface, than can be found several inches beneath the surface. Cut off those surface roots with a broad hoe, or with a harrow, or cultivator, and nature will at once appropriate all the energies of the growing plants to form a new system of roots, near the surface. This fact teaches us that the growing wheat plants do not need root-pruning. If a horse-hoe, or hand-hoes be employed to cut up the surface of the ground between the rows, the surface, or coronal roots will be seriously mutilated, to the injury of the plants. I think that all good farmers and practical gardeners will coincide with me on this point, that after the seed has been put in, the surface of the soil should not be disturbed by implements of husbandry. If noxious weeds and grass spring up among the growing grain, let them be pulled up by hand, and laid between the rows, where they will subserve the purpose of a mulch to the wheat. Weeds may be pulled up, when they appear among the wheat; but they should never be cut up with hoes. The soil should be so thoroughly prepared, that the growing wheat will outstrip the weeds, and maintain the ascendency until harvest time.

It is contended by some writers, that the efficiency of the preparatory tillage is lost by the fine particles of the soil coalescing, or running together, thus forming a crust over the surface, which excludes the atmospheric supplies of nourishment to the roots of the growing plants. In numerous instances, particularly when the soil is very heavy, long before the crop has reached the period of perfect maturity, the soil will be found almost as impervious to water and as firm as it was before the ground was ploughed preparatory to sowing the seed. This is frequently the case. When carting the crop after harvest, the surface is sometimes so firm and indurated, that the tracks of the teams and loaded wheels can scarcely be traced. Instead of cultivating the growing plants, prepare the soil as directed in the second volume of the Young Farmer's Manual, by the author, under the head of Keeping the Best Soil at the Surface.

HARROWING WINTER WHEAT.

The practice of harrowing winter wheat in the spring of the year has been frequently recommended by some practical farmers and certain agricultural writers, while others have denounced this operation as productive of more injury than benefit to the growing plants. It is by no means difficult to explain why harrowing winter wheat in the spring may prove beneficial in one instance and not in another; and it is easy to show when the young wheat plants may be benefited by harrowing and when a harrow would do far greater injury than good. When wheat is growing on a light and dry soil, where the seed was sowed broadcast and harrowed in, as many of the young plants would be found rooted near the surface, a harrowing would be liable to do greater injury by tearing up large numbers of such stools of wheat, than the scarifying of the land would benefit the crop. Again, when the seed has been put in with a grain drill, say two inches deep, and the surface of the land seems to be covered with a hard crust of earth, a light harrowing, when the ground is sufficiently dry to be ploughed, would prove of great benefit to the young wheat plants. But the operation should be performed with a light harrow, having numerous small teeth, rather than with a heavy implement provided with only a few large teeth. When winter wheat has been put in with a drill about two inches deep, all the primary roots will be found at that depth below the surface of the ground, until after the growing season of the succeeding spring has so far advanced as to produce a system of secondary roots near the surface of the ground. This fact suggests why winter wheat—if harrowed at all—should be harrowed very early in the spring, before the growing season has commenced. The object of harrowing so early is twofold: one is to pulverize the hard incrustation that has been formed on the surface, so that there may be a thin stratum of mellow ground between the primary roots of the wheat plants and the surface, instead of a crust of calcareous earth, which is almost impenetrable by the secondary roots of the young plants. This would be eminently essential to the perfect growth and development of the wheat plant, were there no secondary roots to appear after the young plants have attained a growth of a foot or more in height. 'The second object of harrowing the soil is to form a mellow seed-bed at the surface of the ground, around each plant, through which the secondary roots may spread with facility, when that period in the growing·season has arrived for the young plants to put forth their secondary roots. Roots of trees, bushes, vines, or roots of grass or plants that produce grain, spread with the utmost difficulty through clods, or a hard crust of almost any kind of ground. But when there is a liberal supply of calcareous matter in the hard lumps, or crust of earth, roots will not spread through the soil in such a condition much sooner than they will enter soft stones.

Still another object in harrowing winter wheat is to bury the grass-seed, or clover-seed, when the land is stocked down in the spring of the year.

A few years ago, a correspondent of the "Cultivator" wrote thus: "Myron Adams, of East Bloomfield, New York, has for many years harrowed over the whole of his wheat fields every spring, pulverizing the crust and greatly benefiting the crop. If the ground is to be seeded with clover, it is harrowed in at this time. The whole amount torn up by the roots has been found by examination not to exceed the amount of a bushel on ten acres. The wheat looks rather unpromising when thus dusted over with earth; but the first shower washes it off, and leaves it clean, fresh, and vigorous."

WHEAT ON SOD GROUND,

Raising a crop of wheat on sod ground in some sections of the country is practised with satisfactory success, while in most instances, all efforts to produce a fair crop

of wheat on inverted sod have ended in complete failures. In Monroe County, N. Y., one of the noted localities for producing fair crops of winter wheat, many
excellent farmers were accustomed to raise wheat on
sod ground, by preparing the land in the following
manner:

About the first of September the sod is neatly ploughed about eight inches deep, with a lap furrow, after
which a roller is passed over it, when a thin coat of
good barn-yard compost is spread evenly over the surface,
and is either well harrowed in, or is turned under very
shallowly with the gang-plows, which usually cut from
three to four feet in width at one through. The
wheat is then put in about the fifth or tenth of September.

It will be perceived by this system of management
with the soil, that the surface of the seed-bed is prepared in
exact accordance with the requirements of the *habit* of
the wheat plant. Read the remarks under the head of
the Habit of Wheat, on a preceding page.

By passing a roller over the ploughed land, the furrow
slices which lay up loosely, are pressed down firmly
together. Then, by scarifying the surface with gang-
ploughs, or cultivators, so as to pulverize the surface to
the depth of about three or four inches, and fertilizing
the surface with a rich compost, so that most of the roots
will spread out horizontally, instead of striking downward vertically, the young plants will be well prepared
to resist the sinister influences of the cold weather, which
arise from the upheaval and settling back of the surface
of the soil.

But I would not, as a general rule, recommend the
practice of attempting to raise wheat on sod ground, un-

less the land is very free from noxious weeds of all kinds, and grass that will not decay readily, and the soil in an excellent state of fertility. When the land is at all foul, and any kind of grass has taken possession of the soil which will grow up after ploughing, before the wheat can come up, a farmer may about as well sow his seed wheat in a pasture field, with the expectation of growing a fair crop of grain. Wheat will not thrive at the same time where noxious grass flourishes.

Sowing Wheat among Indian Corn.

In some parts of the West, where the soil is so fertile that farmers entertain the erroneous notion that its fertility is inexhaustible, the practice is in vogue of sowing seed wheat among the growing corn, and covering the seed with the horse-hoe and hand-hoes, in the latter part of summer, or even in September. A farmer writes to one of our Western papers, that "sowing wheat among standing corn is an excellent practice when done by competent workmen. The most successful plan will be found to plant the corn in rows five or six feet apart, and the hills in the rows two feet apart. The ploughings, horse-hoeings, and dressing with the steel-tooth cultivator, will all require to be done in one direction across the field, and not in right-angular rows, as is the common practice; and before the wheat is sown, the ground should be made level with a steel-tooth cultivator or harrow. The time for seeding should be the last of August; the quantity sown per acre, two bushels—and the seed should be ploughed in, putting the whole field into lands the width of the rows of corn. The stalks may remain on the ground during winter, and about the first of March be chopped down, and allowed to remain on the surface."

I perceive serious objections to this system of seeding. The first is, the great injury done to the growing corn, by the teeth of the tools and horse implements, which will tear up the roots of the corn, to the great injury of the crop. Indian corn needs no root-pruning. Horse-hoes cannot be employed between the rows after the plants have put out their tassels, without seriously injuring the roots, which often extend two or three feet down the stems. Sowing seed wheat among growing corn may be well for the wheat plants, but it will be exceedingly injurious to the crop of Indian corn.

Another consideration of some little account is this: When sowing wheat among growing corn, the large and broad leaves of the growing plants will gather many of the kernels, and thus prevent their falling to the ground in due time to take root before winter. And much of the grain would be destroyed by exposure to alternate wet and sunshine, while the kernels are lodged in the stems of corn.

Sowing Wheat on Corn Stubble.

The practice of sowing wheat on corn ground, in autumn, used to be more in vogue than it is at the present day. In the Middle and Eastern States, farmers were accustomed to sow winter wheat in autumn, after a crop of Indian corn had been removed; but the practice is now nearly abandoned. A writer in the "Ohio Farmer" states, that "it is still the practice with a *few* farmers, on the rich lands of Ohio, and other States, to sow land to wheat in the fall, on which corn has been grown the same season. A sod is turned over for corn, upon which manure is spread, if the land is not rich enough without it, and as soon as the corn is cut and stooked in the fall, the land is harrowed to level the corn rows, and the wheat is drilled in. The stooks of corn are placed in rows as far apart as possible, and the drill runs close to them, leaving unseeded the space occupied by the stooks, which are set in as straight rows as possible, so as to leave as little land unseeded as possible. The land is seeded down to such grasses as are desired at the same time the wheat is sown.

"It is said that good crops of wheat are grown in this way, but only on lands that are in good fertility, and where the corn has been well cultivated. It saves one season in time, and one ploughing, which are objects of importance; but the unseeded strips where the corn stooks are placed, make this system less satisfactory than it would be, if the entire field could be seeded down at once. The unseeded strips, however, may be harrowed early in the following spring, and seeded down to the same grasses that were sowed on other parts of the field, and after harvesting the wheat the entire field would be uniform."

There is a plausible objection to sowing winter wheat after corn, where the crop of corn is not removed from the ground before the wheat is sowed, which is this: after the wheat has come up, the blades are exceedingly tender; and by driving teams and wagons over the growing plants to remove the grain and the stalks, and by the bruising and crushing of the leaves by the feet of laborers, when husking, the growing wheat is materially injured, so that the yield will be several bushels of grain less, per acre, than if the crop of corn had been removed before the seed was put it.

Some farmers contend that driving over growing wheat and treading the tops down in autumn, does not injure the growth of the plants. I will not occupy space, in these pages, to argue the case, to show that the poaching of the ground by the feet of heavy teams, the crushing of the leaves, which are the lungs of the young plants, with the loaded wheels, and the breaking of the roots of the growing plants, all result in serious injury to the growing crop, for I *know*, that whatever mutilates the growing plants, must have an influence in retarding and diminishing the fructification of the grain. The better way is, to defer sowing winter wheat; and after the corn crop is removed, plough the land in late autumn, and sow spring wheat the next season, instead of winter wheat. I am satisfied that more grain can be raised by sowing spring wheat, than to try winter grain, and tread the tops half to death, while husking the corn and removing the stalks.

ALDEN's THREE-HORSE CULTIVATOR.

This style of cultivator, which represents a wheel cultivator manufactured by Alden & Co., Auburn, N. Y., is a strong, three-horse implement, extensively used in the wheat-growing sections of New York, Ohio, and Canada, for preparing ground for both winter and spring grain. It is a very strong implement; and not very easily broken. The teeth consist of iron standards bolted firmly, and braced securely to the sills of the frame; and the cutting edges of the teeth are made of plate steel, with a cutting edge on each end. After one end of the plates is worn out, the ends can be changed by simply taking out a small bolt, which secures the plates to the cast-iron standards, and turning the dull ends upward. This arrangement provides an econom-

FIG. 34.—Alden's Cultivator.

ical tooth for such heavy cultivators. The teeth can be adjusted to run at any desired depth in a few seconds; and all the teeth and the frame can be elevated above the ground several inches, for convenient transportation.

This cultivator is employed extensively by grain-growing farmers for cultivating stubble ground after harvest, for the purpose of rooting up grass and young, noxious weeds, and covering the seeds of troublesome plants, so that they will readily vegetate, and thus facilitate future extermination. Besides this, the teeth can be put down so as to run six inches deep, thus pulverizing the entire ground quite as effectually as the work can be performed with a plough.

With three strong horses, or with a yoke of oxen and a span of horses attached to such a cultivator, which cuts a through four or five feet in width, one man will be able to prepare a number of acres in a day. The three-horse cultivator requires a strong and heavy team. I would advise a man to be *perfectly satisfied* that he needs a three-horse cultivator before he orders one. But there is no danger that a *two-horse* cultivator will be too large and heavy.

How to Raise Wheat on a Poor Soil.

I fancy that numerous readers will say: "Now, my land is poor, the soil thin and unfertile; how may I raise a fair crop of wheat?" Well, you can't expect to do it in one year, nor in two seasons. In order to bring poor land into the proper condition to give us good crops of wheat, we must adopt a better system of culture. The land must be worked to a greater depth, be more thoroughly pulverized, and have suitable fertilizing material liberally applied. Where necessary, the surface must be underdrained to the better warming, draining, and aërification of the soil. When we accomplish this, we shall find that as good crops will be realized as in former days; and those destructive insect enemies, which are the dread of all wheat-growers, will be defeated, especially where we adopt a system of rotation, raising crops for feeding stock, and manuring with especial reference to this crop, and growing from a less area a greater amount of grain or other crops. We must adopt an alternation of growing the cereals with the leguminous and root crops, and feed them out, applying the manure made therefrom to the soil. Such crops should be raised for feeding as will furnish the elements for the richest manure, such manures being found the most economical for application to the soil. It will scarcely be necessary to say that wheat may be grown on a variety of soils, as there exists a great diversity over the region in which it is a leading crop.

Farmers all over New England may just as well raise their own wheat as to purchase their flour at such an extortionate price ; and often be so scandalously imposed on by those who sell a poor article for a large price. The whole system of wheat growing may all be summed up in a few words, namely : *Cultivate well, and manure bountifully.* Usually the best preparation of the land for wheat, is a dressing of rich, well rotted, or composted, barn-yard manure. Unrotted manure tends to produce a heavy growth of straw, which will be liable to rust, and yield less grain. The best practice is to apply it late in autumn, simply harrowing it in after the land has been well ploughed. By spring it is well decomposed. Where it is desirable to apply the manure in the spring, scrape the hog-yard for it with broad hoes, and use heaps of fine manure previously collected ; and if the soil be compact and heavy, add well-rotted chip manure. On soils in which there is a great amount of vegetable matter, never apply any barn-yard manure, unless it has been thoroughly composted or rotted. On land where there is usually a great growth of straw, wood ashes, either leached or unleached, applied in liberal quantities, will have an excellent influence in producing a bountiful crop of grain. After ten years of thorough cultivation and manuring, the heavy crops of wheat will appear.

Rough versus Smooth Wheat Fields.

Many of our best farmers have of late been accustomed to contend, that the rougher the surface of the ground, where winter wheat is growing, can be left after the seed is put in, the more advantageous the rough land will be to the growing plants in protecting them from the severity of the winter. The "Western Rural" states that "Every experienced grower of wheat knows that this rule is more frequently disregarded than it is observed. A moderately rough surface in the wheat field has many advantages over a smooth one ; for instance, it keeps snow from being blown away, and thus affords protection to the young plants from the alternate thawing and freezing which is so destructive to their vitality. In spring, after the snow has disappeared, the rough surface affords shelter to the plants from the cold winds which prevail during the early part of that season. In every wheat field may be seen in spring, plants growing in little hollows, sheltered by lumps or banks from the cold wind, but enjoying the benefit of the sun's rays. The difference between the growth of these plants and others which have not the benefit of shelter, is remarkable. Smooth, level surfaces are liable to become a mass of soft mud, when the spring thaws take the frost out of the ground, and much wheat on smooth surfaces is heaved out by the sudden change from frosty to mild weather. It need scarcely be stated that a surface may be too rough and lumpy, as well as too smooth and level. A mean between the extremes of roughness and smoothness is the best state of the soil for the wheat crop." A proper preparation of the soil will be found more satisfactory than a rough surface.

GROWING WINTER WHEAT ON CLOVER SOD.

Different management is required to raise winter wheat on red clover sod, than is necessary for spring wheat. There is one great error to be avoided in preparing the ground, which is, turning all the mould, clover-stalks, and vegetable matter, eight or ten inches below the surface. This is the usual practice; but it is decidedly wrong *for winter grain.* The dense growth of the clover has exerted a very ameliorating influence on the surface of the soil, simply by *shading* it, to say nothing of the direct fertilization by means of its large roots and decayed straw. This nicely pulverized soil at the very surface, and all the vegetable matter afforded by the decay of the clover, needs to be kept near the surface of the ground, where it will promote the growth of the young wheat plants before winter. The leading idea is to perform the ploughing in such a manner, that whatever fertilizers may aid the growth of the wheat before winter, whether it be in the form of decayed clover, or barn-yard manure, the whole may be within three or four inches of the surface, so that all the roots of the wheat will be spread out, making a complete mat in a shallow stratum of soil.

The best soil must be kept on the surface. A thin coat of well-rotted barn-yard manure should be ploughed under, in connection with the clover-stalks, not deeper than just specified; and the subsoil plough should follow the common plough, in every furrow. Twice in each furrow is much better than once. See how to subsoil, with illustration of a subsoil plough on a previous page, and also in second volume of my Young Farmer's Manual.

The "Cultivator and Country Gentleman" says:

"Sowing wheat on a good clean clover lea is undoubtedly the best course to pursue, as nearly all the benefits of a clover crop for the season, except for growing seed, or for fall feed, may be had before it is taken for wheat. The best piece of wheat in this section is on a clover sod turned over and sown within ten days after ploughing. But farmers will not generally have such a clover sod to spare, until they come into the practice of seeding to clover with spring crops, instead of ploughing under the stubble and sowing wheat."

Joseph Harris, Editor of the "Genesee Farmer," Rochester, New York, writes in relation to raising wheat on clover sod, that:

"In England, wheat is generally sown on a one or two year old clover sod, the land being ploughed immediately before sowing. As a general rule, this practice does not succeed here, because, for one reason, we sow a month earlier than they do in England, and a clover field ploughed here the last of August is generally so dry that the seed wheat does not germinate evenly; and it is found, too, that the wheat is overrun with weeds and grass the next season. I think, however, if our land were cleaned the way it should be before it is seeded to clover, and eaten down by sheep during the summer, wheat might be raised here with one ploughing, as in England, especially if we used a little Peruvian guano at the time of sowing. In Western New York, manure is seldom applied directly to wheat; some say it is injurious. But I apprehend that, on most farms, the wheat would be very grateful for a little good, well-rotted manure, either ploughed in or spread on the surface just before sowing. Wheat needs something to

give it a good start in the fall, and a little well-rotted
manure, not ploughed in deep, would be very accepta-
ble. A dressing of Peruvian guano, say one hundred
and fifty pounds to three hundred pounds to the acre,
would perhaps be better still. It will pay if we get one
dollar and fifty cents per bushel for wheat. At one dollar per bushel the profits from the use of guano will be
very slight, and may be on the wrong side of the
ledger.

"Gypsum, or sulphate of lime, seldom does any good
on wheat in Western New York, although it has a very
good effect on clover, and sometimes on peas. Some
good farmers sow a bushel of plaster (gypsum) per acre,
on the wheat in the spring; but it is done, not to benefit the wheat, but for its effect on the clover sown with
the wheat."

PLOUGHING IN CLOVER FOR WHEAT.

Clover is an excellent crop to precede wheat. The
heaviest crops of wheat I ever succeeded in raising, were
sown on clover sward. In ploughing under clover I prefer
waiting until it has perfectly matured. Many prefer
ploughing when it is in full bloom, but this does not
coincide with my experience. It is true that there is
apparently a greater amount of vegetable matter upon
the ground at the time of flowering, but it is too sappy,
and disappears very soon after being turned under, in
consequence of a too rapid fermentation taking place.

The objection may be raised to ploughing down a
crop of clover, that it is an expensive mode of manuring;
but this, I think, is incorrect; for the expense should
not be counted at a higher figure than the interest on

the cost of the land, with the value of the clover seed added ; and it is impossible to manure as cheaply and at the same time as effectually in any other manner.

Thaer, in his work on the Principles of Agriculture, after enumerating a number of crops suitable to be grown before wheat, concludes by saying, "Lastly, the best way of obtaining good crops of wheat, is to sow the grain on broken-up clover land ;" and he further recommends that the clover should be ploughed a month previous to sowing the wheat. The recommendation coincides with the practice of many of the best farmers in England, who prefer sowing wheat on a stale furrow, under the impression that land which has become somewhat compact in consequence of having had time to settle, is more congenial to the growth of wheat, than that which has been recently ploughed. It is also thought important not to have the ground too finely pulverized, as the grain is supposed to stand the winter better when the land is somewhat cloddy on the surface. This is also the opinion of many of the most successful wheat-growers in the interior of this State, and it also coincides with my own experience. The reason for preferring a cloddy surface is, that it does not so readily form a crust after showers, and the clods, as they crumble to pieces during the winter and spring, supply fresh, mellow earth to the roots of the plants.—*J. Harris.*

Manuring the Surface for Winter Wheat,

In preference to mingling the manure thoroughly with the soil, as deep as it is ploughed. By ploughing the soil to a good depth once, and by working only a few inches in depth of the surface—rendering it fine and mellow—

and by spreading finely pulverized compost on the surface, and simply harrowing it in about the time the grain is sowed or drilled in, the roots, for the most part, will strike out horizontally, or nearly so, and will become so thoroughly interwoven with each other near the surface, that they are not drawn out at the surface, as they are when they strike down nearly vertically; but the entire soil rises and settles back in the same manner as sod ground does, without heaving out the plants.

I have made particular inquiry of those farmers who have adopted the practice of manuring on the surface, in every locality where I have travelled during the past season, and I have found that in most instances they are satisfied that winter grain will not suffer so much injury from freezing and thawing, when the manure is well rotted and spread thin on the surface, and harrowed in about the time when the grain is put in, as it will if the manure is ploughed under.

Growing wheat on clover lay is practiced in many instances. When the clover is in full bloom it is turned under with the furrow about six or seven inches in depth, during the latter part of July; and if the clover is the large kind, which is considered preferable, it is not ploughed in until the former part of August. Of course, circumstances will determine the most proper time for ploughing it under. If the clover is pastured for several weeks in the spring, it will not have attained its full growth until after the middle of summer has passed.

If the ploughman be expert, and can turn a well proportioned furrow, and make his work uniform, one ploughing for a clover sod is sufficient. But it should be done one month before sowing, to impart to the surface a suitable mellow condition for the seed, and also that

10

portions of the sod may break up and remain on the surface, by the action of the seed harrows, thus securing the same object sought by the second ploughing.

Raising Wheat on Mucky Soils.

In many places, where a black, mucky soil, several inches deep, rests on a heavy subsoil, by turning up two or three inches of the latter in autumn, and mingling it thoroughly with the soil, draining if necessary, and manuring, a very good wheat soil may be formed in a few years. Where the muck is so deep that the clayey subsoil cannot be reached with a plough, and clay can be obtained within a distance of half a mile, it will pay to apply eighty or a hundred loads per acre. The best time to spread it is late in autumn, or in winter, that it may be acted upon by rains and frosts. Still, if applied in the spring, and ploughed in, the effect will be good on the crop the same year. Portions of fields frequently are very heavy, while other portions are composed, for the most part, of vegetable mould. The practice of the writer has been to haul mucky soil and spread it on the heavy clay; and in all cases, the application has produced an equal, or better effect for wheat, than a liberal application of good barn-yard manure. As there is a great difference in muck, this might not always be the case. Compact, heavy soils contain a large amount of wheat-producing material; but they need to be made light and porous, so that the roots of the wheat plants can permeate the entire soil as deeply as it has been pulverized.

On some kinds of soil, a dressing of muck will exert a marvellous influence in producing a heavy crop. Yet, on some kinds of land, it will not pay to cart muck forty rods. Experiments must be made, to determine when muck will operate as a valuable fertilizer, and when it will not.

The very act of exposure of this swamp muck, has caused an evolution of carbonic acid gas: that decomposes the silicates of potash in the sand; the potash converts the insoluble into soluble manure, and lo! a crop. The growing crop adds its power to the geine. If all the long series of experiments under Von Voght, in Germany, are to be believed, confirmed as they are by repeated trials by our own agriculturists, it is not to be doubted, that every inch of every small knoll, on every farm, may be changed into a soil in thirteen years, of half the number of inches of good mould.

Manuring Sandy Soils for Wheat.

In the summer of 1867, I was exploring certain parts of South Jersey, at Weymouth; and I found on the farm of Mr. S. Colwell, that excellent crops of wheat had been growing on light, sandy loam soils, where a man could paw a hole a foot deep with the heel of his boot, with little difficulty. Mr. Colwell stated that his system of management was as follows, in preparing the ground for the crop just alluded to: A liberal dressing of barn-yard manure and muck was applied to the land, ploughed in, and Indian corn planted. The next season Indian corn was sowed for feeding domestic animals. In autumn the ground was ploughed and winter wheat drilled in. As nature has made abundant provision for the draining of the cultivable fields in this part of the State, the freezing and thawing of the soil

during the winter months, does but very little injury
to the growing wheat. On such light, loamy ground,
which never requires under-draining, spring wheat can
be produced with much more profit than winter grain,
if the seed be put in at the very beginning of the growing
season. If such light loam be top-dressed with clay not
more than half an inch in depth, the argillaceous material in the dressing will impart a firmness to the light
land, which is eminently essential for the production of
a bountiful yield of this kind of grain. When a dressing of clay is applied to such loamy ground, or to a soil
where light, black muck is the predominant characteristic, it can be carted during the winter months, when
laborers and teams can find but little employment. In
some localities the clay can be hauled on a sliding
vehicle and spread on the snow. Should the clay be
distributed in clods weighing eight or more pounds each,
two or three frosts and showers of rain will usually dissolve the lumps, so that, when partially dry, the clay
may be spread evenly with shovels, and afterward harrowed into the soil, or mingled with the surface soil by
a two-horse wheel cultivator, which some wheat-growers
prefer to a plough for preparing the ground for a crop
of wheat, after the field has been thoroughly ploughed.
A dressing of marl, or muck, on such land, in addition
to the clay, cannot fail to produce a bountiful yield of
wheat, or of almost any other cereal grain. Farmers
who make and apply large quantities of compost, such
as Mr. Colwell is accustomed to prepare for his fields,
find that they can grow excellent crops of wheat, even
on our lightest loams. But the fertilizers applied to
light soils should be rich in grain-producing material,
and covered with a cultivator, rather than ploughed in.

Wheat on Light Sandy Loam.

In order to raise a fair crop of wheat on sandy loam soils, it becomes necessary to exercise no little judgment in preparing the soil in the best manner for this kind of grain. The element lacking mostly is alumina, which is found in the loam. In many instances, the sandy loam is only four to eight or ten inches in depth, resting on a deep stratum of excellent yellow-clay loam. By bringing up two or three inches in depth of this yellow-clay loam, and mingling it with the fine sandy loam on the surface, a fine seed-bed will be prepared for wheat. Then, by adopting a rotation of crops, such as Indian corn one season, oats or barley, potatoes and turnips, and red clover one or two seasons, with a dressing of rich sheep manure, a bountiful crop of fine wheat can be raised with little difficulty.

On certain fields, the sandy loam is sometimes so deep that it will not be practicable to reach the substratum of clay loam with a common plough, or even with a subsoil plough. But bear in mind the suggestion, that the sandy loam requires a little clay to give the soil solidity and firmness. The correct mode of procedure in such instances, is, to plough the sandy loam in late autumn, turn under a coat of red clover if convenient, or a thin dressing of compost, or both, unless the soil is unusually fertile; then when the ground is frozen, cart or haul on muck and clay, and spread it thin over the entire field. Fifty two-horse loads of muck, and fifty more two-horse loads of pure clay, or heavy clay loam transported from some distant clay-bed, and spread evenly in the winter, would make a seed-bed for wheat of fine tilth, which could scarcely fail to render a light sandy loam eminently productive. In the spring, let the ground be thoroughly harrowed, or scarified with a two-horse cultivator, without ploughing; and wheat will grow heavy and stand up remarkably well.

An important consideration is to be able to cart the clay and muck in the winter, when teams and vehicles will not pack the mellow seed-bed; and also when the labors of the field are not urgent. It is seldom convenient to perform this kind of work during the growing season. Besides this, one grand point to be secured is, the ameliorating influence of the freezing and thawing of the clay, by which coarse clods are all reduced to a fine tilth. When teams and laborers have but little to do, time can be very profitably employed in carting earth to top-dress wheat fields. The dressing of clay, or clay loam, will render the soil more productive for other kinds of grain and grass, also as well as for wheat.

Seeding without Ploughing.

Light soils are frequently ploughed to their serious injury, for a crop of wheat. My father and his neighbors as well as myself, have raised the most bountiful crops of wheat, that any of us ever produced, on land that was simply harrowed thoroughly. We were all satisfied that the crops were much heavier than they would have been had the ground been ploughed. I have in mind numerous instances, in New Jersey, in which the soil was a deep light loam, covered with a very thin mould, where all the vegetable matter was turned six inches below the surface. The result was, that the crop of grain was amazingly light; whereas, had the ground simply been worked with a wheel cultivator, or harrowed thoroughly, the crop would have been much heavier, with half the labor. Were I to manage the light, sandy loam soils· of the United States, where the surface soil and the subsoil are not compact, I should seldom use a plough in preparing the ground for any kind of crop. Such a cultivator as is illustrated on page 142, would be a far more satisfactory implement for preparing the soil for wheat, or for any other crop, than a plough. The object is to keep the best soil at the surface. With a cultivator, it can be readily done. But with a plough, the fertile mould is worked downward farther and farther beneath the surface.

Of all soils to be cultivated, or to be restored, none are preferable to the sandy light soils. By their porousness, free access is given to the powerful effects of the air. They are natural in that state, to which trenching, draining, and subsoil ploughing are reducing the stiffer lands of England. Manure may as well be thrown into water, as on land underlaid by water. Drain this, and no matter if the upper soil be almost quicksand, manure will convert it into fertile, arable land. The thin covering of mould, scarcely an inch in thickness, the product of a century, may be imitated by studying the laws of its formation. This is the work of " Nature's apprentice hand ; " man has long been her journeyman, and now guided by science, the farmer becomes the master workman, and may produce in one year quite as much as the apprentice made in seven.

PASTURING WHEAT, IN AUTUMN OR WINTER.

Many years ago, we used to see it recommended in agricultural papers, " to pasture off wheat in late autumn.". But for more than twenty years past, in which these observations and inquiries have been made on this subject, I have not met with a single instance which afforded any assurance that the practice is at all beneficial. On the contrary, *everything* argues against it. Vegetable physiology is against it, because the leaves of plants are their lungs. Therefore, if they be cropped off, the growth will be checked. And if the growth be checked in late autumn, the plants cannot endure the severity of the cold in winter. Scientific agriculture is decidedly against it ; because every good wheat-grower knows how important it is that the young wheat plants should become firmly rooted before winter sets in, so that they may not be lifted out so readily, and that they should acquire a large growth, for the purpose of mulching the soil in cold weather. The practice also of our best wheat-growers has *proved* it to be a very wrong system of management ; and no good farmer who has tried it once or twice, will be induced to practise it again.

My own experience has always been, that the larger the leaves of wheat are allowed to grow, the more they will mulch the ground, the firmer the plants will be rooted, and the more effectually they will resist the influences of intense cold, and of alternate freezing and thawing, not only during the winter, but in the spring.

If animals of any kind be allowed to crop off the growing plants, their teeth often sever the tender stems close to the ground. Thus the crowns of the growing plants will be exposed to the influences of the weather, and in many instances effectually killed. Besides this, heavy animals will injure the roots of large numbers of the stools, by treading on the plants where the ground is soft. The great injury done to the plants by the feet of animals will often cause more damage to the wheat than the injury arising from cropping off the stems with their teeth.

Pasturing wheat is not to be commended under any circumstances. If there is too large a growth of leaves and stems, let the seed be put in later in the season, rather than to pasture the wheat with any kind of stock.

MULCHING WINTER GRAIN.

Every observing farmer knows that in autumn, or winter, soil that is entirely bare will freeze up solid, while that in meadows, or pasture fields, will not be frozen at all. Now, why is it so? Why will the beaten track of the highway be frozen up solid enough to bear a loaded wagon, while the grassy sides may be ploughed or spaded?

Again: when a portion of a field is covered with a thick coat of grass or clover that has not been fed off nor mowed, why will such soil remain unfrozen, except in very cold weather? Because the coat of grass prevents the rapid radiation of heat from the surface of the earth. A soil that is bare, or nearly so, radiates heat very rapidly during the cold nights of winter; and it will freeze much deeper than if protected by some mulching material that will check the rapid radiation of heat from the surface.

Those farmers who have turned their attention to this subject, cannot have failed to notice how much more red clover is lifted out in pastures that have been fed off close in late autumn than where the surface is

10*

protected by a good coat of stems and leaves. And the same is true of winter wheat. Wherever it has been covered during most of the winter with snow it will not be lifted out, nor winter-killed very much, if at all. But, when the seed was sowed late in autumn, and the leaves have made only a short growth, the soil will freeze very deep and the ground will be many degrees colder where the roots of the wheat are than if the surface were protected. Where there is a thick coating of the leaves of wheat, or straw, over the surface, the plants will be injured but little.

Intense cold injures the wheat plants in two ways. One is, by lifting them out of their bed, and severing the roots; and another, by severe chilling, just as the buds of peach trees are injured by intense cold. Therefore, the more we can protect the wheat plants from piercing winds and intense cold, the better crops of grain we may expect to raise. When wheat was sowed so late in the fall that the leaves do not cover the surface of the ground, it will be an excellent protection to spread straw over the entire field, as soon as the seed is put in the ground, and let the wheat plants come up through the straw. But great care must be exercised in spreading it, lest it be applied so thick as to smother the plants. A covering half an inch thick, where the ground is not excessively wet, will be found an excellent protection on those fields that are not shielded from the cold winds by a forest, belt of trees, or an elevation of the ground. But, a coat of straw will not prevent wheat being lifted out by the frost on wet ground. If the straw were worked into manure, by fat sheep or fat cattle, and covered with a cultivator, the effect would be more satisfactory.

Salt for Wheat.

Although my own experience is not in favor of the application of salt to growing wheat, or to the soil where wheat was sowed, I have reason to believe that, *on some kinds of soil*, a dressing of salt has been, and may be again, of great value to the growing crop. Yet, as a general rule, I think salt will exert such a trivial influence on the productiveness of the land, that the small increase will not defray the expense of purchasing and sowing four to eight bushels of salt per acre. The only reliable way to satisfy any one on this point is by experiment. If alternate strips be dressed with salt; and the straw keeps erect better, or the yield of grain should prove to be heavier than where no salt is applied, no more reliable proof will be required, to establish the value of salt as a fertilizer.

Many farmers will insist that a dressing of salt will exterminate, or prevent the ravages of the wire-worm. But I do not believe that one hundred bushels of salt on an acre will have the least influence in repelling wire-worms, cut-worms, or any other worms, as the exceedingly small quanity that would come in contact with the whereabouts of such worms, would not destroy vegetation of any kind.

J. J. Mechi states that he knew a farmer in Northamptonshire, whose wheat crops could scarcely ever be kept from lodging, until he sowed a liberal dressing of salt in his fields. He even went so far as to salt the manure in his yards. He says it is a most singular fact, that while salt tends to preserve animal substances, it will decompose vegetable matter quite rapidly.

Every farmer must test the efficacy of salt on his own

soil, if he would learn its value; for salt has been employed so extensively as a fertilizer, with no apparent
effect, that it is useless to recommend it, unless a farmer
is satisfied that an application of it will pay. We
know a dressing of manure will pay. Now if a farmer
has such assurance that salt sowed on land will pay, I
recommend a liberal dressing of salt on such land.

CHARCOAL DUST AS A FERTILIZER.

Charcoal is composed almost entirely of pure carbon;
and when small fragments are exposed to the influences
of the weather, they undergo very little change during
a long term of years. Still the roots of growing plants
will lay hold of the small pieces of charcoal, and appropriate the substance contained in the coal to the growth
and development of the stems, leaves, and seeds of grain,
fruit, and vegetables.

Experienced chemists assure us, charcoal, and particularly charcoal dust, has the power of attracting and
fixing large quantities of ammonia, a substance which
enters largely into the formation of useful plants, and
of retaining this fertilizing material when buried in the
soil, until the fine fibres of the roots of growing plants
require it for promoting their growth. Charcoal has the
power of attracting and retaining other gaseous substances besides ammonia, which are highly beneficial to
growing wheat plants, as well as grass, vines, trees, and
shrubs.

Every observing farmer who has been accustomed to
raise wheat cannot have failed to notice the luxuriant
growth of cereal grain round about the places where
charcoal has been burned, even more than thirty or forty

years ago. The growing stems of wheat that are produced on such old charcoal-beds are seldom affected
with rust; and besides this, the straw is always much
stiffer than that which grows where there is not a dressing of charcoal. Before charcoal can promote the growth
of plants of any kind, the particles must be thoroughly
decomposed, and reduced to a liquid condition. For this
reason, previous to the application of charcoal dust as a
fertilizer to any kind of soil, the coal should be run
through a mill that will reduce the small pieces to fine
powder. And even when charcoal is thus finely com-
minuted by some mechanical means, the action of the
fertilizing matter on vegetation will be very slow.

It is said that charcoal possesses the power of absorbing ninety times its own weight of ammoniacal
gases. This fact suggests that charcoal dust, which
may be procured in large quantities, at simply the expense of carting, in and around many of our populous
cities, should be scattered in the stables of domestic
animals, after having been ground very fine, where it
will absorb large quantities of the choicest fertilizing
material, which, if mingled with the soil, would impart
a rich store of pabulum to the roots of growing crops.
But whether a farmer would be warranted in purchasing charcoal, grinding it to powder, scattering it in his
stables, and applying it the soil, is a question that can be
decided satisfactorily, only by well-conducted experiments. The probability, however, is that it would not
pay, for the reason that the decomposition of the fragments of the coal would be so exceedingly slow, from
year to year, that the beneficial effect would not be a fair
equivalent for the expense incurred. Where a farmer
can procure charcoal dust for the carting, he can well

afford to haul it two or more miles for the purpose of applying it to certain kinds of soil.

Where the soil is deep, mellow, vegetable, black loam, or muck, it would not pay to cart charcoal dust to apply as a fertilizer, because there is an abundance of carbonaceous material already in the soil. But where the soil consists chiefly of a sandy loam, a gravelly loam, or is a heavy soil of any character, it *will* pay to cart charcoal dust to mingle with stable manure, to be applied to the soil where cereal grain, in particular, or grass, or any other crops, are to be produced.

As to the proper quantity of charcoal dust to be applied to an acre, there is no rule for determining how much may be used with profit. There is no danger, however, of applying too much. The larger the quantity the better. On those soils where charcoal dust will not be of any advantage to growing crops, a bountiful dressing will exert no injurious influence. The larger the quantity spread around all kinds of fruit trees, the smoother and fairer the fruit will be.

In many fields where cereal grain is grown, the old coal-pit beds should be carted and spread on those parts of the field that are not rich in carbonaceous material. Charcoal dust, finely pulverized, is an excellent material to mingle with the soil where fruit trees of any kind are being transplanted. From five to ten bushels per tree would be a liberal dressing. For an immediate fertilizing effect on the growing crops of almost any kind of soil, it would be more satisfactory to reduce the coal to ashes, and sow what remains, broadcast over the field, while plants of grain or grass are young and tender, as wood ashes are an excellent material for grain and grass, trees and flowers, fruits and vegetables of all kinds.

R. Ranson, Ashtabula County, Ohio, writes, touching pulverized charcoal, as follows : " I tried another experiment in 1860. My lands are coarse or loose gravel of rather poor quality. I sowed an acre of winter wheat (the blue-stem) preparing my ground as follows :

" The field was sown with barley in the spring previous ; yield small (eighteen bushels per acre). I turned in the stubble the last week in August, harrowed it over, then took about eighteen bushels charcoal crushed fine, and top-dressed a strip through the middle of the acre over about one-third of its length ; I then sowed on my wheat broadcast and harrowed it over twice. The result was, the heads when ripe were at least twice as long as where no coal was put on. I harvested all together ; the yield was forty-three bushels. I think by applying about fifty bushels of coal to the acre as a top-dressing, made fine by grinding in a common bark mill, it would increase the yield at least four hundred per cent., if the soil is poor.

" He further states he used burned clay and ashes in the fall of 1860, at the rate of about one hundred bushels of burned clay, taken from a fallow where timber had been uprooted several years by heavy winds. The soil on which the timber grew was burned together with the old roots and clay entwined, and perhaps some muck ; the whole, ashes, clay and muck, after being burned as above, were hauled off in a wagon and put upon the wheat field as a top-dressing, and harrowed in with the wheat. The land was poor quality of gravel ; the yield was about five hundred per cent. over the remainder of the field where no clay was put. I think there is no fertilizer ahead of this as a top-dresser." See Mixing Soils, second volume of Young Farmer's Manual.

HOLBROOK'S DEEP-TILLER PLOUGH.

The figure of a plough shown in this place, represents a "deep-tiller" plough, which has been recently invented by Governor Holbrook, of Massachusetts, and manufactured by F. F. Holbrook, Boston. The form of the mold-board is such as is required for deep ploughing. When

FIG. 35.—Holbrook's Stubble Plough.

ploughing stubble, farmers frequently desire to plough narrow furrows, ten to twelve inches deep. With most of the ploughs, it is extremely difficult to plough more than eight inches in depth; and scores of ploughs are not properly constructed for ploughing over five or six inches in depth.

I have devoted a vast deal of thought to the proper construction of the mold-boards of ploughs, both for deep and for shallow ploughing; and it affords me satisfaction to record in this place, a tribute of superior merit to this plough, which is exactly the implement required in numerous sections of the country, where it

is desirable to bring up a little of the rich, clay loam to
the surface, to be mingled with the light soil or vegetable
mould.   In New Jersey, as well as in other States, the
soil, in many sections of the country, consists of a light,
sandy loam, resting on a fertile, clay-loam subsoil,
. about ten or twelve inches below the surface.   For
almost all kinds of crops, especially for wheat and
other cereal grain, it is important to turn up a few
inches in depth of this subsoil.   With a common plough
it is difficult to do it.   But with one of Governor
Holbrook's deep-tiller ploughs, one span of horses will
open a furrow twelve inches deep, and continue to
plough at that depth, provided the plough is adjusted
to cut only five or six inches wide.   Read the chapter
on Ploughs and Ploughing, in both volumes of my
Young Farmer's Manual.

HOLBROOK'S RIGHT AND LEFT PLOUGH.

The accompanying illustration of a plough represents
a style of ploughs manufactured by F. F. Holbrook,
Boston, Massachusetts, which are gaining favor among
farmers, on account of their convenience in enabling a
ploughman to commence on one side of a field, and
plough back and forth, until the field is finished.   By this
manner of ploughing, the entire field can be finished
without a dead furrow.   Besides this, the surface of the
land is kept level, which is not the case when ground
is ploughed in lands.   Some farmers prefer this style of
ploughs for another reason, which is this : when ploughing land for any kind of grain that is to be drilled in,
they can hitch the team to the drill twice, or more, in
a day ; and put in the grain as far as the ploughing is

completed, thus finishing the operation of seeding as fast as the ploughing progresses, which is often desirable. Besides this, when grain is deposited in soil just ploughed, or recently pulverized, the seed will usually

Fig. 86.—Holbrook's Right and Left Plough.

germinate sooner than when it is sowed in ground that has been ploughed several days, or so long a time that the surface has become somewhat dry before the seed is put in the soil. The right and left plough is also an excellent side-hill plough. Mr. Holbrook manufactures several other kinds of ploughs, which give excellent satisfaction for performing the operations for which they were particularly constructed.

CHAPTER III.

How to Save Seed Wheat.

"Oft have I seen the chosen seeds deceive,
And o'er degenerate crops the peasant grieve,
Save where slow Patience, o'er and o'er again,
Culled yearly, one by one, the largest grain."
                              DRYDEN'S VIRGIL.

JUDGING from the suggestions previously recorded, in regard to seed wheat, one would suppose that we might dispense with all details relating to the manipulations of saving the seed. But I consider the manipulations more important than anything I have recorded, as the directions herewith given are an epitome of all the rest. If a farmer will follow the directions here recorded, when securing his seed wheat, from year to year, he will feel so well satisfied with his efforts to produce a bountiful crop of fine grain, that he will never suffer himself to resort to the slip-shod and unprofitable and unfarmer-like manner, which prevails all over our country.

Let it be borne in mind that *earliness of maturity* is the most important consideration in saving seed wheat. Of course, then, seed should never be taken from a locality where the crops are backward in regard to maturity.

It is not only important to select for seed, the grain that matures first on one's own farm, but from those fields in any other locality in the town or county. My farm was some five or six hundred feet above the level of Cayuga Lake. The wheat growing on those fields near the shore of the lake, usually ripened ten to fourteen days earlier than the wheat on the upland. I always secured my seed from those farmers near the shore, for the first crop; then, at the next harvest time, patches of the growing grain, a few rods square, on the knolls and highest points of the field, were staked off on my own farm and allowed to stand until the grain had matured perfectly. The grain that grew on such elevated parts of the field, would mature sometimes a week before the grain growing on low parts of the same field was fit to harvest.

Such seed grain should always be harvested by itself: stacked or stored in the barn by itself; thrashed by itself; and secured in a bin or barrels by itself. It is folly to attempt to grow a bountiful crop of wheat unless all these directions are followed out, year after year, with scrupulous exactness. When the unthrashed crop of grain is stored in a building, the sheaves should never be put in the bottom of the mow, unless unusual care be exercised in removing the grain that may be placed above the seed grain, to prevent grain that is not fit for seed, from falling down among the seed bundles.

Another important consideration to be kept in mind is, to procure seed that grows on high, dry, and rather heavy soil, rather than to choose grain that was produced on a light, mucky soil. Grain that grows on a light, mucky soil, is seldom as light colored as that which was produced on a fertile clay loam. We always find the choicest and the whitest wheat where there is a liberal proportion of clay in the soil. In every locality, farmers should spend a part of a day, at harvest-time, travelling about the country, for the purpose of seeing where they can secure the earliest seed wheat.

I believe that farmers, almost universally, pay little or no attention to the time when seed ripens. If it is only ripe and bright seed, perhaps not one farmer in a thousand would even think, whether it ripened in August, or in November. We cannot expect that any seed which has come to maturity very late in the season, will produce a crop as early as the same kind of seed will, which ripened in August. By collecting and planting those seeds that ripened very late in the season, we can soon produce a variety that will not ripen at all, unless the season were unusually long and favorable.

For this reason, we select, as far as practicable, those ears of Indian corn for seed which ripen first; and by following up this practice, from year to year, we. produce a kind of seed that will mature in the shortest possible period of time; while on the contrary, if we select those ears for seed that came to maturity last, and continue that practice for a few years, we shall have all roasting ears in October, and no sound corn. My experience on this subject goes to establish this position.

A correspondent of the "Prairie Farmer" wrote to that paper thus: "There is, perhaps, no branch of the farmer's business which is conducted more hap-hazard than the selecting of seed. Many do not realize the importance of selecting the best of seed. To such I propose to offer a word of advice. All small grain may be classed together; for what holds good of wheat is also true of barley, rye, or oats. I verily believe, that a large share of the failure of wheat, in Northern Illinois, is due to the fact, that the farmer simply goes to his bin and cleans over the required number of bushels he wishes to sow. Often, very often, this grain is sown without being cleaned at all. Want of time is urged as an excuse, because the ground is left until it is fitted for the seed. If it is a law of nature that like produces like, what can be expected of such a process but a *constant, certain deterioration?*"

Choose the Heaviest Kernels.

The heaviest, cleanest, most perfect berry should be sown always, of all small grain. One way to obtain this kind of seed is as follows: Clean your barn floor; place your grain in a heap at the opposite door to the one at which the current of air enters; then with a small hand-scoop throw out your grain against the wind, so as to fall a little short of the other end of your floor. Of course the heaviest grain will be that which flies furthest; and this will be clean also. If the screen in your fanning-mill has meshes wide enough to admit of the small grains of wheat passing through, you may succeed in cleaning your wheat fit for seed, also your rye; but for oats and barley this will not be the case, as the small grain cannot pass through the screen.

On this subject of selecting seed wheat, a writer in the "Mark Lane Express" has said: "The varieties of wheat are now so numerous, that much difficulty arises in making a proper choice. Whatever variety may be chosen, the farmer ought to select the best sample of it that he can meet with. I would as soon use an inferior ram to my flock, or an inferior bull to my herd, as to sow an inferior grain, be it from whatever well-known stock. I have derived great advantage from changes of seed, brought from a considerable distance on every side, to the extent of hundreds of miles. But, it was from seed on which I could depend. My favorite change is, from a cold, chalky, district to a mild, loamy soil. In a majority of cases, a change is good on every soil, and under every variation of climate."

VITALITY OF SEED WHEAT.

The old story in relation to the wonderful vitality of wheat taken from the coffin of an Egyptian mummy, 3,000 years old, has been reiterated by the press, until intelligent farmers will not give it any kind of credence. It is sheer folly to repeat such an improbability! I do not believe a word of it. (See p. 107, Egyptian Wheat.) Wheat was undoubtedly taken from a mummy; but there was not a shadow of evidence, that the grain was 3,000 years old. Indeed, the evidence is conclusive, that some shrewd Arab—as they understand how eager white and civilized people are to obtain curiosities—put the package of wheat in the mummy, only a few years previous, as seeds of maize, a plant of recent origin and known in America before it was ever seen in the Old World, were found in the package.

Scientific men in Europe, have made numerous experiments to test the vitality of seeds, all of which tend to show, that cereal grain will lose its vitality in a few successive years.

In the year 1840 the British Association for the Advancement of Science, appointed a committee to investigate the length of time during which seeds retain their vitality. The committee consisted of Professors Danbury, Henslow, and Lindley. They made sixteen reports; the last being for the year 1857, at which time, so few seeds were found to retain their vegetative powers, that it was deemed necessary to consider the object attained.

The results of their investigation are well known, and are exceedingly interesting. Thus, they found that in their hands, the celebrated mummy wheat which had been claimed to have come down from the time of the Pharaohs, had no such vitality as had been claimed for it. After a few years, it entirely loses its vegetative powers. Some seeds, as lettuce, become worthless after a couple of years. Others, as melons, endure for a comparatively long period. A few of the most interesting of these results I give. They found that the greatest age at which seeds germinated are as follows, viz. :

Maize,	3 yrs.	Cabbage,	3 yrs.
Oats,	8 "	Hibiscus,	27 "
Spring Wheat,	3 "	Carrot,	8 "
Rye,	3 "	Beet,	8 "
Barley,	3 "	Lettuce,	3 "

Only two kinds (Colutea and Coronilla) vegetated after a lapse of forty-seven years.

The vitality shown by some seeds is wonderful; and the probability is, that certain kinds of seeds retain their vitality much longer in one climate than in another. I once sowed some timothy seed, which I raised on my own farm, which was six years old, bright and plump when it was sowed. But, not a seed vegetated, although it was sowed on new land, where the soil favored the vegetation of every seed. I also sowed a sack of Russian flaxseed, which appeared bright and heavy; but not one single plant ever appeared.

Professor Lindley says: "There are many cases on record which establish conclusively that, under favorable conditions, the vitality of seeds may be preserved for indefinite periods. 'Not to speak of the doubtful instances of seeds taken from the Pyramids having germinated,' melons have been known to grow at the age of forty years; kidney beans at a hundred; sensitive plant at sixty; rye at forty; and there are now living in the garden of the Horticultural Society raspberry plants raised from seeds 1,600 or 1,700 years old.

"The seeds of charlock buried in former ages spring up in railway cuttings; where ancient forests are destroyed, plants appear which had never been seen before, but whose seeds have been buried in the ground. When some land was recovered from the Baltic Sea, a carex was found upon it, now unknown in that part of Europe. M. Fries, of Upsala, succeeded in growing a species of Hieracium from seeds which had been in his herbarium upward of fifty years. Desmoulins has recorded an instance of the opening of ancient tombs, in which seeds were found; and on being planted they produced species of scabiosa and heliotropium."

A Reliable Rule.

Seeds and grain often lose their vitality; and we cannot determine by the external appearance of a seed or kernel of grain, whether its vitality is gone, or not. It is, therefore, always wise to keep on the safe side, by sowing wheat that has not been kept over more than one winter. Wheat that is sown in autumn, should not be the product of the *previous* year; but grain that grew the same season. Spring wheat should be the pro-

duct of the previous year. Therefore, when seed wheat
or seed rye is obtained from seed stores, or from any
other source, if the grain were not raised the previous
year, a handful of the kernels should be tested, before
the grain is sowed in the field, for the purpose of determining whether the seed will germinate. There is no
reliable rule concerning the vitality of any kind of seed
grain. In one instance, every kernel of seed may vegetate, when it is ten, or more years old. On the contrary, a large proportion of seed only three and four
years old, may, and *may not* vegetate.

LARGE *vs.* SMALL KERNELS OF GRAIN FOR SEED.

"Yet, the success is not for years assured,
    Though chosen is the seed and fully cured,
    Unless the peasant, with his annual pain,
    Renews his choice, and culls the largest grain."
                        DRYDEN'S VIRGIL.

We perceive by the suggestions in the preceding coup-
let, which was penned several hundred years ago, that
the importance of choosing the largest kernels was
understood in those days, as well as now. But, whether
the precept was observed in selecting seed, is a question
involved in some doubt, as cultivators of the soil are
exceedingly apt to neglect the saving of all kinds of
seed. Besides this, many intelligent farmers and gardeners contend that it makes no difference whether the
small kernels of the tip end of an ear, or any others, be
planted; and, to prove it, they refer to experiments recorded by C. L. Flint, secretary of the Massachusetts
Board of Agriculture, in which it is stated, that it has
been proved by experiment that the yield of Indian corn

from the kernels on the tip end of the ears, was *greater* than from seed on the *middle* of the ear.

No doubt Mr. Flint recorded the experiment in good faith; but I have no confidence in the result of it. I do not believe it was fairly conducted. It is contrary to reason, common sense, the experience of good farmers, and opposed to the established laws of vegetable physiology, that a small, ill-formed kernel should produce more and better grain than would grow from the best ones on the ear. All good farmers, in ages past, and even at the present day, have been instructed to plant the best kernels—to propagate from the best kind of everything—because " like produces like," as well in the vegetable as the animal kingdom.

In our efforts to improve our domestic animals, we always choose the very best as a breeder—one that possesses the most good points of form, symmetry, and constitution. By this means our flocks and herds have been brought to their present degree of perfectibility. Now, let us suppose, for example, that we are told by a man, who is considered good authority, that, by selecting the meanest and shabbiest-looking nags that can be found, or by breeding from the veriest scrub of a cow and skalawag bull, we may obtain animals superior to anything that we have ever raised! Every sensible man or woman would say, at once, that the idea is a palpable absurdity. When we breed from ill-favored animals, we never expect to get offspring superior to their progenitors; because it would be unnatural for an animal, or for any kind of seed, to impart to its issue or product, excellencies which itself never possessed. If we can raise more and better grain from the small, ill-formed kernels on the little end of the ear, than from the largest and fairest, then we may sift out all the small grains of oats and wheat for seed, instead of selecting the largest and plumpest with so much care, as good farmers consider to be essential to a large crop.

There are many theories and experiments recorded and promulgated, by men who ought to know better, in regard to planting small, half-ripe seed, or rearing animals from inferior breeders, all of which tends to mislead beginners in agriculture. Any old, superannuated grandmother, in her second childhood, knows better than to recommend planting inferior seed, if we would raise an abundant crop. Scientific writers have done an untold amount of harm by sanctioning such palpable absurdities about the comparative excellence of good and inferior seed. Let our young farmers not be misled by the teachings of scientific writers, when reason and common sense both assure us, that such teachings are erroneous; and, if followed out to the letter, the result will be a serious failure and a grievous disappointment.

How to produce a New Variety of Wheat.

The true way to obtain a new variety of wheat is to go to the field of some excellent farmer, who sustains a fair reputation for raising superior wheat, when the grain is ripe, and select one, two, or more heads for seed. You can select, if you choose, one or two that appear to be quite unlike the great proportion of the heads. The ultimate product of this peculiar head, or heads, of grain will be the new variety sought. If you select a few heads of the best in the field, the product will be only an *improved* variety of grain. Reject such heads as are not well filled out with plump kernels.

Those also that do not have chaff of a uniform appearance should not be selected, as chaff of different colors and forms and partially bearded is a certain indication of a hybrid grain. The aim should be to start with a pure variety, if possible. Then prepare the ground by thorough pulverization and manuring, as for a carrot-bed, and plant the seed about the middle of September in the latitude of New York city. Make a hole two inches deep with one finger, or with a wooden dibble, and one foot apart in rows each way, with one kernel in a place, and cover the seed with mellow, rich soil. See that fowls do not scratch up the grain, nor bite off the tender blades after they have grown two or more inches long. If the ground is rich, every kernel will produce a stem that will tiller so extensively as to occupy the entire ground with large heads of grain. Next season, and the two following seasons, weed the wheat, and reject every head that appears a trifle different from all the rest of the ears. In a few years the identity of the variety will be permanently established, and the quality of the grain and its productiveness will be so greatly improved that one bushel of seed will yield several bushels more of superior grain per acre than can be grown on the same soil from ordinary seed.

After a valuable variety of wheat has been well established, if proper care be exercised in selecting the seed, from year to year, there is no more danger that an excellent variety will degenerate, than that the South Down breed of sheep will run out, when bred and reared with care, from year to year.

The "North British Agriculturist" says on this subject:

"In every field of grain there are to be seen ears differing in size, in form, and in general appearance from those growing beside them. Some of these can be recognized as the ears of established varieties; but a few will be distinct from any of the kinds in cultivation. Farmers usually bestow little attention on the different kinds of ears which may be sometimes seen growing in the same field, and which can be best observed during the cutting and harvesting of the crop; but if one farmer in a thousand would undertake the collection of such ears with the intention of sowing the seed, and thus propagating the kinds, the number of varieties would soon be considerably increased, and the kinds in cultivation would be improved by this selection of the best ears. Those who intend to collect ears of one or more of the cereals should proceed methodically, not only when selecting, but in keeping the ears of the apparently different kinds distinct at the time of gathering them, so that each kind can be sown by itself, and the produce from the seed of the selected ears collected and stored for future sowing. During the time of selecting ears, small bags formed of cloth should be carried, and as the ears are separated from the stalks, they should be placed in one or other of the bags. Care should be exercised to prevent confusion and intermixing of the seeds.

Every circumstance should be noted at the time, such as the field of grain in which the ears were gathered; the characteristic features which the ears presented in growing, such as size, form, whether the ears are close or open, and the color of the chaff and straw, chaff smooth or downy, and other points deemed worthy of being recorded. A written description should be placed with the ears put into each bag for after reference, as it is seldom advisable to trust to the memory as to facts.

The bags containing the ears should be hung in an open place away from mice or other depredators until the period of sowing the seeds.

The amount of trouble which the propagating of varities entails, renders it advisable for experimenters not to attempt too much at one time. Only those who are resolved to bestow minute attention during the whole period from the time of selecting the ears until the quantity of grain produced admits of its being distributed, should undertake the selection of ears for propagating the variety.

Keeping Varieties Pure.

In propagating new varieties, constant attention is essential to keep the variety true to the kind selected, more particularly if it has originated in what is termed a sport, either the result of cultivation or hybridization—the pollen of the ear of one variety fertilizing the seeds contained in the ear of a different kind. This hybridization is sometimes effected by experimenters, but accidental contact is the more frequent cause of the sports which appear in cultivated plants. Every variety of grain in cultivation will occasionally show ears differing from those which possess the characteristic appearances of the variety, while some varieties show red or brown ears, and ears with and without awns. The higher the manurial condition of the soil, the tendency to sporting appears to increase in force. As the soil should be made rich on which the seeds of the selected ears are grown year after year, this tendency to sport is certain to appear; and as the propagating of the selected variety is proceeded with, constant care is essential to cull out the ears which differ from the original standard of the selected ears. If the variety is the result of hybridization, this culling is all-important.

The ears will differ considerably in appearance, some resembling the kind from which the fertilizing pollen was derived, and others more closely resembling the variety which the pollen fertilized. Uniformity is essential to entitle any grain to the term variety; and this uniformity can only be secured by constant care in selection. After the type becomes fixed, sporting and degenerating will almost wholly cease, provided ordinary care is taken by the propagator. But every established variety should be kept up by occasional selection of the best ears.

In an industrial point of view, the propagating of a new prolific variety of any of the grains is of immense national importance. Any new variety which would yield from one to four bushels of additional grain per acre over the ordinary varieties in cultivation would tend thus far to raise the resources of our own soils. In this direction an extensive and most inviting field is open to all cultivators. Were agriculturists to study more closely the operations of horticulturists, much benefit would result to all. Farmers generally not only undervalue, but wholly disregard what horticulturists have done for agriculture.

The pleasure, and in exceptional cases the profit, to be derived is so considerable, that the propagator of new varieties will generally be amply rewarded for the time occupied in conducting the various operations of selecting, sowing, and reaping new kinds of grain. Those farmers who are anxious to improve the varieties of grain in cultivation—wheat, oats, or barley—should adopt

the same means as those so successfully followed out by
horticulturists—hybridizing, and more especially by selecting the best ears, and growing the seed so obtained
until sufficient quantities are secured to seed considerable portions of land preparatory to disposing of a
portion of the seeds raised from the selected ears. The
improvement of the domestic animals and birds has been
mainly effected by selection, and the same principles are
equally applicable for the improvement of the various
varieties of the cereals in cultivation. This field of experiment is open to all, and the persevering may cal-
culate upon success. Where so much can be effected
with even an ordinary amount of attention, the experimenter who possesses a knowledge of the cereals, and
also of vegetable physiology, is certain to reap a good
harvest. (See North British Agriculturist on the
subject of selecting new varieties.)

PROCURING EARLIER SEED WHEAT AT THE NORTH.

Mr. J. W. Clark, of Wisconsin, writes on this subject
as follows : " Why should we suppose southern seed will
give us earlier wheat, when we know our own wheat or
corn cannot ripen so early farther north as it does in our
own latitude ? Do not middle latitudes bear nearly the
same relation to the south as northern ones do to them,
and so in proportion of intermediate differences of distance and temperature ?

" We have good reason to believe there was no such
thing as Dent corn grown in latitudes 42° to 44° north,
fifteen years ago. But when Brigham Young and his
dupes were scattered from Missouri—Yellow Dent, and
subsequently White, in consequence of the Yellow suc-

11*

ceeding—was introduced into these latitudes in Wisconsin and elsewhere, by some of his, or rather Joe Smith's followers. The climate of those latitudes was then much as at present; yet it required full five years to acclimate this favorite and now general variety of the northwest, before it matured sufficiently early to ripen ere severe frosts set in and could be relied upon as a staple crop. Wheat being subject to the same forces of climate, must be therefore influenced in the degree that its new place of growth is dissimilar, or more or less favorable to vegetable development. Mr. Clay's and his neighbor Mr. Howard's experience, though the opposite of each other, both tend to prove that corn cannot mature so early when first grown from southern seed; and the writer used seed from Maryland two years ago, and under the most favorable condition of soil and culture, yet not a kernel of it ripened. If five years are requisite to acclimate corn removed only five or six degrees farther north, and seed raised in Mississippi does not ripen till October in Kentucky, and that grown in Maryland will not ripen at all in latitude 43° north, why are we to expect Kentucky wheat to ripen in Western New York, and the same latitude west or east of it, earlier than native-grown seed?

"If it should be alleged that wheat, unlike corn in this particular, does not require either so high a heat or so long a season to mature it, the fact is admitted; but what is the inference? Is it, that because wheat ripens early, and before the hottest weather has more than half passed, in Tennessee or Kentucky, it will ripen equally early five to ten degrees farther north? If this be the supposition, it must surely be without good reason or theory—the same thing. What can such an inference mean in the light of the fact that peas, strawberries, etc., that have been grown in Georgia and the Carolinas, are seen in abundance in the New York market several weeks, more or less, before the same and similar varieties are even out of blossom eight or ten degrees farther northward. The peas were nearly ripe at the south in consequence of being subject to a sufficiency of heat by a given date, and they were not yet formed in the pod at the north, by reason of not having been subject to any such sufficiency of heat as was necessary to a like result at the same date.

"If wheat seed is taken from south to north, it does not carry any vital force in the seed germ that can modify or resist the force of northern temperatures. On the contrary, northern temperature, or climatic forces, must control the character of the next seed crop, by wholly originating and controlling the growth of the entire plant. Supposing northern fall wheat to be just restarting to grow with vigor at the opening of the Erie Canal, similar fall wheat will be then half-leg high in Tennessee, and this because it was subject to a sufficiency of heat weeks before our northern wheat received any such adequate supply of that thermal element.

" To procure seed from the south will not only not accelerate, but retard the harvest, because such seed will have been acclimated by and be adapted to a higher degree of heat at such and all, or nearly all, stages of its growth, than it can receive in a far northern situation. Having grown under a higher thermal forcing influence, it will not grow, till after several years of acclimation, with equal vigor and rapidity with a lower heat or less forcing.

" But procure seed from Canada, Sweden, or any more northern locality, where the temperature in the average is colder, and the time of first growing later in the spring, and harvest still later, in consequence of the lower average of summer heat, and the more time needed to supply the heat required; take seed wheat from such a situation to one where the growing season commences earlier by reason of the requisite heat being earlier present, and it will not only commence its growth as much earlier as the germinating degree of heat earlier surrounds it, but will ripen much earlier generally, as the average heat is higher by reason of having been subject to the *whole amount* of the great thermal element necessary to its maturity in a shorter or *less period* of time. Thus, on this question, theory and facts appear to adjust themselves consistently together; and our decided conclusion is, that from farther north is the direction seed wheat or corn, or in fact any cereal, should be procured, if the object be to secure earlier maturity in the resulting product. Cereals that ripen *early* far north, will naturally and with general *certainty* mature *earlier* when cultivated considerably farther south." Read Climotology of Wheat, pp. 57, 79.

No Facts to Prove it.

Old wheat-growers will contend earnestly, that facts are against this theory. If they are, I have not had the good fortune to meet those facts. If it can be shown by well-conducted experiments that seed wheat should be procured in a southern latitude, then we will believe it. But, in order to establish such an assertion, excellent seed must be obtained in every instance, and the test made fairly, for several successive seasons.

Degeneracy of Wheat—Cause and Remedy.

From time out of mind there appears to have been a prevalent opinion among wheat-growers that varieties of wheat deteriorate, becoming in a few years so unproductive that other kinds are sought and cultivated. Allusion to this subject is made in Virgil, penned more than two thousand years ago, and the writer speaks of having seen the peasant grieve over the degeneracy of his grain, where the heads had not been culled with care from year to year. We have always observed from boyhood that farmers have recognized this fact, and when alluding to it have appeared to acknowledge that there is no remedy for it. When writers have alluded to varieties of wheat cultivated in different parts of our country, they have almost invariably mentioned kinds that once flourished, but "for some unknown cause have degenerated." The English Agricultural Society, several years ago, issued circulars desiring information on this subject.

It cannot be denied that varieties of wheat do run out. We well remember when a boy, that a kind of winter wheat called Red Chaff, or Bald Wheat, was cultivated quite extensively in that part of the State where we were living; but in a few years farmers discontinued raising it, because, they said, "it had run out." The same was true of the White Flint, Beaver Dam, Wild Goose, and Hutchinson Wheat, most of which yielded well when first introduced; but after a few years failed to return remunerating crops. The identity of the variety appeared to be gone. The heads were of various colors, and the kernels small, of different and varied forms, and the yield was less and less from year to year, until farmers were satisfied that it would not pay to sow that kind of wheat any longer.

The abettors of this theory of degeneracy, maintain that the wheat plant has an inherent tendency to degenerate; and not a few men, who have acquired something of a reputation for being scientific, have also endorsed this visionary theory, and have even affirmed that "the science of botany and vegetable physiology proves that wheat, or any other plant, when grown on the same soil for a long succession of years, will continue to degenerate until it is not worth raising." This theory received the sanction of such men as Hon. Jesse Buel, who moved the world with his agricultural wisdom, and who acknowledged that "the tendency of varieties to degenerate is not a vague opinion, but a fixed fact, and that the duration of a variety in perfection is generally computed at from fourteen to twenty years, though this period is sometimes prolonged by a change of soil or climate." T. A. Knight, the President of the London Horticultural Society, writes: "I believe that almost every variety now cultivated in this and the adjoining counties, has long since passed the period of its age when a succession should have taken its place. It has long been known that every variety cultivated, gradually becomes debilitated, losing a large portion of its powers of producing grain fully equal to previous crops."

We know this is not so. The science of botany and vegetable physiology teaches no such doctrine. Reason, common sense, and the experience of the past are all decidedly against it. It never has been and never can be shown that there is any natural tendency in well-established varieties of wheat, or any other grain, to degenerate, any more than there is in the suggestion that the human race grows imbecile and effeminate from generation to generation. The theory has no facts to sustain it. If properly cultivated and suitable care be exercised in selecting the seed, varieties may be maintained in all their primeval excellency and purity as long as the vicissitudes of the seasons continue. We grant that varieties do degenerate and lose their identity, their "vital energies" and powers of reproduction.

We have due respect for the integrity of such writers as were just alluded to. But when they recorded these suggestions they simply reiterated what they considered to be plausible theories that had been broached by other writers, all of whom had made assertions touching the degeneration of wheat. In this way many vague and exceedingly erroneous theories have been promulgated from year to year by scientific writers on agricultural subjects. But mere assertion of a supposed fact does not constitute a well-established theory on any subject.

On the borders of the River Nile, in Africa, one of the finest regions in the world for the production of excellent wheat, the same varieties are grown, from year to year, without the least deterioration, that were cultivated three thousand years ago. And the same thing may be done in this country by exercising the same care in the selection of the seed that is observed by the farmers in that part of the world.

It is a well-established fact that wheat will hybridize when different varieties are allowed to grow in close proximity. Of course, the product would be a mixture of seed, in which the purity of the variety is gone. Consequently, with a mixture of seed, a farmer would find himself in the same circumstances with reference

to the improvement of his wheat that he is when he
undertakes to improve his domestic animals by breed
ing from mongrels or from grade stock. It is well understood that such animals—grades and mongrels—
when employed as breeders, never transmit the excellent points of desirable form and symmetry to their offspring with reliable certainty, while pure-bred animals
never fail in this respect.

The same facts hold good in the vegetable kingdom,
with seed wheat in particular. When different varieties are sown in close proximity, and the product, which
will be an impure grain, is again employed ·for seed, a
pure variety of choice wheat may be run out most effectually in a few years, so that intelligent farmers who
were only superficial observers would be ready to affirm,
without any hesitancy, that wheat does degenerate.
The cause of degeneracy, and the remedy, may all be
expressed in a few words. We have hinted at the cause,
namely: sowing different varieties near each other, so
that the grain will hybridize; thrashing several kinds
together, and continuing to employ such grain for seed
from year to year. Herein lies the whole secret of the
degeneracy of varieties. If a pure variety be kept by
itself with suitable care, and cultivated on good ground,
and the grain never thrashed with other wheat, the purity of a variety of wheat, with all its excellent characteristics, may be maintained intact as long as wheat
may be cultivated. There is no uncertainty about this
suggestion. The idea is in perfect keeping with the
established laws of vegetable physiology. Cultivating
any variety of grain in a slip-shod, slack, and perfunctory manner, will cause the best variety of wheat the
world ever knew to degenerate and run completely out

in a few years. On the contrary, if the seed be selected every season with the same care that the originator of the Weeks wheat observed for a decade of years, generations unborn would cultivate the same varieties that our fields now produce, without the least deterioration in either yield or quality of grain.

FURTHER TESTIMONY ON DEGENERACY.

I herewith copy the following suggestions from the " Independent :" " If there were an inherent tendency in wheat to degenerate—as many people affirm there is— how is it that no signs of degeneracy are manifest, so long as a well-established variety is cultivated well, from year to year, and kept by itself? No farmer was ever heard to complain that his ' wheat appears to be running out,' until after there has been great neglect in saving the seed.

" Clean, pure, and well-ripened seed is sowed on the best soil for many seasons, after which, many farmers become indifferent about their seed, often sowing that kind of grain which is nothing more nor less than a hybrid. Mediterranean wheat—which is usually a red variety—and the various kinds of white wheat, are often thrashed together. The good, the poor, the well-matured, and half-ripe and shrunken kernels, all go into one bin; and such grain is used for seed. Now, as wheat will sport and hybridize when growing in close proximity, how can we expect, with any degree of confidence, that good grain will be produced by very inferior seed?

" In producing new varieties of strawberries and Irish potatoes, a certain kind is often cultivated for several

successive years, and sometimes abandoned, as un-
worthy of further efforts in endeavoring to establish a
new variety. Therefore, when farmers sow anything
and everything that is called wheat, letting it all grow
together, whether it ripens early or late, and cultivate
it poorly at that, and take no pains to sow the choicest
seed, or to keep a good variety distinct, what can any
one naturally expect, but rapid degeneracy of the grain?
Degeneracy, or 'running out of varieties,' is the natural
and certain result of such bad management in the selection of the seed, and cultivation of the crop, to which
we have alluded.

   " We never hear that a good variety of Indian corn
has degenerated, until it has been planted near other
kinds, with which it has been allowed to mix.   And, if
the same care were exercised in selecting the very best
kernels of a well-established variety of wheat for seed,
and keeping the seed grain separate, in a secure place,
we should have the unbounded satisfaction of seeing our
wheat fields produce, not only larger heads, plumper kernels, and heavier grain in much greater abundance per
acre, but no signs of degeneracy would appear, were the
same kind of grain raised in one locality generation
after generation.

   "Historians inform us that the same varieties of good
wheat are now grown on the fertile soils on each side
of the River Nile in Egypt, with no signs of degeneracy,
that were raised there a thousand years ago.

   " Instead of there being a natural tendency in wheat
to degenerate, if it is cultivated as it always should be,
and none but the best seed put in, there would be a
manifest tendency to improve from year to year. Every
experienced wheat-grower will acknowledge this. Farm-

ers who never save their seed with care will doubt it."

The Commissioner of Agriculture recorded the following fact in regard to the degeneracy of the Hunter wheat, which corroborates what I have penned. He writes: "Hunter's wheat, one of the oldest and most esteemed varieties in Scotland, was discovered half a century ago by the roadside in Berwickshire. Through long culture and want of care this variety has greatly deteriorated."

In searching agricultural documents for facts on this subject, I have been greatly surprised to meet with so long a list of once excellent varieties of wheat, entirely run out, so that they are no longer cultivated. It is a serious and grave accusation against American tillers of the soil, that as a general rule, the wheat crop is neglected and shamefully abused; and I often wonder that we raise half as good crops as we now meet with.

WHEN TO SOW WINTER WHEAT.

Winter wheat may be sowed too early in the season as well as too late. Every intelligent farmer will admit this fact. There must be, therefore, a certain period, midway between the too-early and the too-late time, which may be fixed upon, as the most proper period of all the growing season, to put in the seed. In designating any given period as the best time to sow winter wheat, there are considerations of transcendent importance to be observed, each and all of which will be found to exert more or less influence on the wheat crop. The growing wheat has destructive enemies to encounter, which flourish only at certain periods in the

growing season. The aim of the husbandman, therefore, should be to have his wheat plants grow, as much
as possible, before, and after these enemies flourish and
commit their ravages on the growing plants. Besides
the insects destructive to wheat that must be encoun-
tered in autumn, and those that it is desirable to shun
in the summer, before harvest, there are adverse circumstances which must be foreseen and guarded against, as
much as practicable, among which I may mention
drought, wet weather, and the sinister influence of the
freezing and thawing of the soil in winter. In addition
to these things, the *habit* of the wheat plant should
exercise a controlling influence in the mind of the
wheat-grower, in determining the most proper period
for sowing the seed for a crop of winter grain. The
wheat-grower must encounter hosts of formidable an-
tagonists, in autumn. in winter, in spring time, and in
summer. To outstrip one, dodge the other, circumvent
a third, take advantage of a fourth, to run the gauntlet,
so to speak, from September till the next harvest, literally surrounded by untold millions of insects that find
a rich subsistence on the germinating kernels, as soon
as they exhibit signs of vegetation, and that feed on
the tender blades, and extract the delicate juices from
the growing kernels, and to triumph over all the adverse circumstances and unpropitious influences of the
season, and to be able, by agricultural skill and judicious management, to develop a large field of plump
wheat, waving in the breezes like a sea of gold, is, most
assuredly, a laudable employment. When we consider
how many destructive enemies growing wheat has, and
what a wonderfully fastidious plant wheat is, in regard
to the vegetable nutrition that the soil affords, it seems

a mystery—not that farmers do not grow large crops of this kind of grain—but that they are able to mature any at all.

Now, then, for the best time to sow winter wheat. In the first place, looking forward to the long and dreary winter, we find that the strongest wheat plants, those that are most firmly rooted and that have a system of luxuriant leaves, sufficient to cover the surface of the ground, will endure the rigors of our northern winters with less injury. In consideration of this fact, reason would seem to dictate putting in the seed very early—even in the month of August. But there are destructive enemies ahead. If the seed be put in very early, so that the plants attain a large size in a few weeks, countless hordes of insects, in the form of the wheat fly, will nearly destroy the crop. As this enemy flourishes between the two periods—early seed time and late seed time—we must evade, if possible, its ravages. Therefore, we must choose the *late* seed time; and in order to be prepared to resist the adverse influences of winter, we must plough and harrow and manure the soil, cultivate, pulverize, drain, and fertilize the seed-bed, and by repeated and most thorough mechanical tearing and trituration, get the ground into such a favorable condition for vegetation, that the young plants will spring from seed deposited in the soil, *after* the dreaded foes have run their course, and still have sufficient time to become rooted and topped before the winter sets in. Here, then, we are able to fix upon a point of time for every farmer in every latitude, with the assurance that, if a crop cannot be secured by seeding, at that period, we must meet a failure.

When wheat is sowed so late in the growing season,

that the roots acquire very little toughness, and the leaves attain only a small size before cold and freezing weather comes on, the growing plants will suffer such serious injury by the intense cold, and freezing, and thawing, and upheaval of the soil, that a fair crop of grain will not be produced the next season. Our best wheat-growers understand this point perfectly ; and our horticulturists and pomologists know how eminently important it is, that a plant finish growing and attain a proper ripeness and solidity of juices, and some tenacity of fibre, before the tender plants are exposed to the destructive influences of cold weather. In order, therefore, to be still more definite and explicit, respecting the best time to sow winter wheat, we may fix the time at this period, viz., let the seed be put in as late in the season as it can be, and still have sufficient time to throw out a system of roots and leaves, sufficiently large to cover nearly or quite the entire surface of the ground.

In this latitude, the great majority of wheat-growers agree that about the 10th of September is the most desirable period to sow winter wheat. But, I think, that every intelligent farmer, who understands the habit of the wheat plant, will agree with me, that if the ground be put in such excellent tilth, that the young plants will attain the desired size before cold weather comes on, the first or even the 10th of October will be found a more desirable period for autumnal seed-time than any time in September. But, let it be understood, that unless the soil is in an excellent state of fertility—really rich—friable, and sufficiently moist when the seed is sowed to insure immediate germination, it will not be safe to defer seeding to that late period. Let me assure wheat-growers, however, that in practice, they will find it more profitable to make their soil doubly rich, and pulverize it more thoroughly, and put in their seed as late as the first of October, than to cultivate tolerably well, manure moderately, and sow at an early date.

As we move south of this latitude, the period of seed time should be fixed at a still later date in autumn. We should keep in mind this one great fact, to put whip and spur to the growing wheat plants between the period when insects would injure its growth, and the influences of winter. Then, the crop will be safe, so far as its salvation can be secured by choosing the most propitious period for putting in the seed. But one of the most important consideration in the whole system of wheat culture is to have the soil in the right condition, bountifully fertilized with such pabulum as will develop a healthful and stiff straw and a plump and shining kernel.

It would seem that early sowed grain in autumn would mature the next season just as many days earlier than other crops, as the seed which was put in. But experiments have shown that, in practice, we cannot count upon any advantage, from early seeding, in securing an early harvest, as wheat sowed the middle of September and the first of October, on the same kind of ground, will mature at the same period the next season. If we would have wheat ripen early in the season, an early variety must be obtained, as early seeding will not secure an early harvest.

The following extract taken from the report of a committee appointed by the Kentucky Agricultural and Mechanical Association, will be read with interest. The Committee say:

"The fly, or as it is popularly known, the Hessian

fly, which was not known in our country until the war of the Revolution, was supposed to have been introduced here in the straw of the bedding of those mercenary troops (the Hessians) whom our good mother sent over here to cut our throats. Your committee know of no remedy for this pest. It has been thought that late sowing obviated it to some extent. This is, no doubt, true. But there are several difficulties attending it. First—late sown wheat is more liable to be winter-killed than that which is early sown. Second—it is just as liable to the spring crop of the fly as the other. And third—if it escapes these, it is much more liable to that worst of all difficulties, rust—indeed almost sure to be materially injured. Then the question comes, what shall we do? It would probably be best not to sow early or late, but take a medium, say from the 25th September to 10th October. Very early sown wheat is very liable to be badly injured by the insect."

Moore's "Rural New Yorker," published at Rochester, New York, in the centre of a fine wheat-growing country, says: "If the question is presented to the farmer whether he shall sow his wheat very early in the season on soil hastily and imperfectly prepared, or wait until a later period and expend more labor in the preparation of the seed-bed, let him decide in favor of late sowing and thorough preparation. Under most circumstances early sowing is of no advantage, and often it is highly injurious. The supposed benefit to be derived from it is a large fall growth, and strong-rooted plants which can endure the winter. But it is not always the largest growth of top in the wheat plant in the fall which makes the best root. Early sown wheat may have its growth, by means of warm, wet weather, thrown largely to the top and less to the root, than is desirable, and in this case will not come through the winter as well as that sown later, when the cool weather is favorable to root growth and healthy development of leaf. We do not advise late sowing on poorly prepared ground, and that which is too much impoverished. Sow early on such soil, if you must sow it in, poor condition. But it is preferable to defer the seeding a week or two, and, in the mean time, till and manure the land. A top-dressing of manure or straw, after the sowing, is worth more for winter protection than a large development of the plant leaf; and Western farmers that are in the habit of burning large quantities of straw might find better use for it in shielding their wheat fields.

" This year the Hessian fly has injured the wheat crop to a greater extent than usual. Early sowing induces their attack. Very early sowing, followed by a warm autumn, sometimes causes the seed stalk to start before winter stops the growth of the plant, and thus a portion of its strength is wasted. We do not advocate extremes either way in sowing wheat, but first, a thorough preparation of the soil, then the choosing, if possible, of that medium period which comes after the heat and drought of an early autumn, and gives time for a moderate and healthy growth before winter."

Mr. David Wood, Venice, Cayuga County, New York, who is an excellent practical farmer, communicated to me the following suggestions in relation to wheat culture:—The best time to sow winter wheat with us is, from the first of September to the tenth. If sowed before that period the plants grow too large before winter. Wheat that has attained a large growth in autumn, is more apt to winter-kill than if the stems and leaves

12

were smaller. If sowed later than this period, the plants will not grow enough before winter to insure a good crop of grain.

Sowing Seed Wheat in Winter.

I once tried an experiment by sowing winter wheat after the growing season had ended, and the ground was about to freeze up. The soil was thoroughly prepared, by several times ploughing, and the last ploughing was done about the middle of November. About the fifth of December there were certain indications that winter was about to commence in sober earnest. I then sowed the wheat, and harrowed it in; and the next day the ground froze up tight, and remained till the next March. The wheat did not germinate until the growing season had commenced.

The experiment was exceedingly unsatisfactory, as not more than one-half the kernels seemed to vegetate. I sowed seed at the rate of about two bushels per acre; but the young plants stood unusually thin on the ground—not one of them tillered at all; the straw grew very coarse, the heads were short, the grain shrunken and small, and the stems and leaves were so badly affected with red rust, that I never cared to repeat a similar experiment.

General R. Harmon writes in relation to the amount of seed per acre and time of sowing, that there is some difference in opinion as to the quantity required to be sown to the acre: first, we must take into consideration the soil, its quality (for on that much depends), and the time of sowing—on clay loam soils, the first week in September is the best time for this section of the State. It is important to have it take a good root before winter, and if sown earlier, the fly is very apt to destroy some of it in the fall; and if it should be so large as to nearly cover the ground the last of October, it should be eaten off by cattle or sheep, as it is less liable to be injured by deep snows. Here one bushel of seed to the acre, is as good as more on soils in good condition; if sown ten days later, add one peck more seed per acre. On sandy, gravelly loams, the second week in September is the most favorable time for sowing; if earlier, the fly is very apt to affect it, so as to diminish the crop. Wheat, on such soils, appears to suffer more from the fly, than on clay soils. On these soils, one bushel per acre, and if the soil is not in good condition, one peck more should be sown. The White Flint spreads or tillers more than the common varieties; and when I have sown a bushel and a half the second week in September, it was too thick, the straw fine, the heads short, and the berry not as large and fine as it would have been, if one peck less had been sown to the acre. There is one advantage in sowing thick on soils where it is subject to be affected by rust: it will ripen two or three days earlier. That is an important consideration on soils unfavorable to the early ripening of wheat.

William R. Schuyler, Michigan, recorded the following suggestions in reference to the time of sowing winter wheat in that State:

"It is evident from reports received from other sections of the State, that in several counties the crop will not be more than half the usual average. There is reason to fear that early sown wheat will again suffer from the fall attacks of this insect, unless, as is sometimes the case, it has been followed up and nearly exterminated by its parasitic enemies.   It is to be hoped that farmers who last year finished sowing in August and the first of September, will consult their true interests by deferring the work till a later period in the month.   I am aware that in endeavoring to escape one calamity it is advisable, if possible, to avoid the opposite evil.

" On stiff, tenacious clay loams, especially when not thoroughly underdrained, wheat sown after the month of September, is liable to be injured by the winter and spring frosts ; or if carried safely through the winter, protected by its mantle of snow, it is more endangered by the attacks of the spring fly, it not being sufficiently vigorous to outgrow the effects of the injury.   Late sown sandy soils, also, when not properly tilled, are still more exposed to the attacks of this spring generation. In districts where the midge prevails, it is all-important that sowing should not be at so late a period as to retard the ripening of the crop.   It is a fact, however, no doubt familiar to every careful, observing farmer, that under the same conditions of the land there is scarcely any difference in the ripening of wheat sown in the first or third week of September.   There seems, therefore, to be a necessity for selecting a medium period for sowing as the best protection against the fly, avoiding at the same time other evils incident to the late sowing.

" A single frost is supposed to destroy all the insects while in the state of the fly.   There is, consequently, no danger to be apprehended if the wheat is not sown nor up until after an autumnal frost.   In seasons, therefore, when the fly is known to be prevalent, it would doubtless be the safer plan to defer sowing until even the last week in September, should not a sharp frost in the mean time occur.   In the climate of Michigan we seldom escape a frost through the month of September. Last season was one of those exceptions that will sometimes occur in general rules, the effects whereof cannot be guarded against. If my recollection is right, there was no perceptible frost throughout the month of September, and I have no doubt that the present crop of wheat was materially injured by the insect in consequence of the very warm and unseasonable weather in October and part of November, the very early sown fields, of course, suffering the most."

J. S. Gesner, of Canada West, in a prize article on the culture of wheat, says: "I have found the last week in August and the first week in September, to be the best period for sowing winter wheat in this locality. It is useless to sow any variety—except the Mediterranean —in this vicinity, later in the season than the time just mentioned."

J. Homes, of Chittenden, Vermont, writes : " I know of no better mode to prevent the ravages of the midge than early sowing, and even this sometimes fails. The last week in August, or the first in September, I would prefer, but this depends upon circumstances; if the weather is dry and hot, I would rather wait until October. Some years since I made an experiment to test early and late sowing. One piece was sowed the last week in August, one the last week in September, and one in the middle of October, on the same kind of soil, and treated in every respect alike. There was no difference in the time of ripening or in the quality of the grain ; but the earliest sowed produced the longest heads, consequently yielded more per acre.

Hon. Isaac Newton, Commissioner of Agriculture, recorded the following facts touching the influence of the frosts of winter on wheat that was sowed at different periods, and which had attained greater growth in one instance than in the other. He says : " During the winter, the first or September sowing of the premium white Mediterranean wheat withstood the winter very badly, and during the severe frost in the month of January, it was entirely killed ; whereas the same wheat sown in October withstood the winter much better than the red bearded Mediterranean wheat, kept ahead the whole season, and was harvested on the 27th of June. This seems to be a wheat well adapted to this climate, large berry, well filled and thin skinned ; produced forty-eight bushels per acre. The red bearded Mediterranean wheat sown in October did not stand the severe frost so well as the same kind sown in September, showing that the best period for sowing the red bearded Mediterranean wheat is September, and for the premium white Mediterranean, from Port Mahon, is October. The Tappahannock wheat has been the earliest of all the varieties experimented with, although it does not seem to be so productive as some of the other kinds ; still the fine quality of the grain, and its earliness, is very much to be regarded, as an early variety is much less liable to disease and other contingencies."

Sowing Spring Wheat Early *vs.* Late.

I have observed, for many years past, that wheat-growing farmers seem to be about equally divided, touching the best time to sow spring wheat. A part of our farmers contend that the seed should be put in very early in the spring, even before the growing season has really commenced. And if the soil is not sufficiently dry, plough and sow in the mud, rather than not put in the seed early. On the contrary, others contend, that it is better to put in the seed quite late in the season, even after sowing oats and barley. One party contends that spring wheat should be put in before the ground is done freezing and thawing, as spring frosts greatly improve the productiveness of the soil and increase the yield of grain. Others insist that all these things are decidedly injurious to the crop.

I think the abettors of these theories are both right and both wrong. My own experience leads me to fix upon an intermediate period for putting in spring wheat.

I am satisfied, that if the ground be put in order soon after the growing season has commenced—as soon as may be practicable after the soil has become sufficiently warm to cause germination and growth—that the crop of wheat will be more satisfactory, than if the seed were sowed very early, or rather late. Whether other farmers will admit the assertion or not, I am satisfied that cold, frosty weather often injures young wheat plants, more seriously than most people are aware of. After the young plants have appeared, and a cold, stormy period ensues, the leaves turn yellow, cease to grow for several weeks, become stunted, and will never produce so much grain, as if those same plants had received no check in their growth. If the seed be put in late, the growth is liable to be too rapid and too luxuriant; and the consequence is, that the crop is seldom so satisfactory, as if the seeding had been attended to a few days earlier in the season. Late sowed wheat may—as it often has—succeeded well; but the same crop would doubtless have been much better, had the seed been put in a few days earlier. I do not think that the advocates of late seeding have tested the result of seeding earlier. As their land produced a bountiful crop, they *conclude* that the yield is heavier than it would have been if the seed had been sowed at a former period. The *proof* of the pudding is in eating it ; and not in chewing the string of the pudding bag.

EARLY *vs.* LATE SEEDING IN MASSACHUSETTS.

An experienced wheat-grower in Massachusetts writes : " I never had any luck in late sowing spring wheat, nor did I ever see a good piece, sown as late as the 25th of May. Last year was an exception to late sown grain, which we seldom have. The drought injured early sown grain full as much, if not more, than late sown in this section. Even our late planted corn was a larger growth, and was perfectly sound. Late sown wheat in ordinary seasons, will not be as plump as that sown early. The straw is more apt to be weak and to crinkle down by the late rains, and will turn black, and is more likely to rust. There is more risk in harvesting, to get it in a good condition for the mow. Not so with early sown. The kernel is plump, the head well filled, the straw bright and stiff; and the grain will thrash a great deal easier ; and you will have more bushels from a given quantity of ground. The earlier it is sown, if the ground is dry and the weather suitable, the better. I had rather my wheat would be sown the 25th of March if it could be got in as early, than to be put off till the 25th of May. We have had a heavy freeze on early sown wheat, and no detriment at all. The 25th of April, and from that to the 5th of May, is, in my opinion, the best time to sow spring wheat."

A correspondent of the "Rural New Yorker" wrote on this subject: "The reason why spring wheat growing is attended with such ill success in Western New York is that the fallow was not fall ploughed, and consequently is sown too late in the spring." The great secret of success in growing a bountiful crop of spring wheat is the proper management of the soil, the main point being to plough and fallow in the fall, or before the ground is too hard frozen in winter, so that the wheat may be sown as early in April as the spring rains will admit.

Many farmers who succeeded so early in growing a crop of wheat from the scarified virgin soil in the early days of Western New York, now think that the deterioration in that cereal is owing to the exhaustion of a mysterious pabulum in the soil. Yet, to grow a good crop of barley, requires a finer tilth and a less adhesive soil than for wheat.

J. B. Lawes, the prince of England's experimenters on the farm, avers "that he could supply fertilizers to the wheat fallow to produce a given crop of wheat to the acre, subject only to the risk of hail and violent storms." But in England the wheat plant rarely if ever freezes out, as it often does in winter and early spring in the United States, California and the South excepted. It is the freezing out of this plant that prevents the western farmers of Wisconsin, Illinois, and Iowa from sowing winter wheat. But they have reduced the sowing of spring wheat, as a substitute, into a perfect system that rarely fails to succeed if well done. (Read my notes about spring wheat under the last heading of the second chapter of this book, and How Freezing and Thawing of the Soil injures Growing Wheat, pages 123, 124, and 125.)

THICK AND THIN SEEDING.

Wheat can be sowed too thick as well as too thin. Of course, then, there is a correct quantity to sow per acre, as there must necessarily be a medium between the thick seeding and thin seeding. The quantity of seed alone does not determine how much should be sown on one acre, as the kernels vary in size. If the kernels be very large, a much larger quantity of seed will be required to seed an acre, than if the kernels were very small. There is more danger of sowing too much seed on an acre, than there is of scattering too little. When wheat is sowed too thin, provision has been made by nature, to send out numerous stems, from the single plants that spring from every kernel. (See this subject explained under the head of the Habit of the Wheat Plant.) Seed wheat is often sowed in such absurdly large quantities, per acre, that the soil does not yield but a little more than half the number of bushels that would have been produced, had just enough been sowed and no more. It is exceedingly unwise policy to sow wheat, or any other grain thick, for the purpose of smothering a dense growth of noxious plants.

J. J. Mechi, of England, who has had much experience in growing wheat, writes, that "one kernel in a hole, at intervals of nine inches by four, would, under favorable circumstances, be ample, and produce much more than if four times that number were sown; but then we have rooks, French partridges, birds, mice, and wireworms to contend with." It would be a very dangerous experiment to sow generally so small a quantity of seed as one peck per acre. In highly cultivated, warm, mellow soils, free from weeds and in good heart, where harvest is

ready by the first of August or earlier, such small quan
tities may be sown, provided the sowing is done early.

Thin sowing is the first cause of large and vigorous
ears to select from. On this point, there can be no
mistake, seeing that thick sowing has an exactly reverse
effect, diminishing and crippling the growth of the ear,
until, with extreme quantities, there is scarcely a good
kernel, or a good ear. Therefore, in order to get good
ears to select from, or to be certain of the largest possible
yield of grain, sow only a moderate quantity per acre. I
think that every intelligent wheat-grower will agree with
me, that thin sowing has quite as much or more to do
with a large product of superior grain, as the choice of
a prolific variety. No rule can be laid down that will
serve as a reliable guide for farmers in various portions of
the country in determining the quantity of wheat per acre.
For this reason, I shall not attempt to state how much
this farmer, or that wheat-grower, should sow per acre.

In a letter dated June 27th, Mr. M. says:

" I related last year that a peck of seed wheat per acre,
dibbled at intervals of about 4½ inches, one kernel in a
hole, produced fifty-eight bushels of heavy wheat per acre,
and 2¾ tons of straw; in fact, the thickest and heaviest
crop of corn and straw on my farm. It was seen at
various periods of its growth by many agricultural and
other visitors. During winter, a single stem only having appeared from each kernel, the land at a distance
appeared as if unsown, and we were often asked why we
had omitted to drill that particular portion of the field.
In the spring each stem radiated its shoots horizontally,
to the extent in some instances of thirty to forty-eight
stems, and ultimately became the best crop on the farm,
and, which is often convenient in harvesting, about

four days later than the thick sown put in, in October, at the same time as the rest of the field was drilled with one bushel per acre. In October last, rather late in the month, we repeated the experiment on a heavy-land clover lea, as last year. The ground was rough and hard, and very dry, and although a kernel was placed in each hole, only about one-half, or half a peck per acre, came up. Of course we anticipated a partial failure, but spring came, and each stem threw out horizontally a large number of shoots, so that now it is admitted by all who see it that it will exceed in produce the adjoining crop, drilled at one bushel per acre. It appears to be about four or five days later than the rest."

After inviting all interested to come and examine this crop for themselves, Mr. M. concludes : " According to Mr. Caird, the average increase of our corn crops is eight for one—one million quarters of seed to produce nine millions of corn ! This is discreditable to us, for surely one good seed in properly cultivated soil cannot produce so little, if it be allowed sufficient space to develop its growth. Forty to one is nearer the increase on my farm."

QUANTITY OF SEED PER ACRE.

The quantity of wheat sowed on an acre by one farmer, is no guide at all to his neighbor, unless the soil is similar in all respects, and the period of seeding about the same. Rich land does not require so large a quantity as poor ground. When the kernels are large, the quantity of seed must be increased ; and when they are small, the amount may be diminished, and still have just as many stalks on an acre. Kernels of wheat vary so much in size that figures expressing the number of grains in a bushel only mislead and confuse a beginner. I have in mind one farmer who counted the number of kernels in a quart of wheat; and from the number in one quart estimated the number of grains in a bushel to be 559,288. Another man made 660,000 kernels in one American bushel of wheat; and another 690,960.

I have raised excellent wheat where only one bushel of seed was sowed per acre. My practice was to sow two bushels of wheat per acre; and to drill in one and a half bushels per acre. In some instances, I was satisfied that the grain stood rather too thick on the ground. If the ground is rich, one bushel per acre, if put in evenly with a good drill, is all the seed that should be put on one acre. Every farmer should try experiments, for the purpose of ascertaining how much seed will yield the largest amount of grain per acre. If he can satisfy himself that he can secure a large yield by putting two bushels of seed on one acre, that is the quantity for him to sow. The quantity of seed varies, the country through. Very few farmers sow three bushels of seed per acre; and fewer still sow only one bushel. The majority, I think, sow or drill in about one and a half bushels per acre. Observe the quantity of seed per acre, as stated by the various authors of letters on the culture of wheat in various parts of the country in our agricultural periodicals.

The most sensible way to arrive at a correct conclusion on this subject, is, to weigh the grain that grows on a square yard, where the straw seems to stand very thick as well as where it is thin. Every farmer must study out the correct quantity of seed for his own soil.

In order to aid beginners in their investigations of

278   THE WHEAT CULTURIST.

this subject, I herewith give a table which was prepaied a few years ago, for "Facts for Farmers."

Grains per square foot.	Kernels per square yard.	Grains per acre.
4	36	174,240=1 peck.
8	72	348,480=2 pecks.
12	108	522,720=3 pecks.
16	144	696,960=4 pecks.
32	288	1,393,420=8 pecks.
48	432	2,090,880=3 bushels.
64	576	2,787,840=4 bushels.
80	720	3,428,800=5 bushels.

If a square foot be divided into four equal parts, and one kernel of wheat be planted in the middle of each section, if the wheat be of ordinary size, it will require about one peck of grain per acre. By dividing each square foot into sixteen sections, three inches square, and planting one kernel in the centre of each section, about one bushel of seed will be required per acre. But, if seed wheat were drilled in or sowed broadcast, as thick as this estimate, the growing plants will be found to stand as thickly as they should be in order to grow advantageously, and yield abundantly.

The beginner can enlarge, at pleasure, on these suggestions, as everything seems to be quite indefinite, after making our most satisfactory estimates.

WHAT BECOMES OF THE SEED.

Intelligent cultivators of soil, from time immemorial, have asked this question with much solicitude. From my early boyhood, to the present time, I have been on the lookout for a philosophical answer to this inquiry;

but have met with none. I shall attempt to give a philosophical, and I trust, a satisfactory answer. Farmers *do know one thing*, concerning which there is no guesswork—no uncertainty—which is, that all the seed sown does not grow. Therefore, what becomes of it, is an important inquiry.

A portion of seed wheat never germinates; because the germ of some of the kernels has been injured, and thus deprived of all vitality. Kernels of wheat are injured, sometimes when the grain is thrashed; and in numerous instances, the kernels sprout before the grain is garnered. The tender sprouts perish in the sunshine, when the wheat is dried; but the kernels appear changed little, if any. Yet, the germs are destroyed. Of course, if such grain be employed for seed, it never comes up. Much of the good seed also never comes up, for the following reasons: In some instances, the grain is buried so deep, that the substance of the kernels which produces the stem, is all exhausted, before reaching the surface of the ground. Of course, all such kernels will never come up. Some other kernels are deposited in an unfavorable place, surrounded with lumps and stones, where they sprout, but fail to grow. Birds pick up a share before the grain is buried in the seed-bed. Insects take a share; and where several kernels happen to be planted so closely together that all cannot grow, for want of space, a portion of the young plants must cease to grow, and at length fail and die. The young leaves of wheat, soon after they appear above ground, are very tender and good for birds of various kinds, which often bite off large numbers of the stems, close to the surface of the ground. Such plants seldom recover from the injury thus received. In numerous instances, a thousand crows, or pigeons, descend on a field of wheat, and destroy one fourth part of the young plants. Domestic fowls are frequently allowed to range over wheat fields, when they destroy plants sufficient to make bushels of grain. I might mention other marauders that commit depredations on the growing wheat. But these must suffice.

How to Raise Early Grain or Vegetables.

On the subject of raising plants that mature early, a practical farmer wrote in the " Independent " as follows :

In localities where seasons are comparatively short—where late frost is liable to cut down the young plants, and early frost to damage the fruit or grain—it is of great importance that seed for future crops be raised and secured with great care. It will require the exercise of much good care for many successive years to effect any remarkably *good* change in any crop with reference to its early maturity. But, on the contrary, by exercising *no* care, it will be easy to manage in such a manner as to have plants mature very late in the season, and at the same time to yield an *inferior* crop. If we desire to have crops ripen early, we may have the pleasure of seeing our efforts to secure such a result crowned with good success. But if that is a subject which gives us but little anxiety, our contented desires will be satisfied by seeing our crops come to maturity long after our enterprising neighbors have harvested *their* fields of grain.

Now, if we desire to raise early grain, or early vegetables of any kind, we must select the seed that ripens the very first. The first ripe panicles of carrot seed and parsnip seed, the first ripe pods of beans, peas, or other leguminous plants, and the first ripe pods of turnip seed, if selected carefully every year, will effect a very desirable improvement in the crop, both in its excellence as to quantity and quality, as well as in the period of early maturity. But by planting the half-ripe and late seed the crop will degenerate very rapidly.

By planting only a small part of the seed-end of potatoes for several successive seasons where they will receive the best of cultivation, a kind of potato may be produced that will be fit to dig several weeks before those potatoes would mature that are treated in the usual way. These considerations hold good concerning the entire vegetable kingdom; and the young farmer may avail himself of very great advantages arising from them, if he will commence in good time. By saving the first ripe seed from year to year, all our early vegetables and grain have been brought to their present excellence; and if the first ripe seed be not carefully saved from year to year, we cannot reasonably expect our crops will ripen early, nor remunerate us for the labor bestowed in their cultivation.

Suggestions about Seed Wheat.

No farmer can reasonably expect to raise a bountiful crop of superior wheat from inferior seed, even if his soil be well adapted to the production of this kind of cereal grain, having been fertilized and cultivated in the most thorough manner. The legitimate tendency of every seed possessing vitality, in the vegetable as well as in the animal kingdom, is to produce others like itself; and it is not a common occurrence for animals to beget, or for seeds to produce others of their kind, *superior* .to themselves; for it is not practicable for animals or plants to transmit to their offspring excellent characteristics and qualities which they never possessed, and which have not been common to their progenitors.

Excellent wheat may be raised from shrunken kernels of inferior size, by selecting the best grains for seed for several successive seasons. Yet the improvement in grain the first season will be hardly perceptible. Wheat, as well as Indian corn, will hybridize when different varieties are grown in close proximity; and, though a mongrel grain *may* yield as many bushels per acre as a pure kind of seed, still such seed will not be so good for producing another crop as if the grain had not been mixed. For this reason, mixed grain should be rejected for seed; and none sowed except such kinds as have been grown with great care for several successive seasons. That farmer who practises selecting his seed wheat from year to year, as most people gather their Indian corn which is designed for seed the next season, will always raise more bountiful crops of better grain than he could produce on the same soil, with cultivation equally as good, by using seed that has not been saved with special reference to a future crop. When a large crop of wheat is all thrashed together, the grain of the small, half-ripe heads is by no means suitable for seed. For this reason, many farmers meet with great disappointment in their crop of spring wheat. They sowed poor, half-ripe, shrunken kernels, with the confident expectation that the yield of new grain would most assuredly be of a superior quality.

If seed wheat is only of a common quality, with many inferior kernels among the grain, before seed-time, the whole of it should be run through a good fanning-mill, having sieves and screens with meshes of suitable size to separate the large kernels from the small ones, as the latter will yield quite as good flour, although such grain is not so good for seed.

In every plant of wheat, barley, or oats, there is always one best ear, and in every ear there is always one best grain, which is that one found at the following harvest to produce the best plant, all the grains having been planted in competition with each other.

The best of all the competing plants of any "family" of a cereal is ascertained by the most studious comparison of the good qualities they visibly present, and of the notes of the peculiarities exhibited by each during the whole course of its growth, such as—the rapidity with which the parent seed germinates; the manner, time, and extent of the "tillering" of the plant; the periods of its earing, blooming, and ripening; its power of withstanding disease, frost, wet; the toughness of its straw, and any other characteristics which are essential to forming a correct decision, and which cannot be determined, except by a careful observation of the plant during its entire growth, until the grain is fully matured.

We very frequently discover a head of wheat, a few panicles of oats, a few pods of peas, and such-like, which have come to maturity, while the great bulk of the crop remains quite green. Now, could this seed be carefully preserved and planted by itself, we should perceive a decided improvement in the next crop, not only in the time of maturing, but in the superior quality of the grain or vegetables which sprang from the seed. Were farmers of our country to practise saving their seed grain, the wealth of the nation might be doubled.

The Proper Depth to Cover Wheat.

I believe that every intelligent farmer will admit that wheat may be sowed too shallow, as well as too deep. A thinner covering is required in a close heavy soil, than in one light, gravelly, or sandy. The following experiments were made by Petri, the results of which would vary with the moisture or dryness of the soil. They are given as a specimen of trials of this kind, which if often repeated by farmers, would afford them much valuable information :

Seed sown to a depth of	Appeared above ground in	Number of plants that came up.
1-2 inch	11 days	7-8ths.
1 "	12 "	all.
2 "	18 "	7-8ths.
3 "	20 "	6-8ths.
4 "	21 "	1-2.
5 "	22 "	3-8ths.
6 "	23 "	1-8th.

Judging from the unusually great length of time here recorded for the plants in the foregoing experiments to come up, I think the seed must have been sowed in very dry ground, or the weather must have been very cold, as it is extremely uncommon for wheat, or any other grain, when planted under circumstances at all favorable to vegetation, to be so long coming up. Under favorable circumstances, wheat will come up in six or eight days; and in warm weather, where the soil is tolerably moist, wheat will come up in one week, and make leaves so large that the field will appear quite green.

In order to test the comparative influence of plant

ing seed deep and shallow, on the germination of wheat, on the 6th of July, 1867, I instituted the following experiment: I planted eight rows of wheat, a few inches apart, with fourteen kernels in each row. The ground was in only a moderate degree of fertility, and mellowness. A dibble about as large as my little finger was marked off with cuts one inch apart, from one inch to eight. Fourteen holes were made one inch deep, into each of which a kernel of grain was dropped, and the holes filled with mellow soil. The kernels in the second row, fourteen in number, were planted, or dibbled two inches deep. The same number of kernels was planted three inches deep, in the third row. The fourth row of fourteen kernels was four inches deep. The fifth row, five inches deep. The sixth row, six inches in depth. The seventh, seven inches deep; and the fourteen kernels in the eighth row, were dropped in holes eight inches deep; and all the holes were filled with mellow soil; and every evening, the surface was moistened with water from a rose-spout watering-pot. Now for the result:

On the morning of July 11th, four spears had appeared in the first row, where the kernels were planted one inch deep; and before night, those four stems were each more than one inch high. July 12th, in the morning, two spears more, in number one, were half an inch high. In numbers two and three, the same morning, there were two spears in each; and one spear in number two, more than an inch high. On the morning of the 13th, there were ten spears in number one; four in number two; six in number three; and two spears in number four. In number three one spear was three inches high. At sunset of the same day, this last spear was five inches high, having grown two inches in length between sunrise and sunset. In number five, at sundown, of the 13th of July, one spear of wheat had come up, after sunrise, and had grown two inches high. In number six, one spear had grown one inch high during the day. On the 14th of July, in number one, there were eleven spears; in number two, there were seven; in number three, eight spears; in number four, five spears; in number five, three spears; in number six, two spears. On the morning of the 15th, one spear more appeared in number one; one more in number four; and one more in number six.

It will be seen by this diary, which I recorded with my own pen, that none of the grain was over eight days in coming up. After waiting for more than two weeks for the plants in number seven, planted seven inches deep, and those in number eight, deposited eight inches below the surface, I removed the soil carefully, and found a few of the stems nearly ready to appear above the surface of the seed-bed. But, out of the twenty-eight kernels that were planted, half of them seven, and the other half eight inches deep, not a vestige could be found of only four, the stems of which were exceedingly feeble and slender; and for lack of material to form the stem from the kernel to the surface, vegetation ceased, and the stems died. What ever became of the other kernels, seems to be a mystery.

But the experiment demonstrated one point, most conclusively, namely, that if seed wheat be buried too deep, the kernels may germinate. But there will not be sufficient material in the grain to form a healthful and strong stem to the surface of the ground. It matters not, what becomes of seed planted seven or eight inches deep. Experience proves that such grain seldom comes up. This suggests the fallacy of ploughing-in seed wheat, as much of the seed will be buried so deep that the stems can never reach the surface of the ground.

Winter grain of all kinds, will endure the influences of the freezing and thawing of the soil with far less injury to the growing plants if the seed be put in shallow, rather than deep. I have endeavored to make this subject intelligible, under the head of Injury to Wheat Plants by Freezing and Thawing, on page 126.

CULTURE OF SPRING WHEAT.

There are many erroneous impressions touching the culture of spring wheat, which I desire to correct. But, I don't know as I can do it. And, I believe I shall not make much of an effort to induce men to think, that spring wheat will grow luxuriantly, and yield satisfactorily, where a crop of winter wheat can be produced. But I *know* this to be a fact, notwithstanding it has been controverted, by some intelligent farmers. More than this, I know that under certain circumstances, a bountiful crop of spring wheat can be produced, where the land, in its present condition, would *not* yield a crop of winter wheat worth harvesting. I record it as a rule then, that wherever the land will produce a crop of winter wheat, spring wheat may be grown most satisfactorily.

Touching the subject of the culture of spring wheat, the editor of the "Prairie Farmer" writes that "spring wheat in the Northwest is comparatively a modern crop. Spring-wheat flour has one never-failing characteristic to distinguish it from that of winter wheat:

the dough is soft, and requires much more kneading than that of winter wheat; this occurs from the fact that it contains more *gluten* than the latter, and consequently less starch; it being thus more highly nitrogenized, is very valuable for food, perhaps more so than winter wheat. The yellow cast to some specimens of flour is due to *bearded* wheat, as the *bald* varieties produce white flour. The excess of gluten gives the bread a more brown appearance than the winter wheat, which is nearly pure starch.

"It may be interesting to many of our readers to look a little into the history of spring wheat as used, or its culture. Strictly speaking, we have no natural spring wheat; the variety that is called such is simply an artificial variety of winter wheat that can be readily changed back to its normal condition. It is well to understand this fact, for upon it much may depend. In the culture of spring wheat the nearer approach we make to treating it as a biennial the better will be the crop. To do this, the plant must undergo a rest—that is, at some early period of its growth it should come to a stand for a short period. This answers to the natural condition of the plant.

"Previous to 1834, little attention was paid to this trait in the habit of the plant, most farmers taking it for granted that spring wheat was as distinct from that of winter as an annual was from a biennial. A little reflection would, however, show this folly. Was spring wheat an annual it would produce good crops when sown later in the season, say through the month of April, or after frost has ceased to harden the surface. But we all know that to produce a good crop we must sow as soon as the frost begins to come out, even if we sow in the mud; it is not safe to wait until the ground settles. Should a *cold snap* come so as to freeze the ground a foot deep, all the better; the wheat will come forward with more vigor, and produce a better crop—in fact, the crop can be sown just as it freezes up in December, or at any time when the ground is thawed to the depth of two inches, in January or February. The oat, which is strictly an annual, cannot be treated in this manner, neither can any other annual farm crop. It is true that some of the seeds of annual grains will remain sound through the winter, but should they be started by warm weather, the plants die. Not so of spring wheat when sown; cold and warm weather follows so as to sprout the seed; the plants live through the winter, and thus return to the normal condition. This lets us into the secret of the success of the early sown spring wheat, giving it, to a great extent, the condition of a biennial plant. The occasional freezing spells that occur after germinating arrest growth for a time, giving it a sort of hybernation answering all the purposes of a long winter without subjecting the plant to sudden changes after the roots have run deep into the soil, as in the case with winter wheat sown in August or September, the breaking of which destroys the plant." (See page 126.)

THE DIFFERENCE EXPLAINED.

The foregoing suggestions are orthodox; yet, they need a little explanation. The young plants of certain varieties of spring wheat, are as tender as growing oats, and frost will injure them as soon and as severely, as freezing will damage young oat plants. This applies to such spring wheat as has been so thoroughly changed from a winter, to a spring grain that the plants will not endure severe freezing. Spring wheat of this character, should never be sowed until the ground has become thoroughly warmed. This accounts for the fact, that in numerous instances, certain farmers have always had better success when they have sowed their spring wheat quite late in the spring. On the contrary, when a variety of spring wheat is still so much of a *winter* wheat, that freezing does not injure the young plants in the spring, the seed should be put in as early as practicable; and the crop will be the better for early seeding.

These thoughts will explain why it is best to sow spring wheat very late, *sometimes;* and early in the growing season, at other times. A farmer must know his seed—of what sort it is. Then, he must understand, most thoroughly, the habit of growth, and how far the variety has been changed from a winter to a spring grain. When he possesses a perfect understanding of these points, he will experience very little difficulty in growing fair crops of spring wheat, provided his seed is right. (Read pages 170 and 171.)

Monroe's Rotary Harrow.

The harrow herewith illustrated, represents an implement invented by H. H. Monroe, Rockland, Maine, and manufactured by "The American Agricultural Works," Tenth avenue and Twenty-fourth street, New York city. The arms of this harrow are all united at the centre, and a circular way made of a flat bar of iron is bolted to each arm, near the outer extremity. An iron wheel travels on this way when the harrow is in motion. The object of the iron wheel is to press the teeth on one side of the harrow into the soil farther than the teeth enter on the opposite side. The harrow is drawn by the arm that is bolted to the centre of the implement. As the teeth on the side where the wheel is, take a ranker hold of the ground than the teeth of the opposite side, the teeth that enter the ground the deepest, hold that side of the harrow back, while the other side is drawn forward. By this means, the harrow has a compound movement—a motion forward and a rotary motion. The harrow can be made to rotate in either direction by changing the travelling wheel. The arm that supports the travelling wheel is secured to the middle of the harrow in such a manner that the wheel can be placed on either side of the harrow. In harrowing along a hollow, or dead furrow, this harrow can be made 'to rotate toward the lowest place, so as to fill it up with sods and lumps.

Fig. 87.—Monroe's Rotary Harrow.

When harrowing sod ground, the harrow can be made to rotate the same way the furrow slices are turned, or in the opposite direction. The teeth never clog ; and for harrowing in any kind of grain, this style of harrow is far superior to the ordinary harrow, because this will not crowd the seed into rows, like the harrow that moves straight forward.

Spring Wheat requires Manure.

In the culture of spring wheat, whatever may be the variety, thorough and repeated ploughing, with the application of rich manures, putting in the seed evenly, and then using the harrow or drill for covering it, are the conditions to be fulfilled by man. Then, unless the season should prove to be very unpropitious, a remunerative crop may be expected. Let this system of thorough cultivation become general, and you will not then hear very often of the failure of the wheat crop. A few farmers are pursuing this course of thorough tillage. They devote only a few acres to wheat, but expend a large amount on the cultivation of these few acres. And the result is, just what any sensible man might expect, a bountiful crop rewarding all their toil. The time is doubtless coming, when a kind of necessity may compel many a farmer to adopt a similar course, if he wishes to have good bread to eat.

In England and Southern Scotland, wheat has been successfully and profitably cultivated for centuries. Why may it not in these United States, if similar pains are taken ? Almost all our farms contain at least a few acres on which wheat might be sown and a profitable harvest gathered, if proper cultivation were bestowed on it. Barely ploughing the ground once or twice, and then harrowing in the seed sown, are by no means enough. Let me repeat the oft-reiterated suggestion, that wheat, whether winter or spring grain, requires a kind of mineral manure that will reproduce *grain*, and not straw.

Joseph Harris, of Rochester, New York, writes on this subject: " The introduction of turnip culture and drill husbandry into England banished summer fallows from all but the heaviest clay soils. There was good reason for this: the turnips required and received extra cultivation. As soon as the wheat crop is harvested, the land is scarified and ploughed in the autumn, and two or three times in the spring, and rolled and harrowed, and scarified, till it is as free from weeds and as mellow as an ash heap; then the turnips are sown in drills from two to two and a half feet apart. The plants are singled out by hand-hoes in the rows, from twelve to fifteen inches apart, and the horse-hoe is kept constantly going between the rows, and the hand-hoe whenever necessary. In this way the land is as effectually cleaned and mellowed as if it had been summer-fallowed. Hence turnips have been appropriately termed a ' fallow crop.' But we have as yet no such fallow crop in America. I am aware that Indian corn is sometimes called a ' fallow crop,' because, like turnips, it admits the use of the horse-hoe ; but it is not, strictly speaking, a fallow or renovating crop, because it impoverishes the soil of the same plant food as the wheat crop requires. So much has been said in England against summer fallows, and these opinions have been reiterated so often by the agricultural press of this country, for the last thirty years, that there is a very general opinion that summer fallows are unnecessary. This impression, while it may have done some good, has also done considerable harm. Farmers have neglected their summer fallows."

The Conclusion of Wheat Growing.

Now, if our farmers would only regard their own most important interests, and the interests of those who may cultivate the soil after them, every sheep, every swine, and every bullock would be put in excellent condition for the slaughter-house before leaving the farm. Then there would, necessarily, be something left behind to maintain the fertility of the soil, and thus produce more abundant crops of grain and larger and fatter cattle the next season.

Were I asked by a farmer on the cold soil of Maine how to produce wheat there, I would say, raise mutton. Were the same question propounded by a Canadian, I would answer, make mutton, and apply the manure to the soil. Were the farmers of the West to inquire how to raise better crops of wheat, from year to year, instead of poorer yields, which is now the rule, still my answer would be, make mutton, by feeding coarse grain and turnips. This is what the farmers of our country must eventually come to—making mutton—before they can expect to produce such crops of wheat as once grew on our virgin soils. By making mutton from year to year, and applying the manure thus produced by the sheep, farmers will learn that they will receive more money from their flocks, and the yield of grain will increase from year to year, instead of diminishing.

Some chemists tell us that *ammoniacal* fertilizers should always be covered up with a little earth, to prevent loss by evaporation. This is correct. On the contrary, they state that such fertilizers as lime and potash, or ashes, should be spread on the surface, because such heavy fertilizing material has a tendency to work downward into the soil. The main point, in my own estimation is, to make rich manure, and cover it with a thin dressing of soil. J. Harris says, " *There is not enough ammonia in a ton of such stuff as many farmers call manure, to make hartshorn enough for a lady's smelling-bottle ! ! !* Instead of ploughing in so much clover for wheat, then, let us convert it into wool and mutton; and if we can give our sheep peas, or beans, or oilcake in addition, it will tell wonderfully on the manure, and on the crops to which it is applied."

The illustration herewith given represents a new and eminently useful coulter, to prevent clogging when ploughing stubble ground, or when turning under coarse manure or clover—invented by M. A. Spink, Rensselaer Falls, New York, and sold also by R. H. Allen & Co., 189 Water street, New York city. It can be readily attached to the beam of almost any plough, with the same fastening that is required to secure an ordinary coulter in the desired posi-

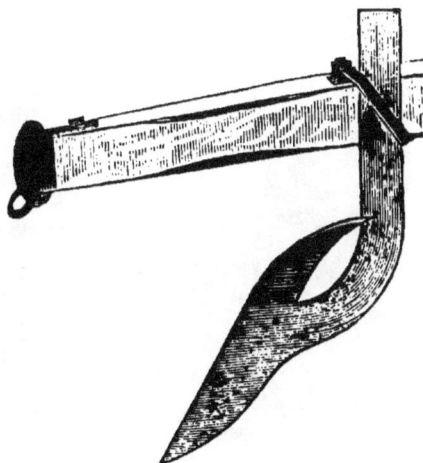

Fig. 88.—Spink's Anti-clogging Coulter.

tion. The shank of the coulter should stand perpendicularly on the beam of the plough, as represented by the illustration. The upper part of the blade is made as represented by the figure, with the upper point bending over to the left three or four inches from a line with the shank. As the stubble or coarse manure is forced·up along the edge of the blade, it is conveyed to the left of the shank and falls off the point of the blade, instead of being gathered beneath the beam to clog the plough.

THE STAR CULTIVATOR.

In some sections of country where wheat is cultivated to considerable extent, farmers like such an implement for preparing the ground, as is represented by the

FIG. 39.—The Star Cultivator.

accompanying illustration of a combined cultivator and seed-drill, which is manufactured by Ewell & Co., Baltimore, Maryland. In the next chapter this cultivator is shown with the roller and seeding apparatus attached.

In this figure the roller and seed-box are not represented ; but in the place of the roller two gauge-wheels
appear.   The implement needs little or no explanation,
as the cut gives a fair idea of the various parts.   The
ploughs regulate themselves, as to depth ; and by means
of the cam lever, they may be raised entirely out of the
ground in an instant, or made to run at any desired
depth.

CAHOON'S HAND GRAIN SOWER.

The illustration given in connection with this article
represents a person sowing seed with one of Cahoon's

FIG. 40.—A Hand Sower.

sowers, for distributing any kind of grain, broadcast, by
means of hand machinery, which the laborer carries,

13*

working it as he travels over the field.   The grain is carried in a receptacle to which the machinery is attached.   At one side of the machine is a distributing wheel, with arms, or flanges, which play in the issue of the grain receptacle.   When the machine is not in motion the grain cannot flow out ; but, as soon as the crank is turned, the grain is scattered broadcast in front of the sower.   If every part of the machine is made perfectly, and if the operator can exercise mechanical skill in managing difficult machinery, he can sow grain evenly and rapidly with such a seed sower.

But there are some difficulties attending the management of such a grain sower, to which it is proper for me to allude, so that a farmer may understand exactly what he is purchasing, when he procures one of this style of machines.   There is the same liability to scatter seed unevenly with this sower as when sowing broadcast by hand.   If the operator does not walk exactly at a uniform gait, and if he does not keep his body in a steady position, without wriggling, and does not turn the crank at a uniform velocity, he will not be likely to sow the seed as evenly as it should be.   By turning the body only a little either way, from a direct, straightforward course, the direction of the falling grain will be changed very much.   By turning the crank faster, the grain will be distributed over a wider breadth of land.   A skilful operator will regulate the motion of the crank by his steps.

A more complete description of this seed sower may be found in R. H. Allen & Co.'s catalogue of his agricultural implements, 189 Water Street, New York city, price $1.   It is sold also by "The Ames Plough Company," 53 Beekman Street, New York city ; and is warranted to operate satisfactorily, which it will do, if the machine be used with the skill required. I have penned the foregoing suggestions, more for the benefit of farmers, than for the pecuniary advantage of the manufacturer of the machine. I have alluded to the difficulties which will be met with in operating such a seed sower, so that a common laborer might not be disappointed, when using it.

Sowing Grain Broadcast.

Every farmer should learn to sow all kinds of grain and grass seed broadcast. I say he should *learn* to do it. Very few men are able to sow anything evenly. On some kinds of land, a drill cannot be used.

In sowing, either by furrows or stakes, always throw the grain *from* the margin of the field; because one can sow much more evenly up to the margin by throwing *away* from it, than he can to throw *toward* it. Let the grain slip off the ends of the fingers, and not *between* the thumb and fingers, nor *between* the fingers. Make calculations how wide to sow at *one through*, or once across; and endeavor to give the grain such a cast that it will come down as evenly as possible.

In sowing by middle furrows and ridges, which, if the ploughing has been done correctly, will be just twenty-two feet apart, I always sow just eleven feet to a *cast*. I can usually sow more evenly by walking about midway from each edge of the strip that I am sowing. It matters little where a sower walks, if he only distributes his grain evenly.

Casting the grain all one way is the most approved manner of sowing, with many farmers. When sowing is performed in this manner, some farmers *mark out* the ground with marks just eleven feet apart; and the sower travels in the marks; and if he commences sowing east and west on the north margin of the field, he starts

Fig. 41.—Sowing Grain Broadcast.

at the east end, travelling on the margin, and casts the grain to the south with his *right* hand, sowing up to the first mark.

The most convenient receptacle to sow from, is a bag

of ordinary size, hung over the shoulder, as shown in the illustration. Read all about the manipulations of sowing grain in first volume of my Young Farmer's Manual, which may be had of the author.

NUTTING'S FANNING MILL.

FIG. 42.—Grain Separator.

Every farmer who raises grain should have a fanning mill that will separate the small from the large kernels. Rufus Nutting, Randolph, Vermont, is the inventor of an excellent fanning mill and seed separator, which is represented by the accompanying illustration. The "Annual Register," when extolling the merits of this mill, states that, at one of the fairs of the State Society, an agent put one of the poorest samples of grain through this mill, returning it to the bag with the large kernels on the top. When the judges saw the grain, they awarded the first prize to the poorest entry of wheat,

not knowing that the large kernels were all on the surface. The screens are so constructed that they have
almost the smoothness of glass, and are made by pressing common wire screens, rendering the meshes im-
movable and always accurate, increasing their durability, giving them the character of glazed muslin, and
allowing the seed to slide over them, when slightly inclined from a level. The latter quality gives them their
preëminent advantage. The seed never falls directly
upon them, but first upon a smooth surface, flat with
the screen, in passing over which and to the screen,
every oblong grain has assumed a horizontal position.
If *longer* than the meshes, it goes over them; if shorter,
it drops through. Such a mixture, therefore, as spring
wheat and oats, often so troublesome to the farmer, is
perfectly separated. Even barley and spring wheat are
separated, the barley grains being slightly longer, and
enough lighter to be driven more by the current of wind.
Wheat is cleaned from chess in a complete manner. J.
J. Thomas says, " For cleaning grass seed, we have never
witnessed anything that would compare with this fan.
A mixture of clover and timothy was run through once
together.; in one drawer was found entirely pure timothy
seed, and in another, clover without a single grain of
timothy; the intermediate drawer had a very small quantity of imperfect seeds of clover, a very little timothy,
and some other seeds of weeds.

"The current of wind is so completely at command,
that all degrees of strength, from the imperceptible breeze
to the blast that sweeps away heavy grain, may be readily
given. This peculiarity, in connection with the screens,
enables the operator to separate any seeds whatever, that
differ either in *shape, size,* or *weight.*

"A most important office performed by this machine is the separation of the different-sized seed of the same grain. Pass, for instance, ten bushels of wheat through the screens; one portion will be found a uniformly small grain; another about medium; a third, large, plump and first rate. The first and third would not be supposed to have grown in the same field. In this way, excellent seed wheat may be obtained from an ordinary crop; and the best bushel in fifty, or the best ten bushels in fifty, may be separated at the option of the farmer."

HARDER'S IMPROVED FANNING MILL.

The illustration herewith given represents an improved fanning mill of a superior kind, manufactured by R. & M. Harder, Cobleskill, Schoharie County, New York. This mill is adapted to cleaning all kinds of grain and grass seeds; and, I believe, gives excellent satisfaction. Every farmer who raises grain should possess an excellent fanning mill, and always clean his seed grain thoroughly.

Fig. 43.—Fanning Mill.

DIBBLING IN WHEAT.

The process of dibbling-in seed wheat consists in simply making a hole in the ground with one finger, or with the end of a pointed stick about as large as a man's

forefinger.   The dibble is put through a hole in a block
of wood about three inches square, which furnishes a
shoulder to prevent making a hole more than two, or two
and a half inches deep.   If no shoulder is attached to
the dibble, where the soil is mellow, there is danger that
the dibble will be thrust into the ground too far.   The
operator carries his seed in a sack or planting-bag
secured to his body, as when planting Indian corn.
The soil is first put in excellent tilth, as the dibbling
process cannot be conducted satisfactorily, where there are
lumps of earth and stones.   The surface of the ground
is made smooth and even, by raking and rolling.   Then
a line is stretched across the piece to be dibbled ; and as
fast as one hand makes a hole with the dibble, the other
drops one kernel into the bottom of the recess ; and each
hole is filled with mellow soil.   This constitutes the entire process of dibbling-in grain.

It has been stated in certain agricultural papers, that
if seed wheat were dibbled in, the yield would be double
the amount of grain that could be raised on the same
ground by any other mode of seeding.   But there is no
reason to believe that one bushel of grain more could be
produced by dibbling-in the seed than by putting in
with a good drill.   The fact that statements have been
made by farmers, to show the superiority of dibbling
over drilling or broadcast seeding, does not make it so.
We want the evidence of numerous well-conducted experiments to prove it.   If the soil is in an excellent
state of fertility, the yield of grain will be as large
when put in with Beckwith's drill (page 306), as if drilled
in by hand.   Indeed, seed is, to all intents and purposes,
drilled in, by such a drill, as I have just alluded to.

Dibbling can be practised advantageously and economically, only where there is an abundance of cheap labor. If a farmer has no drill, and has time to spare, it will pay him to put an acre of land into first-rate condition ; and dibble in the seed. When experimenting on a small scale with the production of new varieties, the seed may be dibbled in.

As the stools of wheat will tiller sufficiently to occupy the entire ground if the soil be rich, if the kernels be planted seven inches apart in the drills and the same distance in the rows, the yield of grain will be fully as large as if more seed had been planted.

In Stephens' "Book of the Farm," an English work, the author has penned a paragraph on dibbling-in grain. But a concluding sentence leads one to infer that he knows nothing practically about this system of seeding ; as he says, "It is asserted by those who have put in wheat by dibbling, that the yield will be five quarters and a half (forty-four bushels) per acre ; and that one bushel of seed is sufficient for an acre."

The "Country Gentleman" contains a brief account of a Michigan farmer, who attempted to dibble in wheat on a large scale, by constructing a roller having ridges and creases, similar to Beckwith's drill (page 306). But the experiment was doubtless too rude to prove anything, either for or against, the system of dibbling.

The superintendent of the County Poor-house, having a large number of men under his supervision, without pay, had an acre of land prepared as for a carrot bed, and the seed dibbled in by hand. It was a tedious process. But the yield was no heavier than if the seed had been put in with a drill.

The idea that by pressing the soil around the seed, or by pressing the soil before the seed is put in, will pro-

duce a larger yield of grain, than if the seed were put
into the mellow ground *without* any such compressing
of the seed-bed, is all moonshine, and unphilosophical.

BECKWITH'S ROLLER DRILL.

The accompanying representation of a drill will furnish

FIG. 44.—Beckwith's Roller Drill.

a fair idea of the style of implement made by P. D. Beckwith, Dowagiac, Michigan.   This drill consists of a series
of cast-iron rollers or wheel, one of which is shown in
the engraving, all placed on a wrought-iron shaft, or
axle, which will roll on the ground, each one independent of the other, and which support the entire frame
and all the machinery of the drill.   These rollers are
twenty-eight inches in diameter, and have a V-shaped
periphery, which, by the aid of the weight of the drill,
form small furrows in the soil to receive the seed.

The rollers are also made with sufficient hub to keep
them the proper distance apart, seven and a half inches

from centre to centre; and each one is loose on the axle and has an independent movement from each other, except the centre roller and one at the end, which are both made fast *on* and rovolve *with* the axle. This end roller drives the distributing apparatus; and by the aid of the centre wheel, will make a uniform motion for distributing the seed regularly upon the most uneven ground. The frame of the drill is made of two cast-iron slidepieces, with rounded corners in front, so as to ward off stumps and other obstructions, when passing them, and still be able to drive the machine very close to the same so as to sow all the ground that can be *ploughed* in new fields or among corn shocks, as many of our Western farmers sow wheat after corn, the same fall, before the corn is removed from the field.

The box or hopper for holding coarse grain is placed behind the rollers, and is made in the usual form, and has two iron plates or jaws at the bottom, one made fast and the other movable. There is a wooden rod placed under these plates, with wire pins projecting up between and about one-half an inch above the plates into the seed. This rod is made to vibrate by suitable lever connections, a cam on the end, with roller. The wire pins running between the plates of the hopper upward into the seed will agitate and cause it to run out between the opening, which can be regulated to sow the desired quantity. The seed from the distributor is con ducted down through iron pipes into the *furrows* made by the rollers. There are inverted iron hoes, or coverers, attached to the frame and drag behind the rollers and conducting pipes, to cover the seed. These cov erers can be raised from the ground, when turning around, by means of a crank attached to the journal.

The grass-seed hopper is placed forward of the rollers and deposits the seed broadcast. The distributor is a slide of thin flat iron, placed in the bottom of the hopper, with suitable holes in it to correspond with the openings in the bottom of the hopper to regulate the quantity sowed. The seed is agitated and made to pass through these openings by a serrated rod made to vibrate in the bottom of the hopper on the thin iron slide by being attached to the levers on the cam of the end roller.

These rollers all being on the one axle, will level the ground similar to a field-roller, and leave the surface in good condition for the reaper and mower; and the rollers being loose on the shaft or axle, may be turned around easily by the team.

Where the soil is light, and mellow, the grass-seed distributor may be forward of the grain drill, as it is better to cover grass seed with one inch or more of earth on very light soils. But as a general rule, especially where the soil is heavy, I think that the grass-seed distributor should be placed behind the rollers, as there is danger of covering grass seed too deep. Grass seed of all kinds requires but little covering. My long experience assures me that a larger proportion of grass seed and clover seed will grow when sowed *after* the last implement has been drawn over the surface than when the seed is harrowed, rolled, or brushed in. There is great danger of covering grass seed too deep. The first shower of rain that falls on the field after the seed has been sown, will cover almost every seed as deep as is requisite to insure germination and luxuriant vegetation.

Another improvement in this excellent drill, besides placing the grass-seed distributor *behind* the rollers, is forming the V-shaped ridge on the surface of a broad thin rim, say five inches wide. This style of rollers would leave the surface of the ground more even, as all the clods would be crushed when they are more than one inch in diameter. If the periphery of the rollers were of this form, the channels made by the V-shaped ridges would all be of a uniform depth; whereas, when constructed of the present form, were the soil very mellow and light, the channels would be made too deep. As this roller drill deposits the kernels of grain about one and a half or two inches deep, the roots of the growing plants spread out nearly in a horizontal direction, more in a mass, and thus withstand more effectually the influences of freezing and thawing of the soil, and the consequent upheaving of the plants in the winter.

I think that all practical wheat-growers, who understand the habit of the wheat plant, and who appreciate the importance of having the seed put into the soil at a uniform depth, will agree that this drill operates on principles strictly scientific, and in perfect harmony with the habit of the growth of the wheat plant. Where there are stones and roots in the soil, to prevent the operation of this drill, a tube drill is preferable.

Practical Advantages of Drilling-in Wheat.

There is great advantage in having seed wheat covered deep and uniformly in dry weather, in order to insure more perfect germination. When wheat is sowed broadcast and harrowed in, in dry weather, much of the seed will never vegetate; but the kernels will absorb a little moisture during the night, which will all be dried out during the daytime. By this alternate wetting and drying of the grain the germs will be destroyed in a few days. If the kernels be buried just deep enough to insure germination, but not having sufficient depth of earth to prevent being dried up by the burning sun, the young plants wither and die for want of depth of earth.

John Johnston, of Geneva, New York, writes: "I noticed last year, on an adjoining farm, where the wheat was drilled in, that it came up much better than mine, where the seed was sown broadcast. In fact, the wheat came up right. I could not account for the difference, at the time, between the appearance of my grain and this in my neighbor's field, as my land is in as good state of cultivation as his; and the seed was put in on both farms at the same time. His field produced a good crop of grain, far above the average crop of this county for several years past. It did not occur to me, till this season, that the great difference between the two crops, was owing to his wheat being drilled in while mine was sowed broadcast and harrowed in. Last season, we both sowed our winter wheat in the former part of September. My ground had been summer fallowed, and I never saw a field in better condition for receiving seed. A dry time ensued at the period of sowing the seed. His drilled wheat came up evenly, and grew luxuriantly; while mine was exceeding thin on the ground. On examining, I found that none of my grain had vegetated, except those kernels that were buried deepest in the soil. It occurred to me then that if I had drilled in my wheat, my fields would have produced five or six hundred bushels of grain more than they did yield. I will drill in my wheat hereafter. Old as I am, I still live and learn. I expect my wheat will yield this season only about twelve bushels per acre.

With the exception of the crops raised in 1828 and 1831, my wheat was the poorest this past season that I have ever raised. The failure was mainly owing to the severe drought in autumn, at seed time. Every wheat-grower knows that it is impossible to obtain a remunerating crop of wheat, when the seed sown in autumn does not come up till after the growing season has commenced the next spring."

THE PHILOSOPHY OF DRILLING-IN GRAIN.

By reviewing what is recorded under the heading of The Habit of the Wheat Plant, page 49, and also page 126, the reader will understand the eminent importance of depositing every kernel of wheat at a uniform depth.

This is aimed at when wheat is put in with an ordinary drill; and, for the most part, the end sought is secured, if the soil be of a uniform quality and condition, so that the teeth will run at a given depth. But when the soil is mellow in some places, and hard in others, some drills will deposit the seed in the mellow places too deep, so that putting in with a drill will have no advantage over sowing broadcast, so far as obviating the injurious effects of freezing and thawing are concerned. The teeth of grain drills should be set to run not more than two inches in depth. One and a half inches deep for winter grain is better than two, for reasons already assigned, except where the soil is light and dry, in which instance the seed should be deposited not less than two inches in depth. Then, nearly all the roots will be so near each other, that the expansion of the soil will neither break the stem nor seriously damage the roots; nor will it cause perceptible diminution of the crop.

The accompanying illustration will furnish a practical illustration of the mode and advantages of putting in wheat with a drill. It will be perceived that the ears of grain are of a uniform size, and all the straws are of a uniform height. The figure shows some of advantages of drilling-in the seed, just as those points are seen in a field of growing wheat. The drilled grain, figure 45, being deposited at a sufficient and uniform depth to receive the moisture and the nourishment of the soil, comes up more uniformly at one time, is better fed and nourished, stands a drought much better, grows more vigorously, ripens earlier and more uniformly, is not so liable to rust, and the heads are larger and better filled.

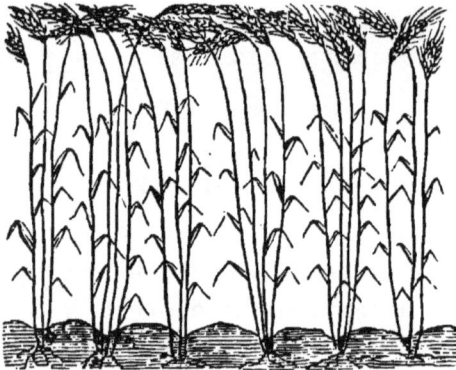

Fig. 45.—Wheat Drilled In.

When seed grain is drilled in, one man will complete the operation, by simply going over the ground once. If sowed broadcast, the ground must be harrowed twice after the seed is sowed. This, in addition to the time consumed in sowing the seed by hand, will require about three times longer than is necessary to drill it in. Moreover, the drill, if properly made and adjusted, will deposit every kernel at a uniform depth; whereas, the harrow covers some of the seed too deep, some not deep enough, and some not at all; and if the soil be deep and mellow, the feet of teams will press a considerable portion of it quite too deep.

Another advantage in drilling-in the seed is, as soon as an acre or two is ploughed, the grain may be put in immediately, thus finishing the work as fast as the ground is ploughed. When grain is sowed broadcast, it is much more convenient, and rather important, to have the entire field ploughed before sowing, so as to be able to harrow both ways. When a farmer has a drill, he can plough an acre, then harrow it, and drill in the seed all in one day, while the soil is fresh, which is the best condition to hasten the germination of the grain. He thus finishes his work as he progresses, and is always ready for temporary interruptions by storms of rain, which are often attended with more or less injury to the crop. Such delays, especially with spring grain, are often fatal to a good crop.

The Disadvantages of Sowing Wheat Broadcast.

The illustration given on the next page is a fair representation of growing wheat where the seed was scattered broadcast and harrowed in. When wheat is sowed broadcast and harrowed, a portion of the seed is left uncovered, exposed to the drying winds and scorching sun, to the fowls and birds; and that which is covered, is at very unequal depths, some very deep, some medium depth, and some so near the surface that in case of drought, it fails to mature for lack of moisture. Winter wheat sowed broadcast is much more liable to be raised by the frost, and be thrown out upon the surface, there exposed to perish, for the reasons already assigned, namely, that a portion of the seed is barely covered with earth; while much of it will be buried four to six inches deep, by the feet of teams, where the soil

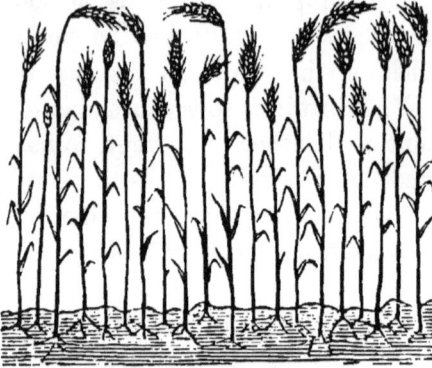

is mellow. If the kernels are not all buried at a uniform d e p t h, the stalks will not grow of an equal height and size. If a farmer will examine growing wheat, after the heads are formed, he will see some large and well-developed

FIG. 46.—Grain Sowed Broadcast.

heads, and some short stems and light, half-matured ears. Of course, there will be a difference in the periods of perfect maturity; whereas, if the kernels are all alike as to size, and all covered at a given depth, the germs will start alike; the stems will grow uniformly; and the grain will ripen all at one time, so that no loss will be sustained in consequence of the late maturity of a portion of the ears.

Brown's Celebrated Grain Drill.

The illustration herewith given represents a transverse section of the distributing apparatus of· a grain drill invented by H. L. & C. P. Brown, Shortsville, New York, which is one of the best tube drills that I have ever met with, as its action is very reliable and uniform. This drill will distribute all kinds of grain with admirable precision. In the box, the stirrer is represented, which consists of an iron rod with wooden pins driven through it, so that the ends of the pins stir the grain near the issue of each distributor, to prevent clogging. Kernels of grain are represented as passing through the run, or passage from the hopper to the issue where the grain drops into the tubes, and is conducted to the bottom of the furrow opened by each drill, before any of the soil falls back over the seed. The teeth on the periphery of the wheel

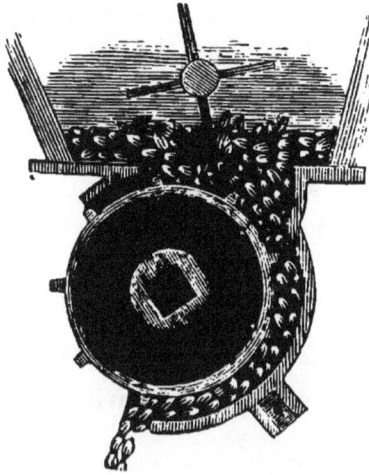

Fig. 47.—Grain Distributor.

which revolves within the case, sweep out a uniform quantity of grain at every revolution. When the team starts the drill, the drill begins to scatter the seed.

Figure 48 represents the opposite side of the same distributor, for distributing peas and beans. Either side, or run, can be shut off at pleasure. Or every other distributor can be adjusted to scatter seed, if it is

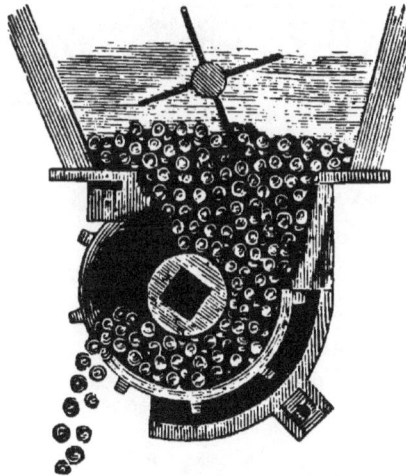

Fig. 48.—For Drilling-in Peas.

desirable. The quantity of seed per acre is regulated

by gear wheel of different sizes. Large numbers of this style of drills have been manufactured by the firm alluded to; and the same drill is made by the following manufacturers: Brown, Adams & Co., Shortsville, N. Y.; Whiteside, Barnett & Co., Brockport, N. Y.; Titus & Bostwick, Ithaca, N.Y.; and Wiard & Waldo, Oakfield, N. Y. I give the names of these firms for the benefit of farmers who want good drills.

THE BUCKEYE GRAIN DRILL.

For the convenience of farmers in different sections of the country, I have concluded to mention the Buckeye Grain Drill, which is represented by the accompanying illustration, Fig. 49. This is a tube drill closely resembling the Brown drill described on previous pages. I can recommend it with all confidence, as

FIG. 49.

large numbers of them have been sold to grain-producing farmers; and I have never heard an adverse report, that this drill did not sustain its high reputation. This drill is manufactured extensively by manufacturers in Springfield, Ohio, and by R. W. Cowan, Fleming, Cayuga County, New York.

CROSS-DRILLING SEED WHEAT.

Some farmers have been accustomed to drill in their seed wheat as oats and barley are sometimes put in—

by drilling-in half the desired amount per acre, by driving the drill in one direction, and the remainder by running the drill at a right angle to the first direction. Some of our wheat-growers repose so much confidence in this manner of drilling-in seed wheat, that they believe it increases the amount of the crop from twenty to twenty-five per cent. But, if any one will take the trouble to decide this controverted point by a few well-conducted experiments, he will satisfy himself that there is really nothing gained, but a loss sustained, by putting in winter wheat in that manner.

The chief objection to cross-drilling of winter wheat is, that the feet of the teams—especially when the soil is mellow and deep—will force much of the seed two or three inches deeper than it was deposited by the drill. Planting a portion of the grain two or more inches deeper than the seed should be covered, and deeper than the larger proportion of the grain is covered, will be found to be decidedly objectionable for winter grain of any kind. Indeed, such an uneven manner of covering the seed will be found more objectionable for any kind of winter grain, than for spring grain. Another objection to cross-drilling winter wheat is, much of the seed that was drilled in the first time will be displaced by the drill-tubes and left partly uncovered. And some farmers contend that the second drilling destroys the little ridges made by the tubes. But this theory amounts to nothing in a practical point of view. Its abettors contend that the ridges made by the drill-tubes are washed down to a level by the snows and rains of winter, thus tending to the accumulation of more soil over the roots of the wheat plants that have been lifted out by the frost.

Fatal Experiment with Seed Wheat.

Farmers should remember that the germs of wheat are organs of exceedingly delicate structure. They are really things of life—little things, and of course, they have but a small amount of vitality. For this reason, it is exceedingly hazardous to tamper with the grain. Let it be always kept distinctly in mind, that it does not take much to destroy the germs of the grain. Young farmers—and sometimes old ones who ought to know better—have a great desire to try an experiment with their seed grain. J. L. Rice, a farmer of Jefferson County, New York, communicated the following suggestions, which will save many a young farmer from falling into a similar experiment. He writes thus to the " Cultivator and Country Gentleman ":

" It is quite common nowadays to try experiments. Some give ' quite satisfactory' results; with others there is nothing perceptible, either good or bad; while a third class often prove very disastrous. The one I am about to give, is of the latter class, and I give it, not because I like to say much about having done a very foolish thing, neither would I recommend it to others—but as a warning to those inclined to try experiments; and, where there is an even chance for a failure, to do it cautiously and on a small scale.

" In the fall of 1857, I had a piece of ground of about four acres, upon which I thought I would risk a crop of wheat. The land was in fine order, it having been well manured previous to the crop of barley, just taken from it—and to make it still better, it had another good dressing after it was ploughed for the wheat. I could see no reason, if the winter was favorable, why I should not have a good crop. But about this time I was seized with an intolerable itching to try an experiment. I wanted to do something that would *destroy* the weevil—keep the wire-worms at a *proper distance*—prevent *smut*, and at the same time make the wheat *grow*, like Jonah's gourd. Now, what would accomplish all this? Be patient, gentlemen, and I will tell you what I did, and what was the result.

"My cow stable is so constructed, that the urine runs back into a gutter by itself, and can be very easily taken up, free from manure. I concluded to give my seed a good wetting with this urine, and dry it off with lime, and then sow it. I did so. It lay about six hours wet, before the lime was applied, and then it was immediately sowed and nicely dragged in. After waiting a suitable time for it to come up, I went to see how it looked, with the bump of expectation considerably enlarged. But I was a *little* too soon—it had not made its appearance—it would come in a few days; of course it would. Who ever knew a field of wheat sown, and not come up? Another week, and I went to take a look—but no wheat! The result was, it *never did come up*. I do not believe, that if all that ever made its appearance above ground, had been left to mature, there would have been as much as a man would take upon a wheelbarrow. It was a *total* failure. This was wholly owing to the *experiment*, for the *seed* was first rate. I sold some to a neighbor, and it grew finely. Now, the application made, like a great many things recommended, was not adapted to the end desired. True, it destroyed the weevil—kept the wire-worms at bay, perhaps. As to the smut, cannot say what the result would have been; but it *killed the germ of the wheat*.

"'Bought wit' is better than *none;* and I am not sure but that it is the *best;* for one is apt to *remember* what he gets in this way. But it should not *cost too much.* Mine, in this instance, cost me about twenty-five dollars, as seed at that time was worth two dollars a bushel; besides not a little vexation and disappointment. I would just say, that I have been rather shy of that puddle behind my cows, ever since its use as above mentioned. Although a very excellent fertilizer, and should by all means be saved, it is better to mix it with straw, and other absorbents, and apply it to the *land,* and not, in its *full strength* and *raw state,* to *seed wheat* or any other kind of seed. So I think."

Brining Seed Wheat.

"Some steep their seed, and some in caldrons boil,
With vigorous nitre and with lees of oil,
O'er gentle fires, th' exub'rant juice to drain,
And swell the flatt'ring husks with fruitful grain."

DRYDEN'S VIRGIL.

Some wheat-growers contend that brining the seed is of no practical utility. But the large majority of good farmers concur in the belief, that washing the seed in brine as strong as it can be made, will prevent smut. It will also enable the farmer to skim out light wheat, chess, and almost anything else that may be in the seed, the strong brine bringing it to the surface much better than mere water. The wheat should, while in the brine, be stirred as long as any foul seed or light wheat rises; one bushel at once in a barrel is sufficient, with plenty of brine; then dip brine and wheat into a basket. When drained a few minutes, empty on a clean floor; take the same brine for another batch, and so on, until you have as much as you wish to sow that day. Then sift on good slacked lime gradually, while another person follows around the heap or stirs it with a shovel, or with a rake. Put on lime until the wheat will not stick together. Then let it be sown and immediately covered. The lime will then continue to stick to the wheat, and furnish fertilizing material to promote the growth of the young wheat plants.

A wheat-grower in Western New York has communicated his manner of preparing seed wheat as follows: " Before sowing, prepare a strong brine. Half a barrel will be needed to pickle as little as four or five bushels of grain, but, of course, would answer for much more, and to this quantity add half a pound of blue vitriol (*sulphate of copper*). A portion is done at a time, stirring it well, and skimming off all that floats, dirt, foul stuff, smutty grains, etc. As fast as each portion is soaked, throw it out into a basket to drain. The pickling should be done four to twelve hours before sowing. Just previous to sowing, the grain should be spread out upon a clean floor and rolled in lime slacked to a dry powder, stirring the heap with rakes."

THE STAR DRILL.

The implement represented by the illustration shown on the next page, is the combined " Star Drill " and Cultivator, a part of which is represented on page 296 of this book. Here the land-roller and the seed-sowing attachment are shown, in connection with the small ploughs.

When this implement is employed for putting in grain, the seed is taken from the seed-box by means of a revolving distributor and dropped immediately behind the plough in the furrow, and covered by the next plough; and so on after each plough, leaving the grain in the last furrow uncovered until the next round. The

Fig. 50.—The Star Drill.

revolving distributor has openings at a given distance from each other, to keep up a continuous stream of grain. The quantity is increased or diminished by the depth of the opening. Resting upon this seed-roller is an elastic substance arranged to distribute the grain in the desired quantity. This is a comparatively new farm implement. But I think, if it is properly made, the machine will operate satisfactorily. Further information may be obtained of the manufacturers, Ewell & Co., Baltimore, Maryland.

Cast Cast-steel Ploughs.

The figure herewith given represents a plough that has become exceedingly popular, and is gaining favor every year. The entire mouldboard, land-side, and share, are made of cast cast-steel. The metal is run in a mould somewhat as ploughs of cast-iron are made.

Fig. 51.—Steel Ploughs.

This style of ploughs is a perfect paragon of neatness and practical utility. Everybody likes them, when they are made right, with a hard temper. They are manufactured by Collins & Co., 212 Water street, New York city. No other plough will excel this implement for working in the light prairie soils of the West. When tempered hard, they never clog; but when the steel is soft as iron, so that it can be cut with the point of a jack-knife, fine soil will adhere to the surface and give as much trouble as is frequently experienced with cast-iron ploughs.

This plough has been before the public sufficiently long to establish the point that steel ploughs, when the parts are hardened properly, are far superior to iron ploughs, as they will draw much easier and last longer.

NISHWITZ'S DISK HARROW.*

The accompanying illustration represents a new style of pulverizer, invented by F. Nishwitz, 142 First street, Williamsburg, Long Island, New York. The principle of construction is quite new; but, by those who have used it, the operation is said to be eminently effective. The wooden frame consists of two pieces of hard, tough timber, about two inches in thickness, by seven or eight inches wide, held in position by the cross-bar, which is firmly bolted to the side pieces, as represented by the illustration.

The pulverizers consist of several sharp-edged circular disks, about one foot in diameter, being concave on one side and convex on the other. When the wheels or disks are cast, a round steel pin, about three-fourths of an inch in diameter, is inserted in the mould, thus furnishing a steel journal for each disk. A bolt with a nut at the upper end is passed through a socket-standard, which holds the disks in their position.

* Was awarded a special gold medal, at trial of plows, harrows, cultivators, etc., at Utica, 1867, by N. Y. State Agricultural Soc.

CHAPTER IV.

Wheat Harvest.

"How the harvest spreads the field!
Waving grain to reapers yield!
Scythes and sickles flash around,
Rakes and pitchforks clear the ground."

EDWARDS.

THE season of wheat harvest, when I was in my boyhood, used to be a joyous and propitious period for poor people. Several days before wheat was fit to harvest, the streets would often be lined with cradlers and rakers and binders, going from those sections of the country where they thought the soil was too poor to produce wheat, to the wheat-growing districts, in quest of labor. For ordinary farm labor, men were accustomed to receive fifty cents in money; or one bushel of Indian corn; or half a bushel of wheat, for the labor of one day. For a day's work in the harvest field, a cradler was accustomed to receive one dollar, or a bushel of wheat; or two bushels of Indian corn. The men who raked and bound after a cradler, alone, received one dollar each, as raking and binding the wheat that a cradler cut down, was considered equal to the labor of cradling the same amount of grain. When two men followed a cradler, they received fifty cents each, per day. A boy who could rake gavels, received twenty-five cents for his day's work, or half a bushel of Indian corn; and the man, or boy, who could bind the gavels, after they were raked, was paid seventy-five cents per day. Cradlers and rakers and binders were required to do their work in a neat and farmer-like manner, or they must find employment somewhere else.

This incentive prompted men to learn how to work with skill and efficiency. Such cradlers and rakers and binders as most farmers are now obliged to rely on, are most inefficient and miserable help. Whether they swing the cradle, or rake and bind, or shock the bound grain, their work is performed in a most perfunctory, slovenish, and unsatisfactory manner. Nothing will have a tendency to make an ambitious and neat farmer so utterly sick of his employment, as to see most of the farm laborers of the present day swing the cradle in grain of any kind, or rake and bind the gavels, and put the sheaves in stooks. When I was a young man, very few of the farm laborers of the present day would have received more than a boy's wages, until they had learned to work in the harvest field with efficiency and in a neat and skilful manner. When a man or boy failed to cradle grain neatly, or rake it clean, or to bind his sheaves tight, and in the middle of the gavel, it was a very common occurrence to hear the proprietor tell him, "You do not work to suit me. You can find work somewhere else." But, at the present day, good cradlers and neat and skilful rakers and binders are the exception—not the rule, as it should be. To aid practical farmers in performing their work in the easiest and most economical manner, is my object, in penning the following pages. Let farmers first learn how to handle tools with skill and efficiency, and then they will be prepared to teach their awkward laborers.

REAPERS AND MOWERS.

Every farmer who raises wheat, or any other kind of cereal grain, needs a good reaper. And while he is procuring one, he may as well purchase a combined machine as to own a reaping machine and a mowing machine in two separate machines. Besides this, it is desirable to get a machine that can be relied on from year to year; a machine that has been brought to the most satisfactory degree of perfectibility. Mechanics will be trying to bring out machines on new principles. The consequence is that a great many imperfect machines must be taken on the farms and experimented with, until all the imperfect points in the machinery have been found and corrected. For this reason, I consider it important to suggest to farmers to purchase such machines as can be used to mow grass, clover seed, flax, and to harvest all kinds of grain; and to choose such machines as have had all their weak points corrected. It takes a vast amount of brain labor and money to make a really good and complete mower and reaper. Either of the firms whose reapers are figured and described in this book have expended a large fortune in bringing their reapers and mowers to their present state of perfectibility.

THE KIRBY MOWER AND REAPER.

This reaper is a combined machine, driven by only one wheel. Some farmers are very partial to a one-wheeled reaper and mower, while others can be satisfied with nothing short of a two-wheeled machine. Whoever has a fancy for a one-wheeled machine, will find all that he can desire in the Kirby. No expense has been spared to perfect every part of it. D. M. Osborn & Co., Auburn, N. Y., told me that their firm expended $20,000 in one experiment to bring out the best labor-saving machine in the county. I merely pen these facts—not to puff this reaper—but to suggest to beginners the importance of getting such machines as can be relied on when grass and grain are fit to harvest.

There used to be, and there is now a serious defect in most one-wheel mowers and reapers, which is this: if the drive-wheel is in a furrow, the weight comes so heavily on the finger-bar, and so lightly on the drive-wheel, that the cutters cease to work. But this difficulty has been obviated in the Kirby, as will appear from the following brief description of the essential parts of this reaper and mower.

The illustration on the next page represents the Kirby combined mower and reaper, with reel-self-rake attachment, set up for reaping.

The drive-wheel is bolted on the axle in the usual manner; but the plate on which the axle is cast, is made to move vertically, in a groove of the frame, so that the drive-wheel has a motion entirely independent of the frame and the finger-bar, and will run into dead furrows, or other depressions, and allow the cutting part to work on the level ground, the motion and power of the cutters not being affected in the least. In running over stony and stumpy meadows also, this method of connection with the drive-wheel gives great facility in raising the frame, and with it the cutting parts, above any obstructions. This is effected easily through the adjustment made between the weight of the driver and

Fig. 52.—Kirby Mower and Reaper.

the weight of the working parts; the one so balancing
the other, that the working of a lever is not necessary
to raise the inner end of the bar, as is the case with
nearly all other machines. The finger-bar is of a greatly improved pattern, giving a cut close to the ground
in mowing. The cutter-bars, or knives, are made light
and strong, of the best cutting steel, and tempered with
great care, so as to give an elastic cutting edge suitable
as well for stony and sandy ground as for the tough,
fine, close bottoms of old meadows. The machine is
made of iron and steel throughout, except the pole, seat,
and track-clearer. The cutting apparatus is the same
as that used for mowing, with the finger-bar raised to
the required height for reaping. The platform is so
shaped as to deliver the grain easily at the side of the
machine. When used as a hand-raker, the person raking off, sits a little in the rear of the frame, having perfect command of the grain as it falls on the platform;
and can bring it off with one easy quarter sweep of his
rake. The reel self rake has recently been attached to
the reaper; and it is operated by simple gearing from
the level wheel-shaft. A small pinion engages the gear
of a circular plate having four radial arms. These arms
are pivoted at their connection with the circular plate,
and are moved vertically by means of cams and ways;
and receive from them all the necessary motions for
sweeping the grain on the platform as it is cut, and raking it off in a gavel, when required. Beaters are attached to three of the arms for gathering the grain upon
the platform; and to the other arm a rake is bolted, to
take the grain off. Rakes may also be attached to the
other arms in place of beaters, so as to deliver the grain
in a nearly continuous swath. This is a very strong

and compact rake, the working parts being all of iron, and put together in a very substantial manner.

KEEPING KNIVES SHARP.

As the cutters of mowers and reapers sever the stems of grain and grass with a crushing stroke, it is of the utmost importance that the cutting edge should be sharp. Besides this, the angles which the cutting sides make with the base must be accurately adjusted to the rapidity of their vibrations, and their temper must be such as to insure the best cutting edge. Experience has shown that, where the whole section is tempered, it is too frangible for practical use. The slightest contact with stones, sticks, or other obstructions, causes it to fly in pieces like glass. The central portion of the section should therefore be left soft, while the tempering is confined to a portion extending from one-half to five-eighths of an inch from the edge. The violent change in the structure of the metal, lying on either side of the line of demarcation (see Fig. 53), often causes a fracture, resulting in loss to the manufacturer or the farmer, according to the time when the fracture appeared.

The illustration on the next page represents a knife, or section, manufactured by Reynolds, Barber & Co., Auburn, New York. The committee appointed by the New York State Agricultural Society to examine these sections, state that "all of the Messrs. Reynolds' sections conformed to their test through ten successive grindings. Several of the others broke when pressed upward at an angle of fifteen degrees. Some of them bent permanently, when pressed upon. None of them except Messrs. Reynolds' showed a good temper after the third grinding. Where a graver was pressed into the section at the centre, and carried toward the edge with a uniform pressure, the groove formed grew grad-

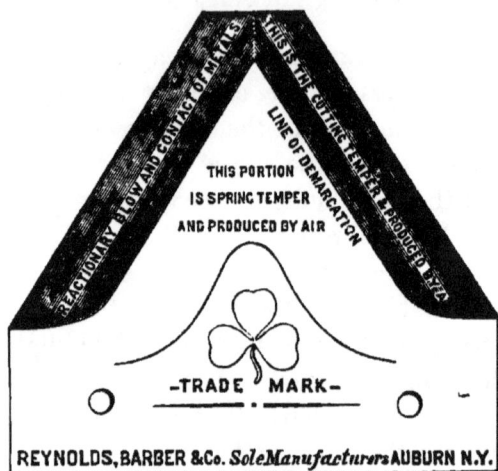

THIS PORTION
IS SPRING TEMPER
AND PRODUCED BY AIR

LINE OF DEMARCATION

REACTIONARY BLOW AND CONTACT OF DIES

THIS IS THE CUTTING TEMPER PRODUCED ETC

-TRADE MARK-

REYNOLDS, BARBER &Co. *Sole Manufacturers* AUBURN N.Y.

FIG. 68.

ually shallower, until it touched the line of demarca-tion—in the Messrs. Reynolds' sections—showing that the hardening was progressive from the centre to the line of demarkation. In the sections made by other firms the groove formed by the graver was of uniform depth until it touched the line of demarcation, when it became at one very shallow. This test shows that the sections of the Messrs. Reynolds grew gradually harder from the centre to the line of demarcation, and that the quality of the metal on either side of the line is not so dissimilar as to cause fractures; and accounted very fully for their absence in the sections.

"Having thus ascertained the superiority of these sections, we were desirous of seeing the processes of their manufacture, and on making known our wishes, the Messrs. Reynolds were kind enough to show us the whole of their works; and we confess to a feeling of great surprise on seeing their sections so perfectly tempered without the agency of any liquid, by percussion, reaction, and cold air alone. We saw over a thousand tempered and ground, not one of which was cracked, or which exhibited any traces of fissure whatever. We believe this process will greatly enhance the efficiency of our reaping and mowing machines; and we rejoice that American ingenuity has perfected so valuable an invention. They are hard and elastic, will break before they will bend, and will carry a sharp cutting edge more than double the length of time of any other section we ever tried. And they all have one uniform temper, which we consider a very essential point to the well-working of any reaper and mower."

REMARKS.—The practical point of first importance to a wheat-grower, when purchasing a machine, is, to ascertain whether the sections, or knives, have a temper equal to those manufactured by this firm.

BEST TIME TO HARVEST WHEAT.

" Shot up from broad, rank blades that droop below,
The nodding wheat-ear forms a graceful bow,
With milky kernels starting full, weighed down,
Ere yet the sun hath tinged its head with brown."
BLOOMFIELD'S *Farmer's Boy.*

It is assumed that every farmer will agree, that there is " a best period " in the growth of the wheat plant for harvesting. In other words, there is a time when, if the straw be cut, the yield of grain will be larger, and

the quality of flour will be better, than if the same
grain were harvested previous to, or after that time.
That is the decisive point for harvesting wheat.   Let us
consider some of the stages of development through
which the wheat passes, as the growing grain approx-
imates the period of perfect maturity.   The first state
is "the milk period."   The heads of grain and the
kernels are now as large and heavy as they ever will
be; and the kernels will measure more at this period
than at any other.   Sometimes the extensive fields of
wheat look like a sea of waving gold.   But the grain is
not fit to harvest.   And if the straw be cut down, more
or less loss must be sustained, as the material that forms
the kernels contains a large proportion of the water
which must be worked out by the vital action of the
growing plants; and its place must be supplied by substances exquisitely fine, which have been collected, atom
by atom, infinitesimally small, and brought to the ears
and deposited in the kernels in the place occupied by
particles of water.   If, at this period, the cradle be thrust
in, and the golden grain be cut down, the water remaining in the kernels will quickly escape, before its place
can be supplied by this fine material that forms the
flour.   The consequence is, the kernels shrink, and the
yield of grain will not reach its maximum quantity.
At this period, most of the leaves may, sometimes, be
entirely lifeless, and the circulation of the vital fluid in
the straw may have ceased.   Yet, the process of changing from thin to thick milk, and from a semi-fluid to a
plastic state, continues until the material in the kernels
is of the consistence of dough when it is put into the
baker's oven.   This period is denominated the "dough
state."   The next is the period of perfect maturity.

This is "the nick of time" to thrust in the sickle and reap the harvest. At this point in the growth of the plant, deterioration commences; and the longer the grain is allowed to remain uncut, the smaller will be the yield, whether the grain be measured or weighed, the larger will be the product of bran, and the smaller the percentage of fine flour. After wheat has passed the milk state, the change to hard grain is usually very rapid. For this reason, grain is frequently allowed to stand several days too long; or until the kernels and straw are "dead ripe." When wheat is allowed to stand uncut through all these periods, a great loss is frequently sustained by the shelling of the grain while the gavels are being bound into sheaves. Still another source of great loss is sustained in the straw, when the grain is not cut until every part is dead ripe. If wheat be cut at the period designated for securing the largest yield of grain, the straw, if properly secured from the influences of the weather, will afford a large quantity of valuable fodder for domestic animals.

On this subject, Agricola, in the "Working Farmer," writes: "There is probably no question in connection with wheat harvest which exercises so much influence upon the quality of the flour, as well as the amount, as the time of cutting. In former years, when we were compelled to depend on the sickle, or later on the cradle and manual labor, there was some excuse for not taking advantage of the proper and best time, but in this fast and improved age, when one man, aided by a pair of horses and a self-raking reaper, can cut and deliver ready for binding, from ten to fifteen acres of wheat per day, there is no excuse for its not being performed at the proper time; the only thing which can interfere to prevent cutting being done on any fixed day is the occurrence of rain, but then, we must remember that our grain ripens very little during wet or cloudy weather. I have often found it to ripen more during one clear, warm day after a rain, than during a whole week of cloudy or showery weather.

" At first glance it would seem that it was but natural that the grain should be. allowed to become dead ripe before cutting ; such would undoubtedly be the case if the whole crop were intended for seed, as is the case in a natural state of the plant; but our object is to attain the greatest possible percentage of flour with the least possible offal ; and not only this, but also to have this flour as rich as possible in gluten.

" All the experiments which have been tried, not only here but in England, have clearly proven that there is a certain stage of the growth of the grain at which it yields the greatest proportion of flour, and that at this time the flour contains a larger percentage of gluten than at any time before or afterward. In order to more fully understand this time, let us go back four weeks ; the first two weeks will represent the time passing between the *green* and *raw* state, and the last two, the time which elapses between the *raw* and *ripe* state, and thus divide the grain into three stages."

Mr. Hannum instituted several experiments to ascertain, if possible, the proper period to harvest the grain ; and his experiments led him to believe that at " about a fortnight before it fully ripens is the proper time for cutting wheat, as the skin is then thinner, the grain fuller, the bushel heavier, and the yield of flour greater." From the report of the miller who ground these samples, it seems that the lot cut raw made eight pounds more flour to every hundred of grain, and corresponding amount of straw. The amount of grain was not materially decreased, showing that the addition to the weight of the grain was mainly in flour and not in bran.

In a similar experiment the result showed a gain of over *fifteen* per cent. in flour, from equal measures of grain, and a gain of *eight* per cent. from equal weights of grain. ' English millers divide the product of the wheat into three classes, styled flour, pollard, and bran ; the sample cut when fully ripe gains fifty per cent. more of pollard than that cut raw. This effect may be thus explained : at the time of the first cutting while in the raw state, the grain contains its largest amount of starch and gluten ; at this period the grain has a thin skin, and consequently less straw ; afterward nature thickens the skin in order to protect the grain, thus changing a portion of the starch into woody fibre.

In a more extended experiment the difference in produce per acre may be thus stated : that cut when raw yielded, per acre, nine hundred and ten pounds more straw ; ninety pounds more flour ; thirty-five pounds less pollard and sharps ; thirty-five pounds less bran ; twenty pounds less waste, than that cut ripe. The real difference in value may be stated at from six to seven dollars per acre.

Nor is this all which we can gain from early cutting. I have heard good farmers admit that they sometimes lost enough wheat by shelling out between cutting and mowing away in the barn to seed the field, or in other words, from one and one and a half to two bushels per acre ; this loss is all prevented by early cutting, for grain cut in the raw state, no matter how thoroughly dried, will seldom if ever shell out if handled in the usual man-

15

ner ; and in addition to this, the sheaf is much pleasanter to bind, load, and thrash, for neither the straw nor beard is so stiff as when the crop is allowed to stand until fully ripe.

In some instances, I have known wheat to be cut on the fourth of July, in Central New York; and the next season, in the same locality, wheat was not fit to harvest till the twentieth of the same month. Therefore, it would be useless to endeavor to fix on any week or day of a particular month ; for one day will scarcely be universal in one country nor with two kinds of wheat.

In favorable seasons the straw commences to ripen from the bottom ; in certain unfavorable seasons the upper joints are ripe first; but the latter case is the exception to the rule. When on examination it is found that the two lower joints of the straw have turned yellow, and the color is beginning to show itself above the *second* joint ; when the field seen from a distance seems quite ripe, but when more closely examined is found still green at the top ; when on crushing the grain between the fingers or teeth, the milk is found to have become so thick as to be fairly called a liquid, *then cut ; but not till then.* My usual rule is to wait until the yellow color begins to show itself almost one inch above the second knot or joint from the bottom ; and then cut the crop. This rule cannot of course be applied universally to the field ; for all the stalks don't ripen equally. But when a majority of the stalks comply with the above conditions, I would cut the field at once ; for though it seems green, the process of drying will ripen it without the loss which ensues when ripened " in the ground." When the weather is unfavorable, let tools and implements be prepared to harvest with dispatch when storms cease.

CUTTING WHEAT IN ENGLAND.

A few experiments have been made and published in this country, showing, by accurate measurement, the advantages of cutting when the chaff has partly changed from green to yellow. We find the following additional proof in Baker's lecture before the Sparkenhoe Club, England, as published in the North British Agriculturist:

"In harvesting wheat, there was a great division of opinion, as well as to when was the proper time and mode of cutting. It was considered a proper time to cut wheat when it had passed from a 'milky state' to a 'doughy state.' Experiments had been made under three heads—first, when it was green; second, when the straw was changing color; third, when fully ripe. The results were in the first case 19¾ bushels per acre, valued at 61s. per quarter; in the second, 23½, at 63s.; in the third, 22¾, at 61s. There was a similar result in the straw. The total value per acre was found to be— on that cut green on 8th August, £12 17s. per acre, or $62.30; second, when cut yellow below the ear one week afterward, £13 7s., or $64.61; third, cut when fully ripe, one week later, £11 12s., or $56.13. This difference arose from that cut first and second producing more fine flour and less bran than that cut last, which proved that the gluten is converted into starch if the wheat stands until fully ripe, the proper time being undoubtedly as soon as either end of the straw has changed to a yellow color, the sap having then ceased to flow; but, on the other hand, it is better to cut early, as no portion is lost by shedding during the process of cutting, or by the effect of high winds. It is also less liable to sprout in the sheaf, and early harvests are also generally best. Besides, a few days gained in the commencement of harvest is of immeasurable advantage, and enables the farmer to take opportunities for effecting other work, which otherwise he could not do."

Signs of Perfect Maturity.

The "Prairie Farmer," in an article headed, "When shall we cut wheat?" says: "In attempting to answer the question, *At what particular period in the condition of the grain shall we cut it?* we shall not refer to our own experience, but only add that our rule is, to cut the grain about *two weeks before it is fully ripe.*

"Prof. Johnston, of the Royal Agricultural Society of England, says, the *rawer* the crop is cut, the heavier and more nourishing the straw will be. Within *three* weeks of being fully ripe, the straw begins to diminish in weight; and the longer it remains uncut, after that time, the lighter it becomes, and the less nourishing.

"On the other hand, the grain, which is sweet and milky, a month before it is ripe, gradually consolidates —the sugar changing into starch, and the milk thickening into the gluten and albumen of the flour. As soon as this change is nearly completed, or *about a fortnight before it is ripe, the grain of wheat contains the largest proportion of starch and gluten. If reaped at this time, the bushel will weigh most,* and will yield the largest quantity of fine flour, and the least bran.

"At this period the grain has a thin skin, and hence the small quantity of bran. But if the crop be still left uncut, the next natural step in the ripening process is, to cover the grain with a better protection—a thicker skin—and a portion of the starch of the grain is changed into woody fibre. By this change, the quantity of starch is lessened and the weight of husk increased. Hence the diminished yield of flour, and the increased produce of bran.

"Theory and experience, therefore, indicate about a fortnight before it is dead ripe, as the most proper time for cutting wheat. The skin is then thinner and whiter, the grain fuller, the bushel heavier, the yield of flour greater, its color fairer, and the quantity of bran less."

Color of the Straw.

When the straw immediately under the head of grain turns from a greenish to an orange hue, for four or five inches in length, it is time to cut the grain. The kernels or berries have then just passed out of the milky state, but are so soft as to be easily crushed between the thumb nails. At this time, some of the leaves on the lower portion of the stem may be dead, but still, that part of the stem remains vigorous for a few days.

Mr. Robert Brown, of Edinburgh, a farmer, and for many years editor of the "Farmer's Magazine," says it is necessary to discriminate betwixt the ripeness of the straw and the ripeness of the grain; for, in some seasons, the straw dries upward; under which circumstances a field, to the eye, may appear completely fit for the sickle, when, in reality, the grain is imperfectly consolidated, and perhaps not much removed from a milky state. Though it is obvious that, under such circumstances, no further benefit can be conveyed from the root, and that nourishment is withheld the moment the roots die; yet it does not follow that grain so cir-

cumstanced should be immediately cut; because, after
that operation is performed, it is in a great measure necessarily deprived of every benefit from the sun and air,
both of which have greater influence in bringing it to
maturity, so long as it remains on foot, than when cut
down, whether laid on the ground or bound up in sheaves.
* * * Taking all these things into view, it seems pru-
dent to have wheat *cut before it is fully ripe,* as less damage will be sustained from acting in this way than by
adopting a contrary practice.

Another authority says that grain, if not reaped until
the straw is wholly yellow, will be more than ripe, as
the ear generally ripens before the straw; and it is observable that the first reaped usually affords the heaviest
and fairest samples.

In the "Farmer's Encyclopædia" it is stated that the
indications of ripeness in wheat are few and simple.
When the straw exhibits a bright golden color from the
bottom of the stem nearly to the ear, or when the ear
begins to bend gently, the grain may be cut. But as
the whole crop will not be exactly ripe at the same
time, if, on walking through the field and selecting the
greenest heads, the kernels can be separated from the
chaff when rubbed through the hands, it is a sure sign
that the grain is then out of its milky state, and may
be reaped with safety; for although the straw may be
green to some distance downward from the ear, yet, if
it be quite yellow from the bottom upward, the grain
then wants no further nourishment from the earth, and,
if properly harvested, will not shrink. The young
farmer should study this subject most thoroughly, with
this book in one hand and wheat in the other. He will
soon learn when is the best time to harvest wheat, and

all kinds of cereal grain. This subject should be studied thoroughly.

TIME TO CUT WHEAT.

Rawson Harmon, an experienced wheat-grower of Western New York, writes, in relation to the best period to harvest wheat: " To be most valuable for millers, wheat should be cut as soon as the berry has passed from the milky to the doughy state. Wheat cut then, contains more gluten and less starch, than if it were not harvested until the grain is fully ripe. If wheat is allowed to stand uncut, until the kernels become hard, the gluten is diminished, and the starch is increased, which reduces the quantity and quality of the flour. But for seed, it should never be cut till fully ripe. Starch is more valuable in its early vegetation than the gluten. One cause of the increase of smut, of late years, is the cutting of wheat intended for seed, too green. Wheat cut before it is fully ripe, should not be sown. If wheat-growers would adhere strictly to the sowing of no seed that is cut before it is fully ripe, they would find smut disappearing without the preparation of brine and lime. The farmer that neglects to brine and lime his seed wheat, does not look to his best interest. Smutty wheat is much improved by not cutting until fully ripe."

CUTTING WHEAT TOO GREEN.

Although there is but little danger of harvesting wheat before the grain is really fit to cut, still wheat *may* be cut before it is really fit to harvest; and instances have been recorded, where the loss sustained from cutting a crop too green, amounted to many hun-

dred dollars. J. P. Lowe penned the following facts:
" A Southern farmer once grew three hundred acres of
wheat, which, in June, had attained a huge growth,
and appeared remarkably promising. The agricultural
papers were then recommending to harvest early, while
the grain was in the milky state. He followed their
advice, and cut the whole three hundred acres as soon
as the juice of the kernel began to whiten. The grain
shrank badly. He estimated his loss, from too early
harvesting, at $5,000. The blunder, as estimated by
the writer, and by the gentleman himself, who, by the
way, appeared very candid, and was willing to take his
full share of the blame, fairly belonged, about one-half
to him, and the other half to the agricultural journals
of the time. The papers had blown too strongly, and
altogether too indiscriminately, on the benefits of early
harvesting, and he had followed their advice to excess
—had cut his wheat in a greener state than they had
recommended—had misunderstood them, to an extent
which he freely confessed was inexcusable."

MANAGEMENT OF WHEAT.

Beginners frequently inquire whether it is not better
to cut down the growing wheat at harvest time, and
allow it to remain in the swath for a day or two, before
it is bound into sheaves. But experience proves that it
is far better for the grain, especially if the straw, when
cradled, is somewhat green, to be bound in bundles, and
put in stooks, than to let it lie in the swath, especially
in hot and dry weather. If the grain be exposed in the
swath to the burning sun, for only a few hours, the
intense heat scorches the soft kernels, and dries up the

moisture in the grain so rapidly, that its quality is seriously injured, for making the best quality of flour. Besides this, the grain shrinks far more than it would, were the heads permitted to cure in the shade. If the straw be bound in bundles, and the sheaves be set in neat stooks and covered with caps of some kind, which shade the grain, the soft kernels will cure gradually, be more plump, and make more and better grain, or flour.

Mr. E. A. King, a practical farmer of King's Ferry, Cayuga County, N. Y., penned the following instructive suggestions for the "Cultivator and Country Gentleman": "I believe it is a conceded fact that wheat, before it is perfectly ripe, gives more and a better quality of flour. Still the yield is owing greatly to the manner in which the grain is cured, after being cut. Every intelligent wheat-grower knows that grain of any kind, cut in a greenish state, and allowed to remain in swath to cure, will cause the kernels to shrink and be of an inferior quality; while if bound almost immediately, or before it gets dry, and put up in round shocks and capped, the grain will receive the juices remaining in the green straw, and become round and plump. To prove the benefit derived from keeping the heads of grain from being exposed to the air, let any one who has practised round shocking examine the heads of the top cap sheaf, and he will find the berries much less plump and heavy than those taken from underneath. Where wheat is struck with rust, early cutting, immediate binding, and round shocking will often save the crop, when if put up in long shocks, as many farmers do, the damage would be great. This is especially the case with spring wheat, as this variety is with us more apt to rust than the winter variety, as the time of ripen-

15*

ing usually occurs later, when there is a greater amount of warmth and moisture, which is no doubt the cause of the grain rusting. To prove this, wheat, oats, or barley, sown on our hilly lake land, where the drainage is quick and immediate, are seldom struck with rust of any kind."

If wheat-growers will observe this suggestion, they will perceive that when grain is harvested and cured in cloudy weather, the yield will always be larger than if the weather were burning hot while the grain is curing. If wheat could be cut when the straw is quite green and cured under shelter, without being put into a mass so large as to heat, we should perceive a vast difference in the quality of the flour which is made of the grain. When grain is designed for seed, I always let it lie in the swath, one day or more, for the purpose of curing the straw as soon as practicable, so that the sheaves might be garnered immediately.

Suggestions about Grain Cradles.

Every man who ever uses a cradle, ought to understand *why* every part is made as it is—with its peculiar form. He ought to be able to tell what is the best form of the scythe, and the best curvature of the fingers, and how the fingers should stand with reference to the scythe. Although the great bulk of harvesting grain will probably be done with horse-power, still grain cradles will always be needed, even if horse-reapers are used to cut nearly the whole crop. Cradles must be employed to cut the grain around stumps, trees, along fences, to cut the corners of a piece of grain, when the reaper is in motion, and so forth. No farmer can get along satisfactorily, without a good grain cradle; and it is important for a laborer to know what constitutes a good cradle, how to put it in good order, and how to use it, so as to cut grain and lay it in a swath in a neat and workmanlike manner.

The most correct form of a cradle scythe is a point which should be thoroughly understood and appreciated, whether one can obtain a scythe of the desired form or not.

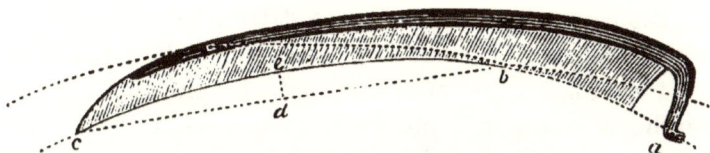

FIG. 54.—The best form of Cradle Scythe.

A very straight scythe is quite as objectionable as one that has too much curvature. When it is too straight on the cutting edge, it will cut too squarely across the standing straws; whereas the cut should be made in a drawing or sliding manner. If the scythe be straight on the edge, the fingers must of necessity be correspondingly straight. The illustration herewith given, Fig. 54, represents a cradle scythe of a good form. It will be seen that the cutting edge from a to b, about one foot in length, is a part of the arc of one circle; and the other part, from b to c, is the arc of another circle of the same size, but in a different position.

It may be seen by measuring, that these circles are about ten feet in diameter, and that the distance from d, in the dotted line, to e, when a scythe is four feet long, is about two and a half inches. A cradle scythe of this shape works well, if it is properly hung on the snath, and the cutting edge kept in order.

The question is frequently asked why a cradle scythe is made broader from the back to the cutting edge, than a grass scythe? The object of this is twofold. The first is to support the grain after it is cut off; and second, to furnish ample room for the straw to slide back from the cutting edge, against the fingers, after it has been cut off. If a scythe, no wider than a grass scythe, is attached to a cradle, as soon as the space from the fingers to the cutting edge is filled with straw, the scythe cannot cut off any more straw ; therefore, as the cradle is "full," it must slide over the rest of the clip.

If the fingers do not correspond with the curve of the scythe, a cradle will not work well, even if the scythe is made according to the most perfect pattern. Fig. 55 represents a scythe of the same form as Fig. 54. The object of it is to show the relative length and curvature of the first finger of the cradle, when compared with the form of the scythe. The inside of the finger should

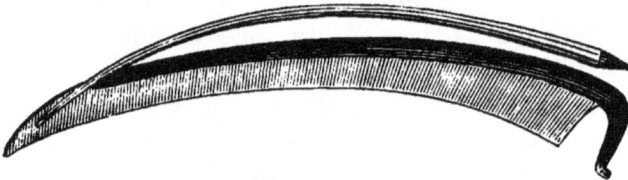

FIG. 55.—Best form and position of lower finger.

extend at least two inches beyond the back of the scythe; and it is best to have the finger from one to two inches shorter than the scythe. The small end should stand over the point of the scythe, as represented in the figure, and be from one to two inches above the blade at the point. If the first finger rests hard on the scythe, it sometimes prevents the grain discharging freely when the cradle is in use. The point of the first finger should always stand as far back as possible, and not catch any straws beyond the scythe. When some straws are pulled down and not cut off, it shows that some of the fingers stand out too far. On the contrary, when the cradle does not gather all the grain that is cut off, some of the fingers are in too far, or are too short. Sometimes every finger stands exactly in its most proper position, and the cradle does not gather all the grain. This can be obviated in two ways: first, by using a shorter scythe; or second, by dulling about two inches of the cutting edge at the point. Sometimes the scythe and lower finger are all right, but the other fingers are so short that the cradle does not gather all the grain the scythe cuts off. This difficulty can be obviated in no other way than by attaching a scythe two or three inches shorter, and cutting off the lower finger to correspond with the scythe, as shown by Fig. 55, and to be also of the correct proportional length with the other fingers. Fingers may be "too crooked," or too much curved near the points. It is a common occurrence to see cradle fingers like a sleigh runner—having nearly all the curvature within twelve to twenty inches of the ends. Cradles having such fingers never work well, as they carry most of the grain, after it is cut off, near the forward part of the cradle, which causes it to work hard, and to hang too heavily on the point, as well as to hold the grain too much, when it is being laid in a swath. When selecting a cradle, it is better to get a short scythe than one over four feet long. These two cuts of scythes and some of the matter, I prepared for the "American Agriculturist" when I was one of the editorial corps of that paper.

GRINDING CRADLE SCYTHES.

"Now, while he brushes the dew from the clover,
　Lay the dull scythe to the steel-gnawing stone;
Turn with a will, boys, over and over;
　Now the edge wires and the grinding is done."
BURLEIGH.

In my Young Farmer's Manual, the reader will find a diagram of a scythe, with more extended remarks about putting a scythe in order, than I shall pen in this place. There, the philosophical reasons are given for grinding a scythe, as directed. But I will simply caution beginners, as well as some old heads, who think what they don't know is not worth the trouble of learning, not to spoil an excellent cradle scythe by grinding the blade too thin. A large proportion of the cradle scythes that are condemned as poor stuff, or as having a poor temper, were ruined by grinding them too thin. Scythes are often ground and ground to death, by men who don't know how to put a jack-knife in order. Then, because the cutting edge fails, after the blade has been ground so thin that there is not steel enough to give proper stiffness to the basil of the scythe, the tool is condemned. Do not spoil scythes by grinding.

HOW TO CRADLE GRAIN.

"All strike as one, with a symphonant cadence;
　All step at once, with a measured advance;
Bowing together the brawny arm's aidance,
　In the slow swing of the shoulders' expanse."
BURLEIGH.

A gang of skilful cradlers, rakers, and binders, such as we used to see before the horse-harvesters took the place of the cradle, is a pleasant and cheering sight.

A good cradler must exercise no little skill in adjusting every part of the cradle to hang exactly right, or he cannot do neat work. Do not put the scythe and fingers out too far, especially if the grain does not stand erect. When all the parts of a cradle are made right, properly adjusted, and correctly handled, almost every straw will be gathered, as the scythe cuts them off.

A good cradler walks close up to the standing grain— within a foot of it. He keeps his body nearly erect. He puts his *right* foot forward when he steps, and never the *left* foot first. There is a philosophical reason for this. I studied it out when I first began to cradle, when I was only fourteen years of age. Point-in low and point-out low. Cut the stubble a uniform height across the swath; and do not scoop out a swath, by pointing-in high and pointing-out high. Keep the scythe level; and bring the cradle around, at every clip, as close to the left leg as you can. Lay the grain evenly at the butts; and do not throw the tops around too far. Let your movements be rather slow and careful, until you can make every clip with as much precision as if the work were done by machinery. There are many things about cradling which I cannot write out; but which can be learned only by the actual use of a good cradle.

CRADLE FINGERS, AND HOW TO MAKE THEM.

There are two kinds of cradle fingers: bent and natural crook. Those having a natural crook are made by first sawing the log into plank thick enough for four fingers, or about two and three-fourths inches thick. Then, pieces are sawed out of the plank, with a scroll saw, of the desired curvature, which are then slitted the other way with a small circular saw. The fingers then have square corners, which are dressed off by hand, or machinery, which does the work very neatly and rapidly.

Bent fingers are made of very tough timber, first sawed into tapering strips just large enough for four fingers. These pieces are then steamed and bent, and sawed into fingers the same as if they were of natural crook. While the wood is still hot and on the form, or clamp, boiled linseed oil is applied to the outside surface, as long as the wood will absorb it. This is designed to prevent the fingers from straightening out, after the cradle is finished. The great objection to straight fingers is, most of the grain that is cut at one clip, will be gathered and held by the fingers so far toward the point of the scythe that a cradle will not work well, unless it cuts short clips; whereas, if the fingers have a proper degree of curvature, the grain will slide back toward the heel of the cradle, as it is cut, thus enabling the cradler to cut a larger clip at once, and to handle the grain with greater facility. Another thing of primary importance in the form of cradle fingers is, they should be more curved than the back of the scythe. See remarks on pages 348 and 349.

Raking and Binding Wheat.

"The reaper binds the bearded ear,
And gathers in the golden year;
And where the sheaves are glancing,
The farmer's heart is dancing."

In order to rake and bind grain satisfactorily, a man must possess a good degree of skill and tact to make every movement of his body and every motion of his rake, feet, legs, and hands aid him in his labor. He must not make any false motions, nor work like a man beating the air. Every motion must be easy and effective. Why will a small, light man frequently rake and bind as fast as two large, heavy men? Because he knows how to do it; while the others alluded to are awkward, and labor to a disadvantage. It used to be a common occurrence to see a small man raking and binding in heavy wheat, and keeping up close to a good cradler. I have frequently heard my father tell of his ambition and skill in raking and binding wheat after a good cradler, when the country was new, and the wheat was as high as their heads over the entire fields; and that often, when on a strife—as cradlers were accustomed to "race it" in those days—he said he has raked and bound the swath alone, and took the last clip off the cradle, as he closed up every sheaf. And it is not incredible; for, when I was a lad, it was an unusual occurrence for two hands to follow one cradler. Sometimes a boy would be employed to rake the swath into gavels, for another boy or man to bind.

I well remember, when I was fourteen years old, as it was considered too hard work for a boy like me to rake and bind, and keep up with a man who cradled wheat, that another boy was hired to assist me. He was to rake the gavels and I to bind. But he was so unaccountably awkward, and made such miserable work at raking, that I refused to have his assistance, as both of us could not keep up with the cradler. He made such ill-shapen gavels, that I was required to spend more time in straightening up the gavels than I would occupy in raking them myself. Therefore, I performed the task alone, in good wheat; have often done it since;

and I never met with a cradler whom I could not follow around a ten-acre field, all day, keep close to him, and do the raking and binding in a neat and workmanlike manner, and help shock the sheaves after the grain was all cut.

I do not record these facts to boast of what I have done, but simply to show the superior skill that was exercised when I was a young man, when compared with what we now perceive among those who rake and bind grain. In order to labor at this kind of work economically and profitably, a man must understand how to take advantage of every circumstance. Raking and binding grain is a part of harvesting that should be neatly performed. If a man binds poorly, or does not rake clean, or makes a great many false motions which occupy time, consume his strength, but do not further his labor, he is an unprofitable hand, and should be taught the first principles of raking and binding skilfully and expeditiously.

THE SIZE OF THE GAVELS.

The importance of making the sheaves as nearly of a uniform size as is practicable, should be frequently impressed on the mind of every man and boy who binds grain, or who only rakes gavels. If the sheaves are to be stacked, it is far more important that the gavels should be of a uniform size, than if they are to be stored in a barn. For this reason, care should be exercised when grain is being cut down with a reaper, to make the gavels—neither too large nor too small— but of a fair size. It is exceedingly inconvenient for a stacker to make a good stack of sheaves of various sizes, as there will be holes where the small sheaves are laid. And if the sheaves are not of a uniform length, even an experienced stacker will be liable to build an ill-shapen stack, that will not turn the rain so well, as if it had been made of sheaves of a uniform size. It is of eminent importance that the man who makes the gavels should understand all the advantages and disadvantages of having sheaves too long, or too large, or too small, and poorly bound.

My own rule always has been, to make the gavels as large as they can be bound conveniently. This thought is always kept in mind when the reaper cuts the grain, as well as when the gavels are raked by hand. If gavels be so large that a binder cannot reach around one without making extra exertions, he will lose time and fall behind. On the contrary, if the gavels be made too small, too much time will be consumed in making bands and binding the sheaves. Many laborers do not seem to consider that it makes any difference whether they make twenty sheaves in going across the field, or whether the same amount of straw is bound into forty bundles, requiring nearly double the time.

If the straw be so short that a double band will not extend around a gavel, of course, the length of the straw must be the guide in determining the size of the gavels. I always aimed to make the sheaves as large as they could conveniently be bound, for the purpose of economizing labor. Raking and binding only a few sheaves is really a small matter. But, when a quantity of grain is bound into 4,000 sheaves, when it might have been put into 3,000, without any inconvenience at all, we perceive a loss of time and expense required to bind 1,000 sheaves. Besides this, there is a loss of time in loading and stacking. If a certain amount of grain sufficient to make 3,000 sheaves be bound into 4,000 sheaves, it will cost nearly one-quarter more to handle it when securing the crop, either in stacks or in barns.

How to Rake Gavels.

Beginners—whether boys or men—should be instructed how to rake gavels neatly, expeditiously, and by exerting the least strength. There is an awkward and laborious way to rake gavels; and there is a neat and easy way of raking. The man who practises the former, will work hard all day and perform but little; while the latter will move along with amazing ease and rapidity, and perform his task in the most satisfactory manner.

Two points should be kept in mind, one of which is to keep the butts even, and the other, to keep the gavel from running out much longer than the straw. In order to rake a gavel easily, keep the rake-handle nearly straight up and down, and move the leg that is against the butts, along with the gavel. This will keep the butts even, and the gavel of a uniform length. But, if a man does not keep one, or both legs against the butts of the straw, the gavel will be much longer than the straw; and the sheaves will be awkward things to stook, as they will not stand erect without help.

When making gavels of grain that is cut by a reaper, if the straw be of a uniform length and weight, it will not be difficult to gauge the size of the gavels, as a little observation and experience will enable an expert workman to make them all of a uniform size. But, if half the gavels be made too large, and the remainder too small, the labor of binding will be greatly increased.

When closing up a machine gavel, or when raking a swath, let the head of the rake be always kept as nearly parallel, as practicable, with the straw. It is far easier to keep the butts of the straw even, when making a gavel, than it is to even them with a rake, after the gavel is made.

MAKING BANDS.

It may seem trivial to dwell on the various manipulations incident to harvesting grain; but laborers should understand how to perform every operation with the greatest possible ease, and in the shortest space of time. Some men will make a band and bind a gavel, neatly, before another man can make his band. Some binders separate a handful of straw into two equal parts, and tie the top ends together. But that is a slow and awkward way. Others double the ears of grain over, and catch them between the gavel and the band. But the lock is liable to become loose, when the gavel is being bound, or when the sheaves are handled.

The mode adopted by all quick binders, and the most expeditious way to make a band is, to take a small handful from the top of the gavel, and while separating it, hold back other straws with the other hand. Then grasp it with the left hand a little below the heads, and, dividing the straw with the other hand, take the half of the band at the right side, carry it quickly to the left side of the other half, so that the left half will rest on the back of the right hand. Now elevate the right hand above the left, thus throwing the butt ends of the branches of the band into the air above both hands. Pass the portion of the band in the right hand around all the heads of grain, and place the right thumb on them, and the lock will never separate when binding, if it is well made.

Binding Gavels of Grain.

I know of but few *little* things that are more perplexing and trying to the patience of an ambitious farmer, than poorly bound sheaves of grain. Sheaves that are poorly bound, will fall apart when one is making stooks. They unbind when the pitcher is heaving them on the load. The bands loosen when the loader is placing the sheaves, and from the time of binding, till the grain is laid down to be thrashed, poor binding is an intolerable nuisance; and every good man whose ambition has not been paralyzed by pitching half-bound sheaves will breathe out grumbling and muttering, and sometimes denunciation without measure, at such perfunctory and miserable work.

I was always accustomed to tell men and boys, who bound grain for me, If you do not bind one hundred sheaves in a day, do put the bands in the middle and bind the sheaves tight. In order to have employés work advantageously, I always would spend an hour with an awkward laborer, instructing him how to make his band; how to put it around the gavel; how to take hold of the ends; and how to form the lock and to make the tuck.

Now, in order to bind a gavel quickly, take the band in one hand, throw it forward of, and around the gavel, while the left hand is passed beneath the opposite side, palm upward, as shown by figure 56, grasping the band in such a manner that its hold need not be relinquished until the sheaf is bound. When the hand grasps the band so that the hold must be relinquished and renewed, it often occupies time enough to finish binding the

Fig. 56.—A Skilful Binder.

sheaf.   When the right hand is passing the band around the bundle, if the stubble is sharp and stiff, keep the band beneath the palm. By this means the tender skin on the back of the fingers and hand, will be protected from the sharp stubble.

There are in common use not less than three different modes of binding. One is, passing the right-hand end over the thumb, with a double twist and tuck; the next is, passing it under the wrist, with a double twist and tuck; and the third is, passing it beneath the left hand, making a nip about the left-hand end of the band, and a tuck beneath it, or, in common parlance, "a nip and tuck." Sometimes binding over the thumb is performed with a single twist and tuck. But, when bound in this manner, unless the bands are drawn very tightly, sheaves are liable to unbind.

Every laborer should learn to bind sheaves *over* the thumb, as he will be able to bind a larger number of sheaves in an hour than if he binds under the wrist. When binding a sheaf *over* the thumb, put one knee on the gavel and draw the band as tightly as practicable, and hold both ends with one hand, and with the forefinger of the same hand grasping the right-hand end of the band. Now, while the left hand holds both ends of the band, whirl the right-hand end of the band around the other end with the right hand, giving them a twist, or two twists, which is better; and tuck the twisted end under the band.

The second mode of binding is done with the left knee on the sheaf; the right-hand end of the band is carried under the wrist of the left hand, and held by letting the wrist drop upon it, until the two ends are twisted together, and tucked under. Sheaves are bound in the "nip and tuck" style by passing the end of the band in the right hand under the left hand, then holding it with the left hand resting on the end of the band, when the right hand releases its hold, and renews it again above the left hand. Then the left-hand end of the band is bent over toward the binder, while the other end is brought around it and tucked beneath the band on the side toward the binder. When sheaves are thus bound, the left-hand end of the band forms a good handle for carrying the sheaf.

LABORING DISADVANTAGEOUSLY.

When a laborer is greatly fatigued by toiling in the hot sunshine, every movement is a tax on his energies. It is fatiguing to stoop down and pick up one's rake. Most binders always throw their rake down on the ground, every time they bind a sheaf. Of course, they are obliged to spend the time and endure the fatigue required to stoop and pick up their rake as often as they make a sheaf.

Now, if an active man will rake and bind one thousand sheaves in twelve hours, and if it consumes two seconds of time to stoop and pick up his rake at each sheaf, he must necessarily endure the fatigue of picking one thousand rakes off the ground, which will consume not less than thirty-three minutes, besides the useless fatigue. During that length of time, he would be able to rake and bind not less than fifty sheaves, which is not a little saving with many hands.

While a sheaf is being bound, the rake-handle should always rest against the shoulder of the binder, as shown by the last figure. This makes it easier work for him than to lay down and pick up his rake at every sheaf. As soon as a sheaf is bound, and the binder straightens

16

his body, his rake is where he can take hold of it, without stooping to pick it off the ground.

A beginner may experience a little difficulty in keeping the rake-handle against his shoulder, while he is binding a gavel; but, by exercising a little patience and perseverance, a laborer will be able to work all day, and not be required to stoop down and pick up his rake a single time. When we have devised every possible means to lighten the labor of raking and binding grain, we find there is a great deal of hard work still to be performed.

When gavels are neatly made, and bound tight with the band in the middle of the sheaf, as represented by

Fig. 57.—A Sheaf neatly Bound.

the accompanying figure of a sheaf of wheat, every sheaf will stand alone, and it will require the force of a strong wind to blow sheaves over. But when the band is placed near the butts of the straw, sheaves will often need rebinding, before they can be stored. Beginners who are slack, poor binders, can imitate this illustration of a sheaf, until they are able to make handsome sheaves which will stand erect without a boy to hold them when no wind blows. The tuck of the band is shown, in this figure of a sheaf, as well as it can be represented on paper. Beginners should see that the ends of the band are thrust under the band, so as to hold well.

A Straw-band Maker.

Many farmers experience great inconvenience for want of long straw for making bands to bind bundles of straw when thrashing grain, as well as for binding stalks of Indian corn. Making straw bands by twisting them out of short straw by hand is a slow and tedious process. But by employing a twister, as shown by the accompanying illustration, straw bands can be

Fig. 59.—Band Maker.

made with satisfactory rapidity. With such an instrument, a man and small boy can make a large number of bands in a day, when they have no other employment; and thus have them ready for use at any future period.

The manner of making bands with this hook and crank is as follows: Secure a handful of straw or hay to the hook, while one person holds it with one hand,

and turns the crank with the other. The person who lets the straw and hay out, should be seated on the floor, with a lapful before him. The twister walks backward, away from the layer, as the length of the band increases. The operation is similar to making ropes. The straw or hay should be wetted before it is twisted into bands, as the straws will not be so elastic as when dry. When wet, the straws will be very pliable; and a very smooth band can be made fifty feet long in two minutes, if a person can lay out the straw skilfully.

Make each band about fifty feet long; lay it down on the ground; let it dry one or two days; then, with a sharp axe, cut the long bands or ropes into pieces of suitable length for binding sheaves. The pieces may be four, five, six, or more feet in length. The desired size of the bundles must determine the length of the bands. After the long hay ropes have become dry, the bands will not untwist when sheaves are being bound.

To make such a straw-band maker, procure a piece of half-inch round iron, twenty inches long. Make a crank on one end and a hook on the other. Any blacksmith will do the work for a dime. The circle of the hook should be about two inches in diameter, formed as herewith illustrated. The length of the crank should not be over six inches. If the crank be too long, the twister will find it far more fatiguing to his arms than if the crank were short.

For a handle, bore a hole through a piece of straight-grained hard wood, shave it true and smooth, split it in two, through the hole, place it on the shank of the twister, and glue the edges together. Put a handle also on the wrist-pin. Persons who have never made bands with such a device, will be surprised to learn how won-

derfully making bands in this manner will facilitate the
labor of binding sheaves of any kind.

A Binder's Day's Work.

Before horse-reapers were employed to cut our grain,.
when young boys were ambitious to rake and bind
grain, six hundred sheaves were considered a boy's day's
work, and a thousand sheaves for a man. But if a man
rakes and binds one thousand sheaves in the course of
twelve hours, he must labor faithfully and understand
how to make his band in the best and most expeditious
manner, and how to bind by exerting the least strength,
and in the shortest period of time. A laborer who receives a man's wages, ought to rake and bind three
sheaves in two minutes, on an average of the minutes in
the working hours. Ambitious men will do more than
this. But muttering laborers, who are always fearful
that they are going to do too much, and who will let a
sheaf drop half bound, when the dinner-horn blows, will
not rake and bind more than five hundred sheaves in a
day; and even one-fourth of those will have to be re-
bound before they are put in the mow. In these days
of agricultural machinery, men and boys ought to edu-
cate their ambition to accomplish as much as laborers
could perform when their fathers were young. But in
most instances, our old men, now in their dotage, will
mow around our common mowers, every ten rods; and
cradle around them twice in cutting across a ten-acre
field; and cut their corners at the end; and then cradle
around to the place of starting, and take a refreshing
nap in the shade before their competitors come up, and
are ready for another start. This is a fact. And I

record it to the shame of our young men, who lack the
promptings of a laudable ambition to be able to do as
much as their fathers could.   A little skill and ambition of a boy with a cradle or rake, will often surprise
a strong man, who is as awkward as a poorly trained
donkey.

SHOCKING OR STOOKING WHEAT.

" Now sheaves are slanted to the sun,
  Amid the golden meadows,
And little sun-tanned gleaners run
  To cool them in their shadows."

The "shocking manner" in which a large proportion
of the wheat of our country is stooked—and in many
instances by farmers who sustain a fair reputation for
being skilful cultivators of the soil—is one of the chief
reasons why the market is often glutted by such a large
quantity of poor and sprouted wheat, and why there is
such a serious complaint about poor bread. It is quite
as annoying and shocking to a skilful farmer, to see his
grain stooked in the awkward and perfunctory manner
that is almost universally practised, as it is to a finely
educated ear, to listen to harsh discords, when harmo-
nious sounds were promised and expected.   Were it not
for the purpose of turning the water from the grain
during showers of rain, the manner in which the
sheaves are set up in stooks would be a matter of small
account.   But, since sheaves may be stooked in such a
manner as to turn all the rain of a moderate shower, it
becomes a subject of first importance to the wheat-
grower to know how to set up the sheaves right.
There is a right way and a wrong way to shock sheaves

of grain; and it is just as easy to adopt the right way
as the wrong, when a laborer knows what is required.
An active boy can be taught, in a short time, to shock
grain so well, that the stooks will stand erect for several
weeks without leaning or tumbling over, thus exposing
the grain to storms.

When I was accustomed to work on the farm, I
shocked every sheaf of grain with my own hands, unless it was not convenient for me to be in the field; and
the result was, that I could often haul my grain to the

Fig. 39.—Setting up Sheaves.

barn, soon after a shower, while the sheaves of certain
neighbors would be wringing wet to the middle; and
many of them would have to be unbound and spread

out before they could be dried. That was because the sheaves were stooked in such a shocking and perfunctory manner. Since shocking grain in a proper manner is a subject of such eminent importance, I deem it proper to lay down the details in the manipulations of putting sheaves in stooks.

How to Handle Sheaves.

When a laborer is carrying sheaves to the place where a stook is to be a made, he should either take hold of the band, or grasp a large handful of the straw near the band. But when the sheaves are to be set up, especially when long shocks or stooks are to be made, each hand should grasp a sheaf as represented by the preceding illustration (Fig. 59). Then the two sheaves should be set down at one thrust, with the tops leaning toward each other sufficiently to settle toward each other. If one sheaf stands erect, and the other leans against it, both will soon fall to the ground.

The accompanying representation of a stook of wheat put up as thousands of laborers shock grain, shows what a complete rain-catcher such a shock of grain is. Look at it! The sprawling tops will not turn rain any better than a binder's old straw hat, when placed bottom-side upward in a hard rain-storm. The gavels were unskilfully made; the binding was only half done; and the sheaves were shocked in a most shocking manner, so that every

Fig. 60.—Badly Shocked.

drop of rain that falls within the area of such wide-spreading sheaves, will be conveyed by the straws down into the middle of the bundles. Look at the cap-sheaf! How much water will that conduct off the sheaves beneath it? Not a single drop. Water always runs down hill. The manner in which that cap-sheaf is put on the stook, will be the means of collecting most of the rain that falls on it, and conveying it toward the band—down hill—and thus down into the sheaves beneath it. Those sprawling tops of sheaves should be gathered into a smaller compass, and placed beneath the straw of the cap-sheaf, which should be spread out so as to carry the rain beyond the sheaves.

The representation of a shock of wheat herewith given (Fig. 61), shows as nearly as is practicable how to stook wheat neatly, so as to turn off most of the rain. There are two cap-sheaves spread out on the tops of the bundles which are set on the buts. My own practice has always been to set about ten sheaves together, in a round and snug compass, and crown them with two caps instead of one, as shown by

FIG. 61.—Neatly Shocked.

the illustration, Fig. 61. Yet the cap-sheaf in this figure is not represented with the tops and butts spread as much as they ought to be. It is extremely difficult to show every important point on paper. But the reader should understand, that it is important to have the straw spread all over the top of the standing sheaves, so that they will conduct the rain to the outside of the stook.

SINGLE-CAPPED STOOKS.

A great many wheat-growers set their sheaves in round stooks; and cap them with only one sheaf, as represented by the accompanying figure 62 of a shock of wheat. But I never approved of this mode of stooking sheaves of any kind; because more skill is required to put on the cap-sheaf, than is necessary when two cap-sheaves are employed, as shown in a preceding figure. In this

FIG. 62.—Round Shock of Wheat.

style of stooking grain, one of the largest sheaves is selected for the cap, and placed with the butts upward. During a heavy shower of rain, that large butt-end of the cap-sheaf will catch, in some instances, more than a gallon of water, all of which will be conducted down into the sheaf, and much of it will pass down among the grain beneath the cap; whereas, the rain that falls on a stook having two cap-sheaves, like the shock on a preceding page, will nearly all be conveyed off the grain to the ground.

Although I prefer making stooks with two caps, still I will pen directions to enable a beginner to shock his grain neatly, with one cap-sheaf.

The number of sheaves in a stook, will depend in a great degree, on the size of the bundles and the length of the straw. My practice always was, when making stooks without assistance, to set up the largest sheaf perpendicularly for the middle of the shock; and then, set eight more sheaves around it, being careful to lean them all a trifle toward the middle sheaf. When setting up the outside sheaves, one hand must support the middle sheaf from being thrust from its perpendicular position, until sheaves have been placed on the opposite side. After the circle is complete, as shown by the accompanying diagram of stars, gather in all the spreading straws and lopping bunches of grain, and form a snug round top. Then, having previously chosen the sheaf having the longest and straightest straw, loosen the band, hold the ends with one hand, and chuck the bundle down on the ground, butt-end first, and bind it again with the band about eight to twelve inches from the butt-end of the sheaf. Now place the sheaf again on the butt-end, and break the straw down horizontally in every direction from the centre of the sheaf. Then place this cap on the stook as represented by the illustration on page 376.

For the purpose of corroborating the excellence of this mode of shocking grain, I copy the notes of J. J. Thomas, of the "Cultivator and Country Gentleman," who writes: "Two years since, when the wheat was almost universally injured or spoiled by rains during harvest, the only exception which we met with was a field belonging to an extensive farmer, the wheat of which was cut *early*—a week before the common time—and well secured in shocks, like that shown in the preceding figure. The grain thus secured remained in the field uninjured through all the rains, and ripened into excellent bright, plump wheat; while all the other fields of this farmer, and all the wheat of his neighbors, were nearly ruined. We will describe a systematic method which we have practised for many years, and *know* that it operates well:

"1. Grain should be firmly bound in smaller sheaves than it is almost universally bound. Loosely bound sheaves cannot be well shocked ; they also admit more rain than tightly bound ones.

"2. Two men can shock better and more advantageously than one.

"3. Let the shocker always take two sheaves at a time, holding them with his elbow against his side, bringing the heads together with hands well spread upon them. Lift them as high as possible, bringing them with force, in as nearly a perpendicular position as can be, to the ground. Never make the second *thrust*, if the sheaves stand erect, for every one after the first, by breaking the butts, makes the matter worse.

"4. Let two persons bring down *two sheaves each at the same time*, as described above, being extremely careful to keep them perpendicular. The form * * * of shock at this period, may be represented * * * thus :

"5. As lastly stated, two more each, thus : * * The reader will perceive we now have ten * * sheaves, forming a circle as nearly as can be. * * * *

"6. While one man presses the head of the * * shock firmly together, let the other *break*, not bend, the *two* cap sheaves, and place them on well-spreading heads and butts.

"The main points are, to have grain *well bound*, sheaves to be stood in an *erect position*, and then put cap-sheaves on *firmly*, and every gust of wind will not demolish your work." Let boys, and awkward men also, observe these directions, till they can shock grain neatly.

How to Make Long Shocks.

When sheaves of any kind are set up in long shocks, the stooks should stand north and south, rather than in any other direction, so that the sun may shine on one side in the former part of the day, and on the opposite side in the afternoon. If the stooks be set up in an east and west direction, the north side of the sheaves get the benefit of very little sunshine, while the south side receives more than an equal proportion.

When those laborers who cannot set up sheaves satisfactorily, carry the bundles together, they should be taught to lay the sheaves in two rows, tops toward each other, with about three feet space between the heads. Then, the operator takes a sheaf in each hand, and chucks them down on the butts, *once only*, on the ground, with the tops leaning inward only a little. The sheaves should not lean as far as the rafters of a house. After they have been set down, press the tops together. Then set up two more sheaves, close to the first pair; and then two more; and so on, until the shock is finished. If a sheaf is chucked down more than once, the butts will be broken and bent around in various directions; and the sheaves will not maintain their erect position so well as they will when jammed down only once. Long shocks may be made of any desired length. But great care should be exercised, that the sheaves do not lean lengthways of the stook. If they be set up correctly, they will stand erect as long as it is desirable to allow the grain to remain in the field. Whether the sheaves be set up in long shocks or in round shocks, a sheaf should never be jammed down on the ground more than once, if we would have it stand up well.

WOODEN GRAIN AND HAY CAPS.

The accompanying illustration represents a shock of
wheat covered with wooden caps, which may be made
at a cheap rate, when lumber and labor are cheap.
They may be made in the following manner: Saw out
a lot of sticks of hard wood, four feet long and one and
a quarter inches square. These are to be employed as
a ridge pole to a barn roof. Select wide shingles, season them thoroughly in the sunshine, until the wood
will not shrink any more; then joint the edges and nail

FIG. 63.—Wooden Grain Caps.

the butts to the miniature ridge-pole. Such a roof will
cover a cock of hay of large size, or a shock of wheat,
keeping it dry through any storm. The only question
is, whether they will not be too costly, and inconvenient
to handle. But tapering shingles would be lighter than
shingles of uniform thickness. Thin boards of bass-
wood, whitewood, or pine, not more than one-fourth of
an inch thick, would subserve quite as good purpose as
wide shingles. Such caps could be carried to and from
the field in a wagon; and packed in a small compass
in a "nest," like wooden bowls. It would be necessary

to make the tops of the cocks of such shape that the wooden caps would fit well, and not be blown off, even by high winds. At times, where there is but little to do, such caps might be made and painted with coal tar, to prevent the shingles shrinking and swelling by the action of showers and sunshine.

If four feet in length should not be of the right length, they can be made five or six feet long; and several caps can be put on a long shock.

CLOTH GRAIN CAPS—HOW TO MAKE THEM.

As there is so much uncertainty about having fair weather during the days of harvest, grain caps, or hay caps, for covering shocks of grain in stormy weather, seem to be almost an indispensable requisite to successful agriculture. Indeed, I think that grain caps are far more important than a mowing-machine, or a reaper. If I could have but one of the two, I should consider it most economical to purchase a hundred dollars' worth of hay caps, rather than a mower and reaper. The chief reason why they have not been introduced more generally is, the expense of procuring the material for making them. Besides this, few farmers really understand and appreciate the eminent value and advantage of such appendages. I think, that if a farmer who has been accustomed to secure his crops without grain caps, will employ them during a wet season, he would ever after be unwilling to dispense with their use. When a farmer has a crop of grain ready to be garnered, and the clouds pour down torrents of rain, so that every sheaf would be wet through and through, and many of them have to be unbound before the grain could be dried, I cannot describe the feeling of transcendent satisfaction which that farmer experiences, when he goes to his fields after a heavy rain has fallen, and finds every sheaf dry enough to cart to the barn! On the contrary, witness the woe-begone countenance of him who fore-sees the hard labor of drying his wet sheaves; and who grieves over the large quantity of sprouted grain, per-haps wheat for his family!

In localities where long and heavy storms of rain are apt to prevail during the haying and harvest season, every farmer ought to prepare a good supply of hay caps, not only for protecting his hay while it is in cock, but for protecting his cereal grain, and Indian corn-stalks, when they are in the shock. Such caps will often pay for themselves, in a single season, in protect-ing hay only. But, after the hay has been gathered, they will be found quite as serviceable for protecting barley, wheat, and oats. That farmer who has never used them has no correct idea of the great advantage of hay caps, both in making hay and in protecting grain from rain.

If, for example, one has a lot of hay that is ready to go into the mow or stack when a heavy rain is at hand,

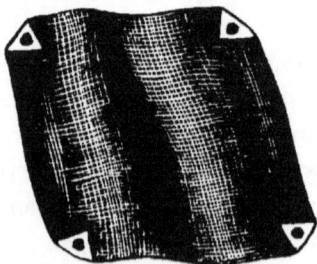

Fig. 64.—Cloth Grain-Cap.

he can put on his caps in a short time, and his hay or grain will receive no dam-age. Then, as soon as the storm is over he can re-move his caps, and go to work immediately at his grain or hay. On the con-trary, had it not been for the protection of his caps, the damage done to his hay or grain might have been more than equal to the value of the caps.

I have examined various ways of making hay-caps, and among them all I can recommend the following mode of making them as the most convenient to handle: Procure common sheeting, or bed-ticking, or any kind of cloth, one yard or two yards wide, and make the caps about six feet square; let the rough edges be hemmed. Now turn up each corner about three inches, and sew them down tightly. Work a small eyelet-hole near each corner, like Fig. 64, for the wooden pins to go through into the hay. The pins may be made of any hard, straight-grained wood, about sixteen inches long. These pins can be made the most expeditiously by sawing off a log of green timber, and split it out, as one would rive out staves. Then shave them, so that they will be about half an inch round at the large end, with a knob on one end, and pointed at the other end. The neatest way would be, to have the pins turned, like the illustration here given.

Fig. 65.
Grain-Cap
Pin.

PAINTING GRAIN-CAPS.

Some people paint their caps; but this renders the cloth rotten, and very stiff. But unless the cloth is very good, they will not turn the rain during a very heavy shower, if the cloth is not painted. Others have saturated the caps with a solution of alum, and some quicklime; but I cannot recommend this preparation. Yet the following preparation I can endorse, even for rather poor cloth. If the caps are made of heavy bed-ticking they will not let the rain through, should it rain a week or more, even if they have not been smeared with any preparation :

Make a paint of three parts of coal-tar and one part of benzole, or benzine, or spirits of turpentine, and apply it to the cloth, in hot weather, and you will have caps that will last as long as one man will need them.

The most expeditious way to put the caps on a cock of hay or stook of grain is, let two men throw a cap over the top, and draw it down, both together, and thrust in the pins into the eyelet-holes, with the points a little upward. Weights in each corner of the caps will hold them well; but they are said to be very heavy to carry around, as one hundred caps must necessarily weigh some six or eight hundred pounds. The editor of the "Cultivator and Country Gentleman" says: "We experimented this season on this modern protect-or, and the result is, that I believe the small caps of three feet square are comparatively useless—those one and a half yards square the best size. Those not oiled did not keep out the wet effectually, but those dipped in boiled oil repelled the rain of nearly a week's duration, so as to require but an hour's airing of the cocks to fit them for drawing. The stones sewed in the corners will, I think, be abandoned on trial, as they make them too heavy to move in quantities; besides proving inadequate in a brisk breeze to retain them in their place; while pegs not only hold them on, but also spike the hay from caking off the top, as it sometimes does, cap, stones, and all. When weights are employed at the corners of caps, one pound, at least, at a corner, will be as light as the weights should be made."

More about Grain or Hay-Caps.

Hay-caps are sometimes made four feet square, having a wooden pin fastened in the middle of each cap, which pin is thrust into the top of each cock. Then, there are pins fastened to small cords at each of the four corners. But the centre pin is of little use, while it increases the expense; and four feet square is quite too small, to protect cocks of an ordinary size; or, to protect shocks of grain.

Experience teaches, that caps will usually be more convenient, when they are made with eyelet-holes at each corner, for receiving the pins, than when the pins are fastened to the middle. When they are made as recommended, the pins can be carried in a basket, and the caps in a large roll, very conveniently; and if the holes be made at the corners, the caps can be used to cover a stack with; whereas, they could not be so employed, when the pins are fastened to the corners with cords. The caps should all be made of a uniform size; and the holes should be marked out by a pattern, so that the caps will all be just alike.

Now, to protect, or shingle a long stack with caps, begin at the top, and lay one cap on one side of the stack, and another one on the opposite side; and, let a pin be thrust through a hole in the corner of four different caps on the top of the stack. Then put another course of caps below the first course, and put a pin at the corners. Round stacks cannot be covered with caps in this way. But, long stacks, and stacks that are only partly finished, which need to be protected from a shower of rain, can be covered with caps made as directed in a few minutes, so as to turn a heavy rain.

Scott's Patent Grinder.

This invention consists of a grindstone turned off true on the side, as well as on the periphery, and supported on a frame, as represented in the figure.

The grindstone is adjustable to any required angle, and the cutter bar, or knife, is securely held in the swinging frame, and placed at the proper bevel. The stone slides the whole length of the frame, and grinds each section to its proper bevel with great accuracy and facility.

Grinding Machine Knives.

Every person who has had experience in grinding the sections of mowing machines, will appreciate the value of such a device. The grinder is manufactured by Richardson & Co., Auburn, N. Y.; and has met with excellent favor wherever it has been introduced.

How to Pitch Sheaves.

There are numerous little considerations which a pitcher must understand perfectly if he would pitch sheaves easily and expeditiously. In the first place, he should have a fork and tines much straighter than for pitching hay or straw. A fork with crooked tines, and spread wide apart, is a disagreeable tool to pitch with, as the tines stick in the sheaf, and require more of an effort to withdraw them than if they were straighter, or not so much curved.

Another thing is, always thrust the fork into the sheaf astride of the band, unless the band be loose, and near one end of the sheaf. Beginners should be instructed how to take up a sheaf with a fork, and how to give it a skilful turn while it is on the fork, so that it will land in the most desirable position. An active boy of only ordinary strength, if he have skill, will pitch sheaves more satisfactorily than a strong, but awkward man.

In order to pitch off a load of sheaves easily, the pitcher should take them up in the reversed order in which they were laid down, as the sides frequently overlap each other. These suggestions, it is hoped, will be sufficient to enable beginners to aim to perform the task of pitching with a good degree of skill.

How to Load Sheaves of Wheat.

When building a load of sheaves on a wagon or cart, there are several points to be kept in mind by the loader; among which are—carrying up the sides uniformly, so that the load will ride safely to the barn or stack, and placing the sheaves in such a manner that the load may be pitched off with facility, carrying all the loose grain with the sheaves. Loading sheaves, so as to save even only a quart or more of the best of wheat at every load, is an item of importance, when the grain is worth three dollars or more per bushel. The first sheaves, when making a load, should not be thrown hap-hazard into the rigging, unless the bottom and sides are grain-tight.

But let the loader take each sheaf as it is pitched and place a course of sheaves across one end of the rigging. Then lay the tops of another course of sheaves on the ears of the preceding bundles. If the sheaves be placed in this manner they will catch all the loose grain that may be shelled out of the other sheaves. One or two courses more will be sufficient to fill the rigging. This rigging, or box, or "shelving," on which the sheaves are carted or hauled, should *not* be filled flush with the outside before the first course of sheaves is laid in the desired place. If the middle be filled even with the outside shelving, the sheaves will be apt to slide off the sides before they can be secured by a middle course. After the middle is filled, lay a large sheaf on each corner first. The object of placing a *large* sheaf on the corner is to keep the corners a trifle the highest. If the corners be carried up true there will be no difficulty in putting a load on square.

A mason, when building a brick house, always carries up his corners first, as the corners are a sure guide. A loader must do the same thing. Let the but ends of the sheaves be laid beyond the shelving, nearly to the bands which encircle them. Place the sheaves as closely together as they can be conveniently pressed. If the ground be rough, so that the sheaves are liable to be jostled out of place, lay the binding course of sheaves in the middle. When loading the *binding* or middle course of sheaves, place the tops of every alternate sheaf in the opposite direction. Select the smallest sheaves for the middle, so as to keep the outside of the load a trifle the highest. When the middle appears too full, let two courses of sheaves be laid around the outside, and only one course in the middle, as fast as the outside courses are laid. It is always better to lay the middle course of sheaves *across* the load, instead of lengthwise, because, when laid crosswise, they keep the outside courses from working outward. If a load be made unusually wide, and the middle sheaves be placed lengthwise of the wagon, upon passing over a rough or uneven way; the sheaves will slip and slide about, and half of them will fall to the ground, when not a sheaf would have moved out of its place, had the middle course been laid crosswise.

When the sheaves are short, the butts must not be laid so far beyond the shelving as when they are long. The load should be so wide that the binding course of sheaves will extend almost to the bands of the sheaves of the outside courses. In order to load sheaves well, the loader should move on his hands and knees, and place the sheaves as close together as practicable.

Another very important consideration is, to have every sheaf pitched clear from the butts of the last course of sheaves, and placed on the top of the load, as no man can make a load with true sides, when the person who pitches thrusts his fork against the last course, so as to displace the sheaves.

When a mason's hod-carrier, through lack of skill, or from heedlessness, knocks the bricks or stones out of place, after they have been laid in the wall, he hears from the "boss" in emphatic language; and he seldom repeats the careless offence. A man or boy who is loading sheaves on a wagon should watch his work as closely as a mason observes the courses of the wall which he may be building. If the foregoing directions are observed, a loader will find no difficulty in building a load that will not tumble off the wagon.

How to Mow Sheaves of Wheat.

There are two modes in vogue of mowing away
sheaves of wheat, colloquially called the "Yankee mode"
and the "Dutch fashion." When sheaves are mowed
according to the Yankee mode, a course of bundles is
laid around the outside of the mow, with the butts outward. Then another course of sheaves is laid inside
of this first course, with about half the length of the
sheaves lapping on the course beneath. The old way
is to lap the *butts* of the second course on the first course
of sheaves, and thus continue to work round and round
until one course laid in the middle covers the surface
of the mow. In some instances the *tops* of the sheaves
are lapped on the first course, instead of the butts.

Those who practise this manner of mowing their grain
aver that when the butts are placed outward, rats and
red squirrels find it more difficult to work into the middle of the mow than when the sheaves are not mowed
in the foregoing manner. But experience proves that
if such animals have access to a mow of grain, they will
destroy as much grain when one style of mowing is practised as another. When a barn is not entirely rat-proof,
or when a stack is not placed on a platform beyond the
reach of rats, it is folly to think of mowing such marauders out of the middle of a stack or mow.

The Dutch manner of mowing is to lay courses of
sheaves back and forth entirely across the mow, letting
the tops of each course overlap about half of the sheaves
of the preceding course. This manner of mowing sheaves
is decidedly preferable to the practice of laying the
courses round and round, until one sheaf will finish in
the middle of the mow. This Dutch system has every-

thing to recommend its adoption over the Yankee mode, as a much larger number of sheaves can be mowed in a given space, and they can also be mowed more conveniently; and when the sheaves are removed from the mow they can be taken up more readily than when they are mowed in the style just alluded to.

Another consideration of no little importance is to work always, except the bottom course, from the back side of the mow to the front. In practice this will be seen to be more convenient than to work from the front to the back side of the mow.

It may seem trivial to expatiate on such minor topics. But laborers who are always seeking the easiest and most expeditious way to perform every laborious operation, appreciate such little details in giving directions for saving labor. When a mow is first commenced, however, the first course should be laid on the front side of the mow, instead of the back side. The object is to save all the loose grain. If the mower begins his work on the further side of the barn, or bay, all the loose grain that falls from the sheaves, both when mowing the bundles and when pitching them off the mow, will fall to the floor. But if sheaves be mowed as directed, and be taken up, when they are pitched off, without turning them over, the loose grain will all be carried along with the sheaves, instead of being left, perhaps, where it cannot easily be collected. Every observing farmer will perceive all the advantages which have been stated, and some others also, by working from the back side of the mow to the front side, after the bottom has been covered with one course of sheaves.

One suggestion further, which few persons ever think of, is this: The mow, for example, is forty feet long.

17

The sheaves are pitched on one side, near the middle. It will be easier for both the mower and the man who pitches the sheaves to the mower, if he will work from each end toward the middle of the mow, instead of mowing from the middle to the end of the course of sheaves. The advantages will be perceived as soon as these directions are observed. The mower should always work toward the pitcher. The man who pitches can make very hard work for a mower by throwing the sheaves wrong end first; or he can facilitate the labor of mowing, simply by the exercise of a little skill in turning the bundles as he pitches them, so that every one will fall directly before the mower, with the heads where they should be.

In order to mow sheaves neatly, and thus be able to get as much grain as possible into a given space, the mower should move on his hands and knees, placing the sheaves as closely together as they can be crowded. Sometimes sheaves can be kept closer to each other by placing a sheaf say ten inches distant from the one beneath the knees of the mower, and then by crowding another bundle between two sheaves and placing the knees on it. By adopting this method a much larger amount of grain can be mowed in a given space than if the sheaves be put in the mow in a perfunctory manner. When barn room is scarce, it is important to know how to make a limited amount of space subserve a given purpose.

The Cayuga-Chief Reaper.

The Cayuga-Chief represented by the cut is a combined two-wheeled machine. It can be changed in a few moments from a mower to a reaper. The cutter-

Fig. 66.—The Cayuga-Chief Reaper.

bar can be set to cut any desired height. The platform and cutters can be adjusted to any angle desired, for the more perfect cutting and easy delivery of lodged as well as standing grain.

The raker's seat is comfortably and conveniently located, and can be adjusted so as to enable the operator to sit in any position he may desire. Many farmers, when using this machine, drive the team and handle the rake at the same time.

The grain is delivered at the side of the swath, giving abundant room for the team and machine between the gavels and the standing grain.

The reel is overhung and driven so as to operate properly at all times. As a harvester, the drive-wheels have a bearing surface of sixteen inches; and the weight is so distributed that the machine will operate successfully on very soft ground. When mowing or reaping, this machine turns as easily as a cart, cutting square corners without any backing of the team, being supported on its own wheels, and balanced independently of the tongue. The raker's seat and platform preserve their proper relations to each other, and the injurious and annoying vibrations experienced in machines balanced by the tongue are prevented.

The best evidence of the success and popularity of this machine is found in the fact that upwards of twenty thousand are now in use throughout the United States.

The Cayuga Chief Manufacturing Company at Auburn, New York, manufacture two sizes of this machine as combined hand and self rake reapers and mowers, and a smaller size.

Mr. C. Wheeler, Jr., the president of the company, a practical farmer and mechanic, is the inventor of the machine; and he makes it his sole business to study and experiment for the "Chief," and keep it fully up in all respects with the improvements of the times. I am assured by this company, that they are taking especial pains in the selection of material for their machines, so that farmers have the assurance that the Cayuga Chief machines will be unsurpassed for *strength of material, workmanship, perfection of finish, and durability.* They say, that they intend that the "Cayuga Chief" shall, hereafter, excel all others in *mechanism and excellent material,* as it has heretofore done in its *combinations of valuable principles.* I can say from personal knowledge of the Cayuga Chief for several years, that I can confidently recommend it to farmers who desire a good mower and reaper. Mr. Wheeler has expended a fortune in bringing the "Chief" to its present state of perfection; and the brain-labor expended, from first to last, in originating, improving, and perfecting the various parts, is truly wonderful to contemplate.

STACKING SHEAVES OF WHEAT.

It requires the combined knowledge of an intelligent practical farmer, a natural philosopher, and the constructive skill of an architect to build a good stack. The chief object to be kept in view is, to place the sheaves so that the straws will conduct the water off the stack. Let me illustrate the idea more plainly: Let a shed be covered with rails, or poles, laid horizontally, as a roof; and, when it rains, all the water will pass down between them; but elevate one end of the same poles to an angle of forty-five degrees, and they will convey nearly all the rain that falls on them, to the lower end.

Straws of wheat represent poles. When the sheaves lie horizontally, the rain will pass readily down between the straws. But elevate one end of the sheaf to the above-mentioned angle, and the straws on the upper side will carry off nearly all the water. Very little of it will find its way into the sheaf. Water always flows down hill.

The Foundation of Stacks.

The first thing in building a stack is, a suitable foundation to keep the dampness from injuring the grain. When rails or poles can be obtained conveniently, they will subserve an excellent purpose. A good foundation may be readily made of plank, by placing four planks on their edges, with other planks or boards resting on these for the stack. A stack should always be so high from the ground that dogs and cats can go under them. This will give a circulation of air under the stack, and the cats a chance to keep it free from mice, rats, gophers, etc. At any rate there must be a foundation of wood sufficient to keep the grain from acquiring moisture from the earth. This done, it is always a good practice to make a round stack about a pole set firmly in the ground. This will keep it erect when it is settling. When making a round stack, where there is no pole in the middle, it will always be found advantageous to stick a fork at the middle, keeping it there as the stack is carried up. Then a stacker can always judge whether he is carrying up the sides true.

How to Place the Sheaves.

In building a stack of any kind, there are two points of great importance to be observed. The first is to

carry up a stack true ; and the next is to place the sheaves
or material in the best position to carry off the rain.
Always begin in the middle to lay the first course of
sheaves. Set a centre pole firmly in the ground, and
brace it securely on four sides. The braces will not
interfere with the stacking. Now set up sheaves around
the centre pole, letting them all lean toward the centre. Place a pole against the centre pole, and carry
the other end entirely around the outside of the stack-
bottom, in order to have the last course of sheaves on
every side of the pole at a uniform distance from the
centre pole.

When the bottom course of sheaves is laid, lay another course on the outer side ; and if the circumference
seems too low, lay two courses of sheaves, one above
the other, and tread them down firmly. Now lay
another course on the inside of the first one, letting the
butts lap on the tops of the outside course, almost to
the bands. The butts should never extend beyond the
bands. Keep the stack nearly level, until it is carried
up to the top of the bilge. The middle should be kept
full, and a few inches higher than the outside ; and the
sheaves should be well trod down. If the middle
be kept much higher than the outside, before the stack
is built as high as the bilge, the outside course of
sheaves will continue to work outward, and the stack
will spread faster than it is desired to have it. The
outside course of sheaves should be placed as close
together as they can be, to prevent large holes in the
outside, where rain will find its way into the sheaves beneath. To prevent the sheaves slipping outward, elevate the top end of every bundle when placing it, as
the stacker is represented as doing, in the figure ; and

thrust the butts on the underside into the course below
it. When they are simply laid down without this secu-
rity, the courses are very liable to slide off. This is one

Fig. 67.—Stacking Wheat.

of the manipulations in stacking that but comparatively
few understand. I have seen half a wagon-load of
sheaves slide at once from the side of a stack built by a
man who was ignorant of this part of stacking. As the
straw of barley and cornstalks is very slippery, it is

difficult to keep the courses from sliding, unless the butts of every sheaf are secured in this way.

To Prevent a Stack from Leaning.

A common and effectual way is to build a stack around a tree. Then it must settle evenly; and maintain an erect position. Another way worthy of adoption is, to set a stiff pole in the ground; and brace it firmly, on four sides, as previously alluded to. This will be as effectual as a tree. If the pole be set two feet in the ground, and the soil be well rammed around it; and braces four feet long be nailed to the pole at the upper ends; and if the lower ends be secured at the surface of the ground by a flat stake, a hurricane would not disturb a stack. When a long stack is made, two or three such poles should be set up. It requires but a little resistance to keep a stack erect. But, after a stack has settled over, it is no easy job to put it back to an erect position.

Bracing stacks, after they begin to lean, is often resorted to, by thrusting rails, or poles, against one side. This practice, however, is not to be commended, as poles thrust beneath the bilge of a stack, will often turn up the courses of the sheaves, so that the straws will slant toward the middle of the stack, in which position they will convey the rain inward, instead of conducting it off the stack.

Another mode of maintaining the erect position of a stack is, to brace one side, with a plank and pole, or with two planks, as represented by the braces shown in Fig. 68.

The upright plank should stand in a perpendicular position, so that the side of the stack may settle down without leaning from its erect position. The brace should be secured in its place by nailing a cleat above the upper end across the upright plank, as represented by the illustration, Fig. 68; and by driving a broad stake at the lower end of the brace. If one such brace be not sufficient, a half dozen may be placed on one side of a stack. Then, after the stack is done settling, the braces may be removed. But if the ends of braces be thrust against a stack, they cannot be taken away at pleasure.

Furthermore, when tall stacks are in danger of being blown over by a high wind, this manner of bracing them will be found more convenient and efficient than any other mode.

What Causes a Stack to Lean.

When a wheat-stack has been built as true as the form of an egg, it will sometimes settle sideways so far as to fall over unless braces are applied in time. This fact is a mystery to most persons; and they often ejaculate, inquiringly, " *What does make it lean ?* "

The prime cause must always be attributed to imperfect workmanship when building a stack. I will mention certain things that cause a stack to lean. When all the grain is pitched on the stack at one side, the heft of the sheaves and the tread of the man who pitches them to the stacker, keeps that side pressed down more compactly than the stack is on the opposite side. Of course the side that is trod down the most will settle least. The settling of the opposite side, more than the side on which the pitcher stood, causes the stack to lean.

Another cause of leaning is, the sheaves are laid out

farther on one side than they are on the opposite side. There being nothing to support the overhanging bilge, that side of the stack settles much more than the other. The consequence is, that the courses of sheaves on one side of the stack will be turned up, at the butts, to such an angle, that the rain will be conducted toward the middle of the stack instead of running off the outside. It is eminently important, that the straws on the outside courses of the stack, should always be so inclined downward, that they will conduct the rain outward, from straw to straw, until the water will all flow off the bilge of the stack.

How to Top Off a Stack.

If the stack is being built of sheaves, the middle must be kept so full that there will be a good inclination of the straw in the butts of the bundles. This is always a much better guide than to attempt to keep the middle of the stack at a certain height above the outside. The stacker should move on his knees, as already stated on a previous page; and, in order to keep the sheaves close together as they can be conveniently, he should lay each sheaf partly on the side of the one last laid; and as it is pressed down with the knees, hold it from slipping with both hands. By this means a much larger number of bundles may be secured in a smaller compass than otherwise. If the straws only have a suitable inclination to carry the water outward, instead of toward the middle of the stack, rain will injure but a small portion of either straw or grain. If one side of a stack should be lower than the other, it may usually be carried up even, by using the large sheaves for the lower,

and the smaller ones for the higher side.   This onesided-
ness should be guarded against before the stack has
become onesided.   The straightest and handsomest bundles should be placed in the outside course, for the
purpose of keeping the stack of the correct shape, as
well as carrying off the rain better, than tangled bundles, which should form the inside courses, whenever
there is any difference in the sheaves.   If it is necessary
to have a man or boy stand on the stack to pitch the

FIG. 68.—A Stack Braced, to Prevent Leaning.

sheaves to the stacker, he should always remain as near
the middle as practicable, and not travel about so as
to displace the sheaves, after the stacker has left them.
Keep the middle full, the form circular, and draw the
courses in gradually.   When the stack is not built
around a pole, sharpen a small rail or scantling, and set
it erect at the centre, by thrusting it in, two or three
feet, so that it will stand while the top is built around
it.   As the area of the top of the stack diminishes, con-

tinue to place the sheaves more erect, until the straws
the last course incline at an angle of about forty-five
degrees. Bind the tops of these securely to the pole.
Then make a large bundle of long rye straw, wet it
thoroughly, so that it will keep in place better; and having bound it with one band, at about one-third the distance from the top to the butts, slip it down over the top
of the stake, and bind the top with several bands, as
represented in the illustration. Spread out the butts
evenly, and rake them down straight. A stack made
according to the foregoing directions will turn heavy
showers almost as well as a shingle roof, and the water
will all fall clear of the bottom of the stack

FURTHER SUGGESTIONS ABOUT STACKING.

A writer in the "Wisconsin Farmer" recorded the
following suggestions about building stacks:

"In the Eastern and Middle States very little grain,
or even hay, is stacked out. In those regions, it is regarded as shiftless for a farmer not to have barn-room
enough to cover all his crops. The sentiment probably
grew, in part, out of the old method of thrashing all
the grain out by the flail, which required a barn-floor
and high guards on either side, to keep the grain from
flying over and wasting; and partly from the small cost
of barns in early times.

"But most of our farmers are from the East, and
never learned to build a stack, to do which, or to make
an axe helve, requires either a man of genius, or a good
deal of training. But the less a man knows about either,
the more apt he is to *think* he can do it first rate; and
the consequence is, that large quantities of grain are

spoiled every year by bad stacking, especially of wheat.
A farmer should never attempt to stack his own grain
unless he is sure he knows how; and he can never be
sure of that until he has a vivid recollection of the time
when he *did not* know how. In Great Britain it has
long been the custom to secure grain in stacks; and they
have brought the art to a great deal of perfection; and
every farmer who has not learned the art himself, should
secure the services of some English, Welsh, or Scotch
farmer to do that job for him until he has thoroughly
acquired the art himself.

"A man may understand something about the theory
of stacking without being an adept in the business.
Building a stack correctly can only be acquired by practice under the eye of a competent instructor. But the
theory is useful, if for nothing but to enable the farmer
to know when he has found a competent practical man.
This theory, as we have seen it practised by English-
men, is substantially as follows:"

Topping Out a Stack.

"When laying sheaves above the bilge of a stack, the
same writer says, commence in the centre by setting
up sheaves as for a round shock, adding course upon
course, setting the butts of each succeeding course a
little more out, so as to have the outside course at
about the angle of a quarter-pitch roof, being careful to force the butts down on the next course so they
will not slip and flatten down as weight is added. Let
this last or outside course, in working from the centre,
serve as the first course in the layer which you
make back to the centre, laying the butts of the next

course about even with the bands of the course under it, and thrusting the butts of each bundle, as you lay it, into the bundle under it, to prevent its slipping outward by pressure. Go round with a single course, keeping your work before you and pressing down the bundles with your knees. Then lay another course in the same manner, lapping at the same place, and so on till you get to the centre. Then commence again at the outside, leaving the butts of the first course even with those of the lower course, or projecting a little over, being careful as before to catch the butts of the new course into the lower one, and work inward as before. The outside should be as little pressed as convenient, in building, and the inside packed as close as possible, so that the pitch of the bundles outward will be increased rather than diminished as the stack settles. If the heads of the bundles do not keep up the pitch of the sheaves equal to that of an ordinary roof, when above the bilge of the stack, put in extra sheaves, in any way which will keep the surface regular in form.

"The butts of each outside course should project a little over the course below it until you are ready to draw in, so that the stack, when done, will have the shape of a hen's egg, a little flattened at the large end. A little marsh hay makes a good cap, which should be secured against the winds by ropes made of the same, placed over the top and held by weights at the sides. When you see a man build a stack in this way, you may know he understands his business; but do not imagine you can do it yourself at the first or second trial." I have given these rather tautological directions, in the stacker's own language, that beginners may understand them the better.

Dodge's Ohio and Buckeye Reaper and Self-Raker.

FIG. 69.

The beautiful illustration on this page represents an excellent combined mower and reaper, made by Dodge & Stevenson Manufacturing Company, Auburn, New York. This machine is a neat mower, and can be rigged for harvesting in a few minutes. Large numbers of this style of mowers and reapers have been manufactured; and wherever they were introduced, farmers have been well satisfied with their operations. The workmanship is of a superior character; the draft is light; material is good and durable; and the machine is well adapted to all kinds of work. The self-raker consists of four independent rakes, so constructed as to allow all of them to be in use for reeling on the grain, or, by a slight movement of the hand or foot, causing either rake to rake off the cut grain, in any sized gavels required.

WARNER'S SULKY RAKE.

This wooden rake combines all the advantages of both the Sulky and Old Revolving Rakes. By means

FIG. 70.—Sulky Rake.

of the lever with its cams and stops, the driver has more perfect control over the rake than can possibly be had over the old-fashioned revolver. It does not dust the hay as wire teeth usually do; is easily handled by a boy; and the inclination of the teeth is easily regulated, so as to pass over any obstacle, or dip into a

swale.   The draw-bars are jointed, so that the rake can
be folded up, upon the sulky, and thus be easily transported.   This rake is made by H. N. Tracy, Essex Junc-
tion, Vermont ; by Blymyer, Day & Co., Mansfield,
Ohio ; and Blymyer, Norton & Co., Cincinnati, Ohio.

ALDEN'S WHEEL RAKE.

The illustration herewith given (Fig. 71), represents
an excellent spring-tooth rake, which I can recommend

FIG. 71.—Alden's Wheel Rake.

as being a valuable, labor-saving implement.   The cut
furnishes such a correct idea of it, that I shall give no

description of it.   M. Alden & Co., Auburn, New York, are the only manufacturers that I know of.

THE BUCKEYE MOWER AND REAPER.

The illustration accompanying these notes represents the celebrated Buckeye Harvester with the self-raker attachment, which is very light, simple, and compact, its weight being no greater than that of an ordinary hand-rake attachment. It does not interfere in the slightest degree with the simplicity of the machine as a mower, and is very readily and easily attached and detached. The following is the description of the Self-Raker given in the official report of the great Auburn trial, when the Buckeye won such world-wide fame:

"A disk with four joints carries four rakes or sweeps with rollers at right angles, which work in inclined ways, with a switch, which makes them act as beaters or rakes at pleasure. The rake-teeth drop down nearly to a level with the guards to catch lodged grain, and pass over a rake-guard, to prevent the teeth from springing down on the guards in rough ground, the rake rising quickly afterward. The inclined ways are adjustable, to give different motions to the rake. The ability which this arrangement gives to the machine, to cut long or short grain with equal facility, without making tedious adjustments, constitutes its greatest merit. It will deliver the gavels in regular intervals of space when the grain stands equal in height and thickness, or the rakes may be regulated by the hand or foot of the driver so as to deliver any size of gavels that may be desired, or by fastening the switch open, it will deliver the grain in swath. It has cleaners hinged so as to brush back the grain which collects on the dividers while acting as reels, leaving it in good shape for the rake to deliver."

The "Buckeye" is still manufactured by Adriance, Platt & Co., 165 Greenwich street, New York city; and the best thing I can record for this reaper and self-raker is to mention the fact that, after having been put to the most severe tests in mowing and harvesting heavy and tangled grass and grain, it was driven into a field of heavy rye, which was seven feet high, and every part, self-rake and all, worked as beautifully as a lawn mower. The "Buckeye" needs no words of commendation from my pen. American farmers are familiar with its worthy record.

The Montgomery Fork.

I give an illustration of this celebrated fork, made by the Montgomery Fork Company, 254 Pearl street, New

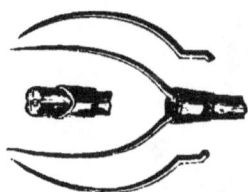

Fig. 78.—The Montgomery Fork.

York city, because it is just such a fork as farmers will find to please them. The illustration shows how the tines are secured to the handle. Some of the merits of this fork are these : In case a tine breaks, another can be replaced instantly at a trifling cost, and without loss of time. In repairing one tine of a common fork, the other tine is invariably spoiled, rendering the fork good for nothing. Should the handle break, the tines can be refitted to another handle in a few minutes. The handle is not tapered at the end near the fork ; but, the whole strength of the wood is left ; and when the ferrule is in its place it binds the whole together, as if one solid substance. The process of manufacture gives a more uniform texture of steel than can be produced by any other method. The weight is no more than the common fork. The tines are warranted not to work loose. This fork took the first premium at the New York State Fair at Buffalo, 1867.

CHAPTER V.

MILDEW IN WHEAT.

THERE have been volumes penned about mildew in wheat, and other plants; but I am sorry to be obliged

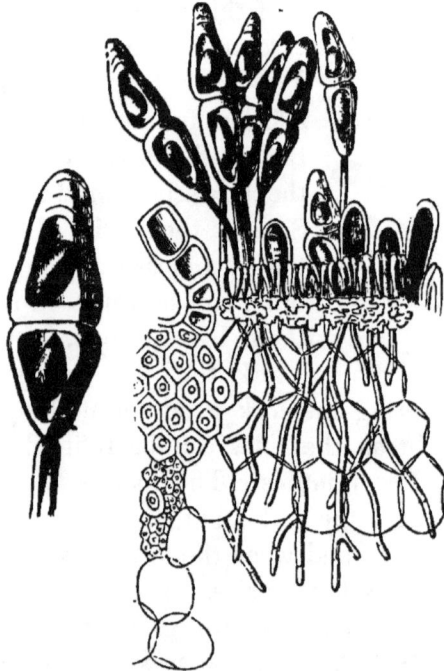

FIG. 74.—Mildew in Wheat.

to record that, after all that has been said, we know very little about it. In order to give wheat-growers something of an idea of mildew, I herewith furnish an illustration (Fig. 74), which represents the mildew of wheat, greatly magnified. To the naked eye these beautiful fungi seem more like the minute particles of dust on a miller's hat, than anything else.

To the practical wheat grower the great question is: *What is mildew? what causes it?* and, *what is the remedy?*

I answer in brief: Mildew is a disease of the growing wheat. The plants are covered with a white substance, which is made up of minute fungi, which appear in spots on the straw. These parasites, represented by Fig. 74, are minute plants, growing on the wheat plant, and extracting the juices that should be appropriated to the development of the grain. After reading scores of pages about mildew, in which various plausible theories are broached by one author, and the same theories controverted by another author of equally reliable authority, I have to again acknowledge that we know little about the cause, or the remedy.

By referring again to Fig. 74, it may be seen, that the ends of the delicate creeping threads bear *spores*, or *sporules*,

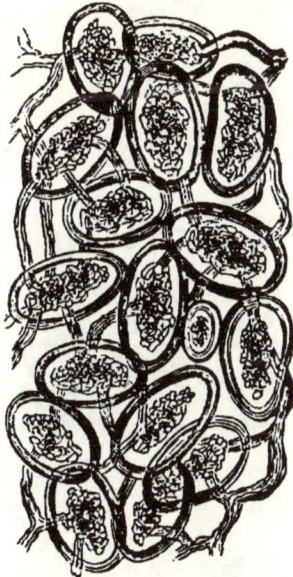

Fig. 75.—Rust magnified.

which fall off, and fly like dust, in the air. Sometimes these spores form quite a little cloud. Strange as it may appear, these infinitesimally small particles of dust are seeds, so to speak, from which millions of plants spring. The spores are borne along in the wind, among the growing wheat; and wherever the straw is not perfectly healthy, and able to resist the attacks of such parasitic fungus, the seeds adhere to the diseased leaves and stems, germinate, grow, and tend to destroy the crop.

There are many kinds of mildew and rust, which originate from spores. Fig. 75 represents a magnified view of a small portion of what is scientifically called *uredo rubigo vera*, in which the spores are represented with a sort of basket-work extending from one to another.

SMUT IN WHEAT.

The illustration herewith given (Fig. 76) represents a magnified view of what is scientifically known as *uredo caries*, which is common to wheat; and seldom attacks any other cereal plant. The dark-colored excrescences represent the spores or seeds of the uredo caries. Unlike other maladies, this one takes its origin in the interior juices of the wheat plant; and affects the kernels, instead of the straw. The pericarp of the kernels of wheat contains a black material, greasy to the touch, instead of flour. The dust of caries, unlike that of smut, emits an unpleasant odor; and the nauseous smell is sometimes perceived in wheat bread. The semeniform grains of the caries (Fig. 76) attach them-

Fig. 76.—Smut magnified.

selves to the minute hairs that are usually seen with the naked eye on kernels of wheat. Machinery will seldom remove these spores. Therefore, their removal must be effected by soaking the grain, and applying some chemical substance, that will decompose the sporules, without injuring the germs of the kernels of wheat. Those spores adhering to the sound grains at the time of sowing, remain in that state, till the young plant starts its growth, when they are supposed to enter the spongioles of the roots of the young plant; and, with the ascending sap, are propelled through the tissues of the plant, till they reach the young ovum, where they find a suitable place for vegetation, rendering fecundation impossible. Yet the grains continue to swell; and when harvest comes, they are perhaps larger than the healthy ones; and curiously enough, the stigmata of the flowers are not destroyed.

Pickling Seed Wheat.

In this important operation the science of chemistry affords the practical wheat-grower important aid. We have seen, on the two preceding pages, how smut or "bunt" is propagated. The object now is to destroy it. The basis of all pickling or dressing consists in converting the greasy, oily sporules which adhere to the sound grains into a soap, which facilitates their removal.

Sulphate of copper (blue vitriol) is sometimes employed for pickling wheat, in the following manner: Four pounds of the vitriol should be dissolved in about two gallons of boiling water; and when fully dissolved, placed in a large tub—an old hogshead cut through the middle answers the purpose very well; and add about

18

twenty gallons of cold water. Procure a wicker basket, of suitable shape to go into the tub, large and strong enough to hold a bushel and a half of wheat. Place the basket in the liquid, and gently pour into it the wheat. By adopting this precaution, the light and imperfect grains, chaff, or small seed will float at the top; and may be skimmed off the surface. Having proceeded thus far, lift the basket, and allow it to drain over the tub. Empty the same, and proceed with the next lot.

While the seed is soaking, let it be stirred with a stick, for a few minutes. By this means, all the light and imperfect kernels may be worked to the surface, and skimmed off the surface of the water. For each four or five bushels of wheat, dissolve one pound of blue vitriol in water sufficient to cover and properly soak the wheat. Some farmers say, let it remain in this soak twenty to twenty-four hours, and sow immediately after taken out of the soak. But there is great danger of soaking the seed too long. It requires but a short time to destroy the sporules of smut. So soon as the spores are destroyed, the seed should be removed from the soak, or steep. The seed should not be kept in the liquid long enough to moisten the germs. The main point is to remove the material that adheres to the exterior of the kernels. Spread the wet seed on a floor, and sift lime, or gypsum, or ashes over the surface; and rake it in. This will render the seed dry, so that it can be sowed, or drilled in, without difficulty.

A North Carolina farmer says, that the best preventive of *smut* is, to make a brine strong enough to bear an egg; pour this as hot as the hand can bear into a half-barrel tub; put in half a bushel of the wheat you are about to sow; stir it up well in the tub; let it settle two or three minutes; skim off all the light grain and chaff that rises to the top; stir it up again; repeat skimming; then pour off the brine, which can be warmed again, and used for another lot of wheat. Now spread the wheat on clean boards or a cloth in the sun, or on the barn floor, or any convenient place. Take slacked lime and sift enough over the brined wheat to cover it well; and as soon as dry, put it into a bag or basket for sowing. Some farmers damp the wheat in a heap on the floor, and mix up two or three quarts of lime with it, and then spread it out upon boards. If in the sun, it will dry in half an hour; if in the shade, it sometimes takes two or three hours. But, let no man suppose that his crop will be safe from smut, unless he has first secured a hardy variety of wheat, as laid down in another part of this book. Various preparations of vitriol, nitre, sulphur, and arsenic have been tried, in some instances, with considerable benefit. Our agricultural papers and books are full of directions for the treatment of seed wheat. But let the reader beware of puerile experiments with his seed, such as he will find recorded on page 318.

Experiments with Smut in Wheat.

For the purpose of determining the influence of smut on sown grain, Mr. Bailey, of Chellingham, tried experiments on seed in which were a few balls of smut. One third of the seed was steeped in urine, and limed; one third steeped in urine, dried, and not limed; and the other third sown without steeping or liming. The result was, that the seed which had been pickled and limed, and that which was pickled and not limed, was almost free

of smut, while that which was sown without under-
going this process was much diseased.   The following
experiments were made at Lord Chesterfield's farm of
Bradly Hall, in Derbyshire : The first was on a peck of
very smutty wheat, one-half which was sown in the
state it was bought, and the other washed in three
waters, steeped two hours in brine strong enough to
float an egg, and then limed.   The result was, that two-
thirds of the wheat grown from the unwashed seed was
smutty, while that produced by the steeped and limed
seed had not a single ear of smut.   The second experiment was made upon some very fine wheat, perfectly
free from smut.   A quart of this was washed in three
waters, to make it perfectly clean ; it was then put for
two days into a bag in which was some black dust of
smutty grain ; and the result was, that a large portion
of wheat thus sown was smutty, while out of twenty
acres sown with the same grain, not inoculated, not one
smutty ear was found.   Mr. Taylor, Jr., of Ditching-
ham, near Bungary, rubbed a number of ears of wheat
with the powder of smut, having moistened them to
make the powder adhere ; one-half of these were washed,
wetted with chamber lye, and limed.   A similar quantity of dry wheat was then procured, the whole being
dibbled, each parcel by itself.   The produce of the infected wheat was three-fourths smut ; the same infected
wheat, steeped and limed, was perfectly sound.   The
contagious smut-powder adheres to sacks and barns with
which it has been in contact ; it attaches itself to the
straw and chaff, and is thus probably in many instances
carried from the barn and stable doors, when the dung
is taken green to the fields, without being properly
turned and fermented.   The infection may indeed be

carried by the wind from other fields, and in various ways which cannot be guarded against. But no person, who is duly sensible that the disease may be checked, if not wholly eradicated, by careful attention, should hesitate to employ all those means of prevention which may be in his power. The barn in which wheat has been either stored or thrashed, should therefore be thoroughly aired, and every corner swept; if also the walls of the interior were well washed with strong lime-water, the precaution would not be improper; and sacks which have held the infected grain should be immersed in a similar solution."

ERGOTED WHEAT.

A writer representing the Botanical Society of Canada West, records the following suggestions concerning the ergot in wheat, in that province. But little is known of ergot in wheat in the States, except in certain localities. The writer says :

" In addition to the various pests that have already been noticed as affecting the wheat crops this season, there is one in more than usual abundance, viz.: Ergot. This is a very remarkable fungus, *Claviceps purpurea*, Fr., which swells up the grain into an enlarged, black, tough mass. If a field of wheat be examined, it will be seen that some of the ears have one or more large, black, horn-like processes projecting from among the grains. These are the ergoted grains. This disease is common in many parts of this province.

" Ergot of wheat has similar properties to ergot of rye, but is by no means so common in Europe. On the American continent, however, it appears to be more abundant, and especially this season. The ergot now present in the wheat fields will, of course, damage the sample of grain by blackening, and render the flour to a certain extent unwholesome, if not separated. Fortunately, the ergoted grains being much larger in size than the uninfected ones, there is no great practical difficulty in separating them during the cleaning of the grain. The wheat ergot has no disagreeable taste, in fact no decided taste of any kind, only a slight flavor of mushrooms is perceptible, after chewing for some time. When we reflect on the energetic physiological action of ergot, it will be seen how important it is that the ergoted grains should be carefully cleaned out, not only to improve the sample, but to render the grain and flour wholesome. Bad grain is apt to be given to pigs and other domestic animals. Ergoted grain cannot be used with impunity in the preparation of food for either man or beast."

Whatever may be the cause of ergoted wheat, the *remedy* is effectual and practicable, which is this : procure hardy and prolific varieties of wheat ; save the seed from year to year as directed in this book ; cultivate thoroughly on rich ground ; and put the seed through a pickle, as directed on preceding pages. If a man sows the wind he reaps the whirlwind. If he sows smutty or ergoted wheat, the product will be smut and ergot, just as certainly as he will be able to raise good grain when superior seed is employed.

Rust in Wheat—the Remedy.

Without occupying space in attempting to tell what rust is, and how it is produced, I shall endeavor to point out the remedy for it. The reader can find all the theories about rust that he will care to read, in works on agriculture, where the remedies are not recorded. The forlorn farmer often rails at the climate, and cries out that his wheat is killed by rust, while in fact it has died from starvation—from the want of that food which, as a provident husbandman, it was his duty to have provided for it.

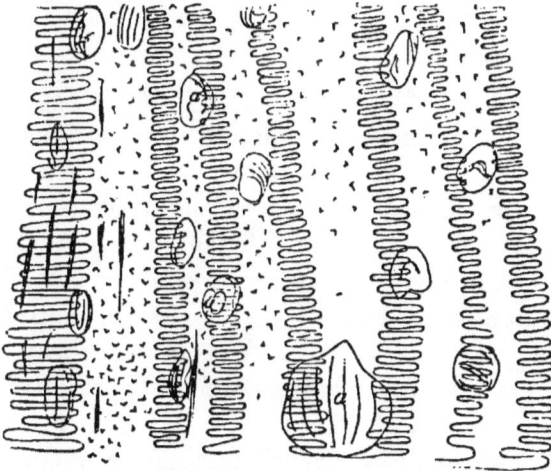

Fig. 77.—Magnified section of Straw, showing Silica deposits.

The illustration herewith given represents a small section of the thin pellicle, or skin, of the stems of growing wheat, highly magnified, and showing the manner of depositing silica in the epidermis of the stalk. Silica is a substance that imparts stiffness to straw. The liquid silica is deposited all around the straw, similar to enclosing it with a thin glass tube. Silica is what renders wheat straw so harsh and stiff.

Now, then, the practical consideration is to supply the roots of growing wheat, in large abundance, with such materials as glassmakers use for making glass, which are sand and potash, or soda. The potash can be obtained most economically by the application of wood ashes. By this means the growing stems will be enveloped in a glass-like covering, which will resist the attacks of rust and mildew. The more ashes, with a dressing of sand, that can be applied to wheat soil, the less liable the growing wheat will be to suffer injury from rust, mildew, or insects.

Insect Enemies of Wheat.

The principal insect enemies of wheat are the midge, the Hessian fly, the chinch bug, and the weevil. As almost every agricultural paper and book contains descriptions and illustrations of the insects injurious to wheat, I shall pen but brief remarks about any of them. The main point will be to offer suggestions relative to an effectual preventive of the ravages of the wheat insects.

Every successful wheat-grower will readily admit that one of the most effectual preventives of the ravages of wheat insects, is a rich soil thoroughly tilled. It invariably happens that the crop is most seriously injured on lands that have been carelessly tilled, and have become impoverished by an exhausting course of cropping. The thin, puny plants on such soils, that are not entirely destroyed, are left still more enfeebled; whereas, when the fly-time has passed, on the well-tilled fields, properly enriched, the wheat, in a great measure, recovers from the slight injury. I might pen a score of pages about the habits of wheat insects, and their mode of propagation and ravages; but I will cut everything short by simply stating, that the correct way to avoid injury from wheat insects is, to commence with the seed first, as directed in the chapter on Seed Grain. Follow all the minute directions about cultivating and fertilizing the soil, so as to produce a luxuriant and healthy growth of both straw and grain; sow the seed at the most propitious period; and the growth of the grain will be so healthful and rapid, that the insects will do but little damage. Read the remarks about The Best Time to Sow Wheat, on pages 260–269.

Levi Bartlett, an experienced farmer of Warner, N. H., writes:

"To avoid injury from the ravages of the midge, some farmers, when the season will permit, sow early, sometimes in the latter part of April. In favorable seasons the wheat gets into blossom before the fly makes its appearance, and thus the grain mostly escapes the midge and rust. Others prefer sowing their wheat late, say from the 20th of May till 1st of June, the midge having generally disappeared before the wheat comes into bloom. But late-sown wheat is more liable to suffer loss from rust, mildew, etc., than the early sown. From better manuring of the land, and more care in its preparation for the reception of the seeds, wheat-growing is evidently upon the increase in this State; though much of this increase is derived from the more extended culture of winter wheat within the past ten years. Winter wheat can be grown, yielding good crops, on low-lying farms, where it was useless to attempt the raising of spring wheat, for the reason that the winter wheat would, when sown early, and on suitable soil, get so far advanced in growth before the appearance of the midge fly, as to entirely escape its ravages, provided the soil is filled with grain-producing pabulum."

Habits of the Wheat Midge.

This insect remains in the earth in its larva state, at least ten months in the year, and buries itself in the soil from half an inch to two inches in depth. This is true, at least in regard to the larger number of them. Others remain in the chaff of the wheat, and are conveyed to the grain-mow, or the stack. But there is no positive evidence that these ever become sufficiently vitalized to perpetuate their species, although, according to experiments made by Dr. Fitch, of New York, there is reason to believe that they do. Certain kinds of wheat are less liable to injury from the attacks of these insects than others. See page 47. Dr. Rathvon is of the opinion that the larvæ of the wheat midges do not imbibe the milky fluid of the young wheat grains; but feed upon the epidermis or outer integument, and that the destruction or injury of *this*, is what causes the ultimate depletion of the grains.

Mr. Rathvon is also satisfied that the wheat midge has not the power to puncture or penetrate the chaff of the wheat with its ovipositor, for the purpose of depositing its eggs upon the grain; nor do the larvæ reach it through such a puncture. But the grain is reached through the separation, or opening of the valvules that enclose the grain, generally when it is in bloom. The largest number of the eggs of the insect are deposited on the outside of the chaff, where they are either washed off by the heavy rains, or are burnt or dried up by the hot sun. But, in whatever way these insects may injure the growing wheat, the only effectual remedy has already been given, on pages 415 and 416.

WHEAT WORMS.

In several States, numerous farmers have observed a kind of minute caterpillars on their growing wheat, such as are frequently seen on red clover. The editor of the " Western Rural " states that they are supposed to be identical with the clover worms, which may be seen spinning down from lofts on which clover has been stored. The caterpillars assume the form of chrysalids in September and October; and the perfect insect appears in June, and deposits its eggs on the wheat, shortly after the ears have shot out. These worms are called by various names, in different localities. In some places they are spoken of as gray worms, and in other localities wheat worms. It is not probable that any of the eggs are attached to the ripened grain; but in order to guard against danger from this source, and also to kill any of the insects that have not been separated from the grain by the fanning mill, the seed should be steeped in a strong brine, and afterward mixed with dry lime. By this treatment, insects and their eggs will be destroyed, and smut prevented. Chaff which contains large numbers of these caterpillars, should be burned.

The true remedy, in addition to the foregoing suggestions, is, to fatten the soil, so as to make the wheat grow so luxuriantly, that the little which the insects consume will not be missed in the growth of the wheat.

THE CHINCH BUG.

This pernicious insect is a very small bug, of a black color, with white wings. In some localities they are called " Mormon lice." See Dr. A. Fitch on Insects, and Klippart's Wheat Plant.

Dr. Sherman, of Waukegan, Illinois, after a patient series of microscopical observations, made a discovery which will surely interest wheat-growers who have been troubled by the chinch-bug pest. His investigations have shown that the seed wheat or kernel was used as a sort of "foster-mother" by the bug ; and that in all wheat grown upon land where there are bugs, there is deposited, in the fuzzy end of the kernel, a large quantity of eggs, which produce the bugs next season. It follows that, if the kernel of seed wheat is the general depository of the eggs of the chinch bug, our farmers have been sowing the pest each year, as regularly as they have their wheat ; and if such is the case, the eradication of the bug will be easily accomplished—either by sowing no wheat that has been in contact with the bug, or by steeping the seed in some solution before sowing, which will destroy the larva. If this remedy fails, when the seed has been selected for a few years, according to directions in Chapter III., the wheat crop must fall a prey to these devouring insects.

It will be an interesting exercise to read all that may be said about the numerous insects injurious to growing wheat, in the books alluded to above. But, after all that can be said, the practical consideration is, *What can be done to prevent or escape their ravages ?* I answer, for the third and last time, *Save your seed with care ; select varieties that are insect-proof, if possible ; sow the seed at the most auspicious period ; and fatten the soil with rich manure.* Let wheat culture receive the same attention that breeders of choice animals give to rearing improved stock.

IMPROVED THRASHING MACHINES.

The illustration shown on this page represents a

Fig. 73.—Improved Thrashing Machine.

new style of thrashing machine, made by Wheeler, Melick & Co., Albany, New York, for thrashing wheat and long rye without breaking, or tangling the straw. This thrasher is one of the most ingenious labor-saving machines that I know of. It is similar to a thrasher invented by Rev. N. Palmer, Hudson, New York, which operated with two long cylinders about five and a half feet long and fourteen inches in diameter, made to revolve toward each other.

The unthrashed grain is fed sideways into the machine, instead of lengthways. If some of the straws enter in a diagonal direction, they will be brought out straight. The straw is carried by the carrier beyond the rear end, where it is deposited in gavels of any desired size. When the machine is in operation, two active laborers will bind the straw as fast as the machine thrashes it.

Straw thrashed with such a machine is much more valuable in market than if it had been thrashed with a machine that breaks it into short pieces; and more than this, the bundles can be stored in a smaller space, and it is more convenient for being fed into a straw-cutter after being thrashed. This machine will thrash all kinds of cereal grain as fast as spiked machines; and when the straw is long and heavy, I think it will thrash faster, with the same power, than the other thrashers which shell out the grain by means of spikes. Two horses will drive such a machine, when attached to a railway power, and do a fair business; but a three-horse railway power will give the cylinders a furious velocity; and an active man will be obliged to work lively in order to feed the machine to the capacity of the thrasher.

The reason why such a machine will thrash long heavy straw more rapidly than a spiked thrasher, is, that a large proportion of the effective force of the team is absorbed in breaking the straw to pieces by means of the spikes, while the corrugated cylinder works the long straw through the machine with the expenditure of little power.

THE NATIONAL FODDER-CUTTER.

The accompanying illustration of a fodder-cutter represents a machine of great superiority, made by J.

FIG. 79.—Fodder-cutter.

D. Burdick & Co., New Haven, Connecticut. These machines are made of several different sizes, to suit the requirements of small as well as large farmers. The small ones are worked by hand, and the large sizes can be driven by horse, or steam power.

I consider a good fodder-cutter to be an implement that every successful wheat-grower needs. In order to raise wheat successfully from year to year, a farmer must keep neat cattle or sheep; and if he makes such use of his wheat straw as will be necessary, in order to maintain the fertility of the land, he must cut his fodder and make rich manure by feeding cattle, or sheep. In order, therefore, to be able to cut straw or any kind of fodder economically, one must have a first-rate machine. I know of no kind better adapted to the wants of common farmers than the National Cutter.

MANAGEMENT OF WHEAT GLEANINGS.

The grain that is gleaned with horse rakes in wheat stubbles, after the crop has been harvested, should never be mingled with the other grain, as the gleaned grain is seldom fit for seed, and never suitable to be ground into flour for human food. When the scattered heads of grain are gathered with the horse rakes, the teeth of the rakes will always tear up sods, grit, and small stones, much of which will be collected with the gleanings. Then, when this unthrashed grain is put through the thrashing-machine, small hard stones are liable, in many instances, to injure the machine more than the value of several bushels of gleaned grain. Gleaned wheat is only fit for cattle feed, because the heads have usually lain in the rain, dews, and sunshine, until the kernels have been swelled and shrunken and dusted over with grit which is dashed over the straw during showers of rain. This alternate wetting and drying of the grain injures the germ of every kernel. Therefore, if the grain be mingled with clean grain for seed, a loss must be sustained equal to the value of such grain. Such kernels will make meal for domestic animals; but if employed for seed, they will not vegetate. When such grain is ground into flour, after having been mingled with clean wheat of a bright color, a small quantity will injure the excellence of the bread, by rendering the white flour dark-colored and the bread gritty. The truth is, that no one can make light white bread, such as an ambitious farmer would place on a table before his guests, when a portion of the flour is made of grain that has been gleaned. If such grain be ground into Graham flour, the bread made of the unbolted flour will be dark-colored, heavy, and gritty. The most skilful baker in the land cannot make excellent bread of any kind, nor pie-crust, nor cake, out of the flour of gleaned wheat that has been wet and dried.

Most farmers contend that such grain will sell for just as much per bushel, if mingled with the crop—which is all true. But dealers ought to make a deduction in the price of every bushel of wheat, which has gleaned grain mingled with it. The large quantities of gleaned wheat that are gathered with horse rakes, in the wheat-growing districts of the country, is one prime cause of so much dark-colored flour and heavy, soggy, and clammy bread, of which the great mass of people have just cause to murmur. Farmers alone are the parties on whom the blame ought to rest. And farmers are the persons who should correct this world-wide evil, of which so much complaint is constantly made in relation to dark flour, heavy and gritty bread.

Wheat gleanings should be kept entirely separate from the clean wheat, and thrashed separately, or be thrashed with other cereal grain that is to be employed for feeding domestic animals. Gleaned grain will make excellent chicken feed; and if the gleanings be thrashed with oats, barley, or rye, which is to be ground for feeding stock, its value will not be lost. And although a person may not realize quite so much money per bushel for his gleanings, when used up in this manner, as when the gleaned grain is sold with the crop, still, he would have the satisfaction of knowing that his wheat went to market in a merchantable condition, and that the flour produced from it, would not fail · to make excellent bread, both for the rich and the poor, who depend on the farmers to deliver them a good article of food, which no one would hesitate to set before his guests.

When grain has been gleaned with horse rakes, the wads or rakefuls should be shaken apart with much care, for the twofold purpose of removing all stones and sods that may have been gathered by the rake-teeth, and for exposing the damp straw to the influences of the sun and drying wind. In case of a storm of rain before gleanings can be secured in the barn or stack, let the windrows be forked into large cocks and covered with hay caps. Then as the gleanings are usually hauled to the barn after the sheaves have been gathered, they can be thrashed and kept separate from the clean grain with little or no difficulty.

CUTTING VEGETABLES FOR STOCK.

Every careful farmer who has been accustomed to feed fruit and vegetables to any kind of stock understands and appreciates the importance of reducing all kinds of vegetables to small pieces, before feeding them to any kind of domestic animals, except horses and mules, which have front teeth on both jaws, with which they can nip their food. When neat cattle and sheep are required to eat pumpkins, turnips, carrots, potatoes, or apples, when the pieces are so large that they cannot be placed readily between the double teeth, the animals are exceedingly liable to get choked. Besides this, if an animal's teeth are poor, they are required to make a great exertion to eat vegetables unless they are cut into small bits.

The accompanying illustration represents a vegetable cutter, which has given excellent satisfaction, for cutting pumpkins, turnips, and all kinds of roots into small

FIG. 80.—Excelsior Root Cutter.

pieces for sheep or cows. I think it is the best cutter in market, at the present writing, as J. S. Robertson, Syracuse, N. Y., the inventor, has received many premiums and medals from Agricultural Societies, on this cutter. At the State Fair, Buffalo, it cut a bushel of potatoes fine enough for sheep in twenty-six seconds.

The pumpkins or roots to be cut are put in the box so that they come in contact with the cylinder, the upper side of which is shown in the figure. The cylinder is hollow, being made of hard iron. Small gouge-shaped cutters are secured to the surface of the cylinder, which gouge out pieces of the vegetables about as large as a man's thumb. Such pieces are of convenient size for sheep or any other stock to eat with facility. A small lad or girl can cut a bushel of roots in about one minute, with comparative ease.

The cutters can be adjusted to cut very fine, or coarse. If the knives become dull, the edge can be put in order in a few minutes with a round file. If vegetables and apples could be reduced to a fine pulp before they are fed to stock, the animals would extract more nourishment from the feed, than if such coarse materials were simply run through a vegetable cutter.

It is an excellent practice, when feeding stock of any kind with cut or pulped vegetables, to mingle meal of any kind of grain with the pulped feed, as there is always more or less advantage in mingling several kinds of food together, before animals are supplied with their usual allowance. Every wheat grower should have such a root cutter. When raising roots, feeding stock, and growing wheat are properly combined, our country will be noted for beautiful crops of excellent wheat.

THE END.

INDEX.

www.ingramcontent.com/pod-product-compliance
Lightning Source LLC
Chambersburg PA
CBHW032305280326
41932CB00009B/705